Seeds of Genius

This book would not have been possible without the generous financial support of the Central Arkansas Planning Development District, the Black History Commission of the Arkansas History Commission, and the Arkansas Black Hall of Fame Foundation.

Seeds of Genius

Twenty-Five Years of the Arkansas Black Hall of Fame

Charles O. Stewart

The Butler Center for Arkansas Studies
Central Arkansas Library System
100 Rock Street
Little Rock, Arkansas 72201

Cover Design by Henri Linton, Jr.
Original Painting by Henri Linton, Sr.

First Edition: September 2017
ISBN 978-1-945624-08-7

Cataloging-in-Publication data is on file at the Library of Congress.

Printed in Canada

INDUCTEES BY YEAR

My years have largely been filled with uneventful hard work, the challenges of everyday life, and the ebbs and flows of an academic career. I have endured through many setbacks and missteps in my professional life and have learned to remain steady and constant despite the adversities that any given day may bring. Then, occasionally, the routine of everyday life receives a welcome disruption. The hard work leads to blessings of success and joy for my family and me, and the years of dedication and perseverance result in a moment of public recognition. In 2006, I experienced one such instance of public recognition. Within the space of a few months, I was privileged to join the Yale University Department of Physics as a faculty member, and, subsequently, was honored with an induction into the Arkansas Black Hall of Fame.

The Induction Ceremony itself was incredible. My wife and two daughters were treated with the honor of meeting Governor Michael Huckabee and many state and city officials. We enjoyed limousine rides to and from the Governor's Mansion in Little Rock and indulged in food and drinks that still rank among the best we've ever had. Family members and friends joined us in Little Rock, traveling from places as varied as Texas, California, and Tillar and McGehee, Arkansas. Our hotel was one of true elegance and charm, a beautiful and historical venue with a mother duck and her ducklings parading through the lobby in the mornings and evenings. During the ceremony, we were presented with a lavish dinner, and we heard speeches—and even a lovely musical performance—from the inductees. To this day, I fondly remember the ceremony, the looks of pride my family members displayed as I gave my own speech at the podium, and the celebration we had afterward.

Envisioned by Charles O. Stewart and Patricia Y. Goodwin more than twenty-five years ago, the Arkansas Black Hall of Fame now includes honorees from the diverse fields of education, medicine, politics, sports, science and technology, mathematics, law, music, entertainment, literature, the military, community service, the arts, and religion. The inductees have applied their crafts not only in Arkansas, but also in numerous communities throughout the United States. It was a pleasure reading about my fellow Arkansans and an honor to be listed alongside those who paved the way for me to do what I love in the field of physics.

While the biographical sketches presented in this book do a wonderful job of explaining the background and accomplishments of each inductee in turn, the sketches do not, in every case, necessarily make plain that spark, that ignition which set each inductee on the path to his or her life's work. However, while reading this book, I immediately noticed that there is at least one trait that the inductees all share: the ability to overcome obstacles, challenges, and disadvantages in order to achieve their dreams. It is quite possible that these very trials are what brought out their creativity, their resourcefulness, and their genius.

In a recent *National Geographic* article entitled "What Makes a Genius," the author, Claudia Kalb, aptly notes, "Natural gifts and a nurturing environment can still fall short of producing a genius, without motivation and tenacity propelling one forward." Kalb goes on to reference Leonardo da Vinci, who reportedly wrote: "Obstacles cannot crush me." Several additional examples of people crowned with the title of genius—people who all share that same tenacious quality—were highlighted in the article, from Michelangelo and Marie Curie to Albert Einstein and Charles Darwin. The pages you are about to read are filled with geniuses and visionaries who stand alongside these historical figures as paragons of grit, fortitude, and endurance under pressure.

This quality of genius struck me as *comme il faut* in referencing the Arkansas Black Hall of Fame inductees. Of course, the Arkansas Black Hall of Fame inductees over the past quarter century certainly do not represent an exhaustive list of pioneers and leaders from this great state. Many more will be honored over the coming decades. What is most exciting to me and what will make this particular book that you are about to read truly rewarding is that when the next foreword is written for the 50th Anniversary of the Arkansas Black Hall of Fame, that writer will refer to inductees who haven't even been born yet. And their seeds of genius will yet again inspire the next generation of Arkansans.

—Dr. Oliver Baker

ACKNOWLEDGMENTS

A work of this kind is not achieved without the assistance of a cast of many who helped to make this book a reality. *Seeds of Genius: Twenty-Five Years of the Arkansas Black Hall of Fame* is the culmination of a vision that has existed now for approximately five years in the run-up to our 25th Anniversary Celebration. I would like to thank the outstanding Arkansans who have been inducted into the Arkansas Black Hall of Fame during the first quarter century of its existence. For those who have been inducted posthumously, we are indebted to family members who have shared their stories and photos with us to then share with the world. We are ultimately thankful to God for planting seeds of genius within all of us. To Patricia Goodwin-McCullough, the co-founder without whose collaboration in the early years, the Black Hall of Fame would probably be yet a vision, we extend our sincere gratitude. This book would not have been possible without the generous financial support of the Central Arkansas Planning Development District, the Black History Commission of the Arkansas History Commission, and the Arkansas Black Hall of Fame Foundation, as well as the many sponsors who annually support the ABHOF Induction Ceremony. It has been a pleasure to work with the Butler Center for Arkansas Studies, Butler Center Books, and the Encyclopedia of Arkansas History & Culture—all part of the Central Arkansas Library System (CALS)—and we are most appreciative to all who have played a significant role in updating the entries for each inductee in the book. We are deeply indebted to Georgia C. Walton for sharing her amazing editing expertise in the making of this book.

Finally, sincere thanks must be extended to the Arkansas Black Hall of Fame Steering Committee. Without the commitment and dedication of the Steering Committee, the Arkansas Black Hall of Fame could not exist and do its important work in recognizing the achievements of these outstanding African Americans with Arkansas ties. Thanks to Sylvia Smith, Paula Patterson, Paulette Lawson, Myron Jackson, Michelle Smith, Ventrell Thompson, Rodney Parks, Gemessia Hudson, Angela Newkirk, Carmen Portillo, Kimara Randolph, Yana-Janell Scott, Danyell Crutchfield Cummings, Chauncey Holloman Pettis, Judith Kanu, Victoria Brown, Denise Ennett, Shanda Macon, Ganelle Blake, Taren Robinson, Theresa Timmons, and all the other persons over the years who have labored with love and dedication to the cause of the Arkansas Black Hall of Fame. Special acknowledgment is extended to John Bangert, Arnessa Bennett, Barbara Abraham, Tommy Farrell, Michael Tidwell and the Tidwell Project, and the late Donna Grady Creer and Oscar Washington.

HISTORY OF THE
ARKANSAS BLACK HALL OF FAME

The Arkansas Black Hall of Fame (ABHOF), founded September 9, 1992, by Charles Stewart and Patricia Goodwin-McCullough, has become a highly respected Arkansas institution. The ABHOF's mission is to annually recognize the accomplishments and contributions of black Arkansans who have achieved national and international acclaim in their chosen fields of endeavor.

The ABHOF was initially founded as a fund-raising mechanism to support the work of the Arkansas Minority Business Supplier Development Council. At the time, Patricia Goodwin was the executive director of the Council and Charles Stewart was a member of the Board of Directors of that organization. Goodwin had attended an event in Atlanta that recognized the achievements of African Americans, and it made an indelible impression on her. Stewart had been nurturing a concept for an event to honor the achievements of Arkansans, and the two married their ideas and concepts to become the Arkansas Black Hall of Fame. In order for the Arkansas Black Hall of Fame to succeed, the very first event had to be a resounding success and the very first class of inductees into the ABHOF had to be made up of exemplary figures in Arkansas and American history. The first class of inductees included John Harold Johnson, Daisy Gatson Bates, Maya Angelou, Ernest Green, Lottie Shackelford and George William Stanley Ish. The first induction ceremony took place in the Robinson Auditorium Exhibit Hall and attracted more than 400 people in a very successful and well-publicized event. The first induction ceremony was attended by Governor Jim Guy Tucker and

other leading political and civic leaders, as well as Bill Dillard, founder of Dillard Department Stores, Inc., who was a personal friend of John H. Johnson. Since the ABHOF's inception, the induction ceremony featured Honorary Co-chairmen Governor Jim Guy Tucker, Governor Mike Huckabee, Governor Mike Beebe, and Governor Asa Hutchinson. They each have welcomed the honorees and guests at a VIP Reception at the Governor's Mansion.

Today, the ABHOF maintains permanent exhibit galleries in the Mosaic Templars Cultural Center, a museum of the Department of Arkansas Heritage. It also features a portrait gallery in the rotunda of the Statehouse Convention Center in downtown Little Rock. The ABHOF operated in partnership with the Council for the first ten years of its existence. In September of 2002, the ABHOF separated from the Council and formed the Arkansas Black Hall of Fame Foundation, a 501 (c)(3) non-profit organization, to broaden the mission of the ABHOF to include supporting other non-profit organizations working to improve education, health/wellness, youth development, and economic development in minority and other under-served communities throughout Arkansas. In October 2002, President Bill Clinton became the first and only Caucasian to be inducted into the Arkansas Black Hall of Fame. This action recognized the historically close relationship that Clinton had with African Americans and played off of author Toni Morrison's portrayal of Clinton as "America's First Black President." This action gained international attention and placed the ABHOF on a global stage. The TV game show *Jeopardy* had the following as a question: "The only Caucasian to be inducted into the Arkansas Black Hall of Fame." The correct answer: "Who is William Jefferson Clinton?" The 2002 induction ceremony attracted over 1,100 guests and moved to the Wally Allen Ballroom of the Statehouse Convention Center.

In February of 2010, the ABHOF inaugurated the Distinguished Laureate Series. The Laureate Series brings back the distinguished inductees of the ABHOF to present lectures on current events and offer concert performances and master classes to high school and college students throughout Arkansas.

The Distinguished Laureate Series, which attracts approximately 700 participants each year, has featured:

- James McKissic Concert presenting the works of Schumann
- Dr. James E. K. Hildreth, "The War Against HIV/AIDS—Are We Winning?"
- Amina Claudine Myers playing a jazz concert

- Dr. Oliver Keith Baker, "Understanding Higgs-Boson (the "God Particle")"
- Haki Madhubuti, *The Diary of Malcolm X*
- Dr. Robert L. Williams, "On Race in America"
- Judge Timothy Evans, "After Ferguson, Race and the Criminal Justice System"

In 2012, the Arkansas Black Hall of Fame received the ACHANGE Founder's Award for community leadership and contributions. The Association of Fundraising Professionals–Arkansas Chapter named the Arkansas Black Hall of Fame Foundation as the 2014 Outstanding Foundation in Arkansas. Previous recipients of this prestigious award have been the Rockefeller Foundation, the Walton Family Foundation, and the Sturgis Foundation. This puts the ABHOF Foundation in great company, and it is an honor to be among those working to bring positive change to Arkansas and to cultivate an environment where future ABHOF inductees may be nurtured.

1993

Maya Angelou

Daisy Gatson Bates

Ernest Green

George William Stanley Ish, MD

John Harold Johnson

Lottie Shackelford

Maya Angelou

(1928–2014)

Maya Angelou was an internationally renowned bestselling author, poet, actor, and performer, as well as a pioneering activist for the rights of African Americans and of women. Her first published book, *I Know Why the Caged Bird Sings* (1970), was an autobiographical account of her childhood, including the ten years she lived in Arkansas. The popular and critical success of the book was the foundation of her career as an author and public figure, as well as the basis of her identification as an Arkansas author. She held over fifty honorary university degrees, along with many other awards recognizing her accomplishments in the arts and her service to human rights.

Angelou was born Marguerite Annie Johnson on April 4, 1928, in St. Louis, Missouri, to Bailey Johnson, a naval dietitian, and Vivian Baxter Johnson, a nurse. Angelou had one sibling, her older brother Bailey Jr., who actually started calling her "Maya," his version of "my sister." After their parents divorced, the two moved to Stamps in 1931 to live with their paternal grandmother, Annie Henderson, and their uncle, Willie. Henderson owned the only grocery store in the small town and reared the children according to the strict Christian values

common in the rural South at that time. The family encountered the racial prejudice of the white customers in the store and of the community leaders generally. In her autobiography, Angelou recounted chafing at the attitudes she encountered of people who seemed to condone the limited opportunities available for black high school graduates of the time. Later, Angelou suggested that her faith and Christian beliefs—as well as her strong sense of fair play and realization of her own and others' inner beauty—stemmed from these early experiences.

In 1935, the children returned to live with their mother in St. Louis but were sent back to Stamps after it was discovered that Marguerite had been sexually molested by her mother's boyfriend. The man was tried and convicted but then released; he was found dead soon after. The eight-year-old girl felt guilty and believed that her voice had caused the death of the rapist, so she became mute and remained so for several years.

Later the two children moved again to live with their mother—this time in San Francisco, California. After dropping out of high school, Marguerite was briefly employed as a cable car conductor, the first black person ever to hold that position. She returned to Mission High School and earned a scholarship to study dance, drama, and music at San Francisco's Labor School, where she also learned about the progressive ideologies that may have served as a foundation for her later social and political activism. In 1944 three weeks after graduation, she gave birth to her son, Guy. She had no further formal education.

At age sixteen to support herself and her son, she worked in many capacities: cocktail waitress, dancer, cook, and sex worker—all before the age of twenty-five. She used these life experiences to serve as themes in her works of prose and poetry.

At age twenty-one, she married a Greek sailor, Tosh Angelos; they divorced in 1952. While singing at a San Francisco nightclub, she created her professional name, Maya Angelou, using a variation of his surname and her brother's nickname for her. Eventually, she legally changed her name.

In 1954–55, she toured Europe and Africa in a production of *Porgy and Bess*. In 1955, she and Guy moved to New York City, where she studied modern dance with Martha Graham and Alvin Ailey. She appeared in television shows and released an album called *Miss Calypso* in 1957, also appearing in the film *Calypso Heat Wave* that year. From her teen years, she continued to develop her writing skills, including poems and song lyrics.

She met prominent members of the African-American creative community and performed in Jean Genet's *The Blacks*. With Godfrey Cambridge she produced *Cabaret for Freedom*, a fundraiser for the Southern Christian Leadership Conference (SCLC). Martin Luther King, Jr., a leader in the SCLC, recruited Angelou as its northern coordinator in 1960.

In the early 1960s, she met South African freedom fighter and civil rights advocate Vusumzi Make, a leader of the Pan Africanist Congress who then lived in New York City. They moved to Cairo, Egypt, where she became editor of the weekly newspaper the *Arab Observer*. In 1963, she and Guy left Egypt for Ghana, where she met Malcolm X. She became an assistant administrator at the University of Ghana's School of Music and Drama and later a feature editor for the *African Review*, as well as a feature writer for the *Ghanaian Times* and the Ghanaian Broadcasting Company, where she also recorded public service announcements.

While residing in Africa, she studied several languages: Fanti (a West African language), French, Italian, Spanish, and Arabic. Her time in Ghana was chronicled in *Essence* magazine and was published in 1986 as *All God's Children Need Traveling Shoes*. When she returned to the States, she resumed her civil rights activities.

In reaction to these events, Angelou—encouraged by novelist James Baldwin—began writing the first installment of her life story, including an account of her years in Arkansas. *I Know Why the Caged Bird Sings* was first published in 1970 and has since been translated into more than ten languages. Her experiences in the civil rights movement were a focus of a later autobiography, *The Heart of a Woman* (1981). Enjoying her burgeoning career as a writer, lecturer, and public personality following the publication of *I Know Why the Caged Bird Sings*, she wrote the screenplay for *Georgia, Georgia*, a Swedish-American film; it was the first screenplay by an African American to be filmed. A collection of her poems, *Just Give Me a Cool Drink of Water 'fore I Diiie*, was nominated for a Pulitzer Prize in 1972.

Winning much critical acclaim and becoming a much demanded national figure and speaker, she continued to maintain her political activism. The running themes in all of her works dealt with the individual's wish and right to survive in a non-hostile world

In 1973, Angelou married Paul du Feu, a Welsh writer and cartoonist from whom she was divorced in 1980.

In 1975, President Gerald Ford appointed her to the Bicentennial Commission. In 1981, she received a lifetime appointment to the Reynolds Chair of American Studies at Wake Forest University in Winston-Salem, North Carolina. She read her poem "On the Pulse of Morning" at the Inauguration of President Bill Clinton in 1993, her poem "A Brave and Startling Truth" at the fiftieth anniversary of the United Nations, and her poem "From a Black Woman to a Black Man" at the Million Man March in 1995.

Angelou had a distinctive speaking voice, and, at six feet tall, was a powerful physical presence enhanced by her training in dance and stage performance. She was nominated for a 1977 Emmy Award for her compelling performance in Alex Haley's miniseries *Roots*. Angelou appeared on many daytime and morning talk shows. She also started a Hallmark greeting cards line called Life Mosaic. The movie *Poetic Justice* (1993) featured Angelou's poetry. In 1998, she made her film-directing debut with *Down in the Delta* (1998); in 2006 starred in *Tyler Perry's Medea's Family Reunion*; and in 2002 won a Grammy for Best Spoken Word Album for *A Song Flung Up to Heaven*.

Angelou was awarded the National Medal of Arts in 2000; the Presidential Medal of Freedom by President Barack Obama in 2011; and the Literarian Award from the National Book Foundation and the Mailer Prize for Lifetime Achievement from the Norman Mailer Center in 2013.

Her body of published works includes autobiographies, numerous poetry collections, a book of essays, several plays, a screenplay, and a cookbook. Among her many works are *Gather Together in My Name* (1974), *Singin' and Swingin' and Gettin' Merry Like Christmas* (1976), *The Heart of a Woman* (1981), *All God's Children Need Traveling Shoes* (1986), *A Song Flung Up to Heaven* (2002), *Hallelujah! The Welcome Table: A Lifetime of Memories with*

Recipes (2004), and *Mom & Me & Mom* (2013).

After being in poor health, Angelou was found dead by her caretaker on May 28, 2014. In June 2014, the town of Stamps renamed its only park in her honor. On April 7, 2015, the United States Postal Service released a first-class stamp in her honor. In March 2016, the U.S. House of Representatives passed a measure to rename a post office in Winston-Salem after Angelou.

✦ ✦ ✦

Daisy Gatson Bates

(1913?–1999)

Daisy Gatson Bates was a mentor to the Little Rock Nine, the African-American students who courageously integrated Central High School in Little Rock in 1957 amid national and international recognition when then-Governor Orval Faubus ordered members of the Arkansas National Guard to prevent the entry of black students. She and her husband, Lucious Christopher (L. C.) Bates, instituted the *Arkansas State Press*, a weekly newspaper dealing primarily with civil rights and other issues in the black community.

Daisy Lee Gatson's birth parents remain a mystery. Before age seven, she was taken in as a foster child by Susie Smith and Orlee Smith, a mill worker, in Huttig, Arkansas, just three miles from the Louisiana border. Gatson attended the segregated schools in Huttig, but the extent of her formal education is unknown. It is unlikely her education went beyond the ninth grade and may have been less than that.

At age fifteen, she met her future husband, L. C. Bates, then a traveling salesman living in Memphis, Tennessee, where she had moved in 1932 after the death of her foster father. Little is known about her until she and her future husband moved to Little Rock in 1941 and started the *Arkansas State Press*. Gatson and Bates were married on March 4, 1942, in Fordyce, Arkansas. Although she rarely wrote for the paper, Bates gradually became active in its operations and was named by her husband as city editor in 1945.

As ardent supporters of the National Asso-

ciation for the Advancement of Colored People (NAACP), both Bates and her husband were active in the Little Rock branch. In 1952, she was elected president of the Arkansas Conference of Branches, the umbrella organization for the state NAACP. She and L. C. worked closely with other members of the Little Rock branch as the national strategy of the NAACP shifted in the 1950s from advocating a position of equal funding for segregated programs to outright racial integration.

Although well known in the black community, Bates came to the attention of white Arkansans as a civil rights advocate in 1956 during the pre-trial proceedings of the federal court case *Aaron v. Cooper*, which set the stage for the 1957 desegregation of Central High. Bates once engaged in a fiery exchange with an attorney for the Little Rock School Board when he called her by her first name. She quickly let him know he was out of line in doing so and demanded that he refrain from it. This challenge to one of white supremacy's oldest traditions—that of controlling and intimidating African Americans by treating them as though they were children—became part of the front-page story in the next morning's *Arkansas Gazette*.

The federal courts at the time allowed the Little Rock School District to set its own pace for desegregation of its public schools, but they could not prevent Bates's involvement with the first nine students who attended Central High School during the school year 1957–58. Although local NAACP attorney Wiley Branton of Pine Bluff had handled much of the litigation, Bates, in her capacity as president of the Arkansas Conference of Branches, was recognized as the principal spokesperson and leader for the forces behind school desegregation. In this role, she was in constant contact with NAACP leaders and in constant conflict with segregationists using intimidation in Arkansas. For much of the school year, she was in daily contact with the national office of the NAACP in New York as segregationists battled to destroy the NAACP in Arkansas as well as to intimidate her, her husband, and the Little Rock Nine and their families into giving up the struggle. On occasion, individuals attacked the Bateses' home in Little Rock, forcing them to stand guard nightly.

In recognition of her leadership, the national Associated Press chose her in 1957 as the Woman of the Year in Education and as one of the top ten newsmakers in the world. In 1959, as a result of intimidation by news distributors and a boycott by white business owners who withheld advertising, the Bateses were forced to close the *Arkansas State Press*.

Bates remained at the center of the desegregation battle on behalf of the NAACP and the civil rights movement in Arkansas until June 1960 when she moved to New York to write a memoir of her desegregation experiences in Little Rock, *The Long Shadow of Little Rock*. She remained president of the Arkansas Conference of Branches until 1961, when she was succeeded by George Howard, Jr., who later became a federal judge. Chosen to fill a vacancy on the national board of the NAACP in 1957, Bates was re-elected to successive three-year terms through 1970.

Her prominence as one of the few female civil rights leaders of the period was recognized by her selection as the only woman to speak at the Lincoln Memorial at the March on Washington on August 28, 1963.

In 1968, Bates moved to the all-black town of Mitchellville, Arkansas, to become executive director of that community's Economic Opportunity Agency, a federal anti-poverty program. She remained there until 1974. This began a new phase in her life that was marked by a commitment to

demonstrating that poor African Americans could achieve economic self-sufficiency in partnership with government. Bates secured grants and donations for several improvements in the community, including a sewer system and a Head Start program.

Bates revived the *Arkansas State Press* in 1984, but it was financially unsuccessful. She sold the paper in 1988 to Darryl Lunon and Janis Kearney Lunon.

In ill health the last years of her life, Bates died of a heart attack on November 4, 1999, at Baptist Medical Center in Little Rock. She is buried in Haven of Rest Cemetery in Little Rock.

In May 2000, a crowd of more than 2,000 gathered in Robinson Auditorium in Little Rock to honor her memory. At this event, President Bill Clinton acknowledged her achievements, comparing her to a diamond that gets "chipped away in form and shines more brightly." In 2001, the Arkansas legislature enacted a provision that recognizes the third Monday in February as "Daisy Gatson Bates Day." Thus, her memory, along with those of American presidents, is celebrated on that date as an official state holiday. There are streets in various towns in Arkansas, including Little Rock, which bear her name. In February 2012, PBS broadcast the documentary *Daisy Bates: First Lady of Little Rock*.

Ernest Green

(1941–)

Ernest Green made history as the only senior of the Little Rock Nine, the nine African-American students who desegregated Central High School in Little Rock in 1957. The world watched as they braved constant intimidation and threats from those who opposed desegregation of the formerly all-white high school. Green's place in Arkansas's civil rights history was solidified when he became the first African American to graduate from the now historic landmark.

Ernest Gideon Green was born in Little Rock on September 22, 1941, to Lothaire Green and Ernest Green, Sr. Green has two siblings: brother,

Scott, and sister, Treopia Washington.

An active member of the community from an early age, Green regularly attended church and was involved in the Boy Scouts. He eventually became an Eagle Scout. He was a student at Dunbar Junior High School until he transferred to Horace Mann the year before volunteering to integrate all-white Central High School. Green persevered through a year of daily harassment by some of his fellow students to become the first black Central High graduate on May 27, 1958. Sitting with Green's family at the event was Martin Luther King, Jr., who attended the graduation virtually unnoticed. In an interview, Green said, "It's been an interesting year. I've had a course in human relations first hand."

After he graduated from Central, Green attended Michigan State University. He earned a Bachelor of Arts degree (BA) in social science in 1962 and a Master of Arts degree (MA) in sociology in 1964. Afterwards, Green served as the director for the A. Philip Randolph Education Fund from 1968 to 1977. He then was appointed as the Assistant Secretary of Labor during the Jimmy Carter administration from 1977 to 1981. In 1987, Green joined Lehman Brothers, an investment banking firm in Washington, D.C., where he became a Senior Managing Director. He has served on numerous boards, such as the National Association for the Advancement of Colored People (NAACP) and the Winthrop Rockefeller Foundation.

In 1958, Green, along with other members of the Little Rock Nine and Daisy Bates, was awarded the prestigious Spingarn Medal, which is presented annually for outstanding achievements of African Americans by the NAACP. In 1999, President Bill Clinton presented one of the nation's highest civilian awards, the Congressional Gold Medal, to the members of the Little Rock Nine. He is married to Phyllis Green, with whom he has a daughter, in addition to two children from a previous marriage. Green is the subject of a Disney movie entitled *The Ernest Green Story*, produced in 1992 starring Morris Chestnut and Monica Calhoun. In 2011, Green was awarded an honorary doctorate by the University of Arkansas at Fayetteville.

◆ ◆ ◆

George W. S. Ish, MD
(1883–1970)

George William Stanley Ish, MD, was a prominent black physician in Little Rock who cared for citizens of the capital city and inspired members of both races. He graduated from Harvard Medical School and was instrumental in founding both United Friends Hospital and the J. E. Bush Memorial Hospital, primary centers for the medical care of black patients. He was also largely responsible for the inception of the McRae

Memorial Tuberculosis Sanatorium in Alexander, the state's separate black sanatorium. Physicians of both races held him in high regard, and he was a staff member at predominantly white hospitals in Little Rock.

G. W. S. Ish was born in Little Rock on October 28, 1883, in the house that his parents built at 1600 Scott Street. He was the son of Jefferson G. Ish and Marietta Ish, prominent Little Rock educators. Ish attended high school in Little Rock and graduated from Talladega College in Talladega, Alabama, in 1903, with a Bachelor of Arts degree (BA). From Talladega College, he went to Yale University's Collegiate Department and graduated in 1905 with a second BA. Ish had originally aspired to become an engineer; but knowing the need for healthcare practitioners, he chose to pursue medicine. He entered Harvard Medical School and graduated with a medical degree in 1909. Dr. Ish served a fourteen-month internship at Freedmen's Hospital (now Howard University Hospital) in Washington, D.C., after which he returned to Little Rock to practice general medicine with a surgical specialty.

Dr. Ish married Lillie Johnson in 1915, and they had four children: two sons and two daughters. His first wife died in the late 1930s; he married his second wife, Ercell Tucker, in 1941.

Dr. Ish was instrumental in founding the J. E. Bush Memorial Hospital in 1918 and served as both the administrator and a physician there for many years. The hospital was located at 908 Arch Street but closed in 1927. Dr. Ish also served as director of United Friends Hospital, which was founded in 1922 and was located at 714 West Tenth Street. He was director of that institution until his death in 1970. He was also active in the Lena Jordan Hospital, a charity hospital whose second location had been the Ish home on Scott Street.

Additionally, Dr. Ish was a member of the Board of Directors of McRae Memorial Tuberculosis Sanatorium from its establishment in 1923 until its closure in 1967. Through his efforts and persuasion, McRae was the first institution in Arkansas and one of the first in the nation to use isoniazid and streptomycin in the treatment of pulmonary tuberculosis.

Dr. Ish was a staff physician at the Arkansas Baptist Medical Center and the St. Vincent Infirmary. He was a life member of both the Pulaski County and Arkansas medical societies. He was a school physician and instructor in health education at Philander Smith College from 1934 to 1965. Dr. Ish was esteemed by the white medical establishment, as evidenced by his membership in largely white medical organizations, which was virtually unheard of at that time.

Dr. Ish lived most of his life in the house his parents built on Scott Street. The house was damaged by fire in 1996, and efforts to rebuild it were unsuccessful. Finally, the house was damaged beyond repair by a tornado in 1999.

Dr. Ish died on March 15, 1970, and he is buried in Haven of Rest Cemetery in Little Rock.

John H. Johnson
(1918–2005)

John H. Johnson rose above abject poverty and racial discrimination to build a publishing empire that helped forever change the perception of African Americans in the United States. Johnson Publishing Company became the largest African-American-owned and -operated publishing

company in the world and launched *Ebony* and *Jet*, two very successful magazines that gave a voice to millions of black Americans.

Born Johnny Johnson on January 19, 1918, in Arkansas City to Leroy Johnson and Gertrude Jenkins Johnson, a cook at a Mississippi River levee camp, Johnson was a third-generation descendant of slaves. After the death of Johnson's father in a sawmill accident when Johnson was eight years old, his mother married James Williams, who helped with young Johnny's upbringing.

During the six weeks the family lived on the Mississippi River levee following the Flood of 1927, nine-year-old Johnson watched the constraints of race disappear when all people, black and white, were forced to work together in their struggle to survive. It was also there that young Johnson developed a keen eye for news—a desire to learn what motivated people, what their desires were, and why they wanted what they wanted.

Because African Americans had no chance for an education beyond eighth grade in Arkansas City, Johnson attended DuSable High School in Chicago, Illinois. After his high school graduation and at the suggestion of a teacher that he adopt a more adult-sounding name, Johnny Johnson became John Harold Johnson. In 1941, he married Eunice Walker. They adopted two children: a son, John Harold, Jr., and a daughter, Linda.

Johnson worked part time at Supreme Liberty Life Insurance Company in Chicago, while attending classes at the University of Chicago. He rose to the position of editor of the company's monthly newspaper and quickly saw a need and an opportunity for a magazine targeting a black audience—news and thought about how black Americans were gaining respect. In 1942, using his mother's furniture as collateral for a $500 loan, Johnson mailed out the first issue of *Negro Digest*, which became an instant hit and led to the creation of Johnson Publishing Company. Two other magazines, *Ebony* and *Jet*, were initiated in 1945 and 1951, respectively.

Ebony became the number-one African-American magazine in the world, with two and a half million monthly readers. It emphasizes positive aspects of black life in America and provides inspiration to all African Americans. *Jet* became the number-one newsweekly magazine, with more than nine million subscribers. This magazine provides coverage of current news as well as reports on events or individuals. The influence of *Ebony* and *Jet* was immediate and widespread as articles covered black history, culture, and demand for equality in American life. The magazines covered important events, including Martin Luther King, Jr.'s March on Washington and the 1957 desegregation of Central High School in Little Rock and answered the call of leaders of the civil rights movement for reporters to attend and report on unrest in cities throughout America. Both magazines were read with great interest by black Americans across the country.

The success of Johnson Publishing Company can be attributed to Johnson's determination to break down racial barriers and to convince major advertisers of the huge, untapped black consumer market in the United States. He also succeeded at overcoming long-held discrimination against African Americans in the banking and real estate industries to obtain bank loans, own property, and build offices in elite regions of Chicago and other cities in the United States.

Johnson initiated the Ebony Fashion Fair, the world's largest traveling fashion show, which was produced and directed by his wife, Eunice Walker Johnson. This fashion show has raised over $50 million for charity since 1958. The fashion show led to the opening of a cosmetics division of Johnson Publishing Company called Fashion Fair Cosmetics, which provides high-quality beauty and skin care products for black women.

Johnson, who was named to the Forbes 400 richest Americans, served on the boards of directors of several Fortune 500 corporations, including Twentieth Century Fox Film Corporation, Chrysler, Zenith, and Continental Bank. He was often in prestigious company and advised many VIPs, including civil rights leaders and several presidents. He served as a special United States ambassador for Presidents John F. Kennedy and Lyndon B. Johnson and accompanied Vice President Richard M. Nixon to Africa and Europe in 1957 and 1959. In 1996 on the fiftieth anniversary of *Ebony* magazine, President Bill Clinton presented Johnson with the Presidential Medal of Freedom, which is one of America's highest civilian honors. He also received over thirty honorary doctorate degrees from such universities as the University of Arkansas in Fayetteville, the University of Arkansas at Pine Bluff, Harvard University, and Howard University.

In 2002, Johnson appointed his daughter, Linda Johnson Rice, CEO of Johnson Publishing Company. The company, renamed Ebony Media, was sold to CVG Group; in 2017, Johnson Rice became CEO of Ebony Media, returning a Johnson to the helm of the company. His wife was the producer and director of the Ebony Fashion Fair until her death in 2010.

Johnson died on August 8, 2005, and is buried in Chicago. In January 2012, the U.S. Postal Service released a first-class stamp honoring Johnson as part of its Black Heritage series.

Lottie Shackelford

(1941–)

Lottie Shackelford is a prominent African-American political leader who became the first female mayor of Little Rock and commanded leadership roles in the national Democratic Party for three decades. She was an Arkansas delegate to every Democratic National Convention from 1980 through 2012, often as a so-called super-delegate, and was chosen to be an automatic super-delegate for the 2016 convention. In addition, she was the longest-serving national vice chairman in the Democratic Party's history.

Lottie Lee Holt was born on April 30, 1941, in Little Rock, one of four children of Curtis Holt, Sr., and Bernice Linzy Holt. Her father was a porter and chef for the Union Pacific Railroad and a truck driver. Her mother worked in a school cafeteria and at an Ottenheimer Manufacturing Plant, which was one of the first Arkansas industries to employ African Americans in anything other than custodial jobs. She later worked as a laboratory assistant in the state milk-inspection program. Lottie Holt graduated in 1958 from Horace Mann High School, Little Rock's all-black high school at the time.

Intending to become a microbiologist, she enrolled at Philander Smith College, the school having developed a reputation in the sciences. When her father became ill and died in 1963, however,

she left school. In 1958, she married airman Calvin Henry Shackelford, Jr., of Little Rock and traveled with him to several assignments at U.S. Air Force bases. They eventually had a son and two daughters. They divorced in 1984.

She returned to Philander Smith when her oldest child was a senior in high school and received a bachelor's degree in business administration in 1979. She worked for the Urban League of Greater Little Rock; the Economic Opportunity Agency of Pulaski County (part of President Lyndon Johnson's War on Poverty); the Opportunities Industrialization Center, which was formed to promote job opportunities for African Americans; and the University of Arkansas for Medical Sciences as a computer laboratory specialist.

In 1974, she ran for a position on the Board of Directors for Little Rock in a citywide election; she finished third in a field of five. The seat was won by a white businessman. Four years later, the board appointed her to a vacant position for two years, and she ran for the seat in 1980 and won. It was the first time that a black candidate won a majority in a citywide race. She was re-elected twice, and in

1987 the board elected her as Little Rock's second black mayor. (In 1981, Charles Bussey had been elected the city's first.) As mayor (a position she held until 1991) she held leadership positions in the National League of Cities.

Shackelford became increasingly active in the Democratic Party in the 1980s, starting with her work in the campaigns of Bill Clinton and her selection as a delegate to the 1980 Democratic National Convention. She served as secretary, vice chairman, and chairman of the Democratic State Committee. She became a member of the Democratic National Committee in the early 1980s and served as a co-chairman of the Platform Committee of the Democratic National Convention in 1984 and co-chairman of the 1988 convention, as well as of its Rules Committee.

As the vice chairman of the Democratic National Committee starting in 1989 and continuing into the second decade of the twenty-first century, her roles evolved. As vice chairman for voter registration and participation in the early 1990s, Shackelford participated in political forums in several European and Asian countries and went to Balkan and Baltic countries to observe elections in emerging states after the breakup of the Soviet empire. In 1989, she embarked on a six-week lecture tour on women in politics in southern and western Africa.

Shackelford was deputy manager of Governor Bill Clinton's campaign for president in 1992 and a member of the president-elect's transition team. President Clinton appointed her as a U.S. delegate to the United Nations Commission on the Status of Women in Vienna, Austria, and as the first African-American woman to the board of directors of the Overseas Private Investment Corporation (OPIC), an independent federal agency that encourages U.S. businesses to invest in developing countries and gain footholds in emerging global markets with insurance and financing guarantees. In 1994, she became executive vice president of Global USA, Inc., an international business facilitator that promotes business opportunities in high-technology industrial sectors.

In 1998, she was a founder of the Women's Foundation of Arkansas, which is dedicated to the advancement of women in the state. In 2014, she led the Women's Caucus of the Democratic National Committee. Shackelford remains active in civic and political endeavors to this day.

1994

Evangeline K. Brown

Judge George Howard, Jr.

Ernest P. Joshua, Sr.

James McKissic

Art Porter, Sr.

Debbye Turner

Evangeline K. Brown

(1909–2001)

Evangeline K. Brown was a longtime educator and activist in the Arkansas Delta who served as a plaintiff and witness in a lawsuit that helped create new majority black districts in the state. She was inducted into the Arkansas Black Hall of Fame in 1994.

Evangeline Katherine Johnson was born in Norwood, East Feliciana Parish, Louisiana, on February 23, 1909, the fourth child of James M. Johnson and Mamie C. Gilmore Johnson. Her father was a farmer who owned the family's farm, which was fairly uncommon that time. The family frequently moved, and Johnson attended high schools in Portland, McGehee, and Dumas, Arkansas.

She eventually married and became a teacher, and settled in Dermott, Arkansas. She was chairman of the Teachers of English Council for the Arkansas Teachers Association, was a board member of the National Council of English Teachers for nine years, and served as president of the Arkansas Education Classroom Teachers Association and the Desha County Teachers Association.

Evangeline Brown was among the plaintiffs in the 1989 court case *Jeffers v. Clinton*. A federal court later ruled on behalf of the plaintiffs, finding that the state's 1982 redistricting plan had diluted black voting strength. Subsequently, the court ordered the creation of new majority black districts for the Arkansas House of Representatives and the Arkansas Senate. In the following election, the number of African Americans in the Arkansas General Assembly reached twelve—double what it had been.

Brown was active politically and was a local coordinator for Bill Clinton's 1990 gubernatorial campaign. She also coordinated the first Head Start program for Chicot County and served on the Southeast Community Action Board. An April 26, 1994, article in the *Arkansas Democrat-Gazette* described Brown as "the most outspoken black activist in Dermott." The article went on to say, "She is widely admired as a good-hearted person, but widely disliked for irritating the white establishment." An article the following year called her "the gadfly, the eternal campaigner, the apostle of desperate causes" and wrote of her: "Even when buying the poor's political support was an accepted arrangement in Chicot County, a place that places a high value on discretion and tradition, Brown assumed the role of loud disturber, railing against buyouts of hearts, souls, votes." In one of her noteworthy fights, she challenged the local hospital for refusing to provide rape examinations to African-American women.

Brown served as director of Dermott Concerned Citizens, which changed its name to Dermott Community Action, Inc., and formally incorporated in 1985. The nonprofit agency served low-income people in Dermott and surrounding communities. She was also a member of Seven Star Missionary Baptist Church and served in a variety of leadership roles. Over the span of her life, she reared more than forty foster children and received many awards for her community service. The Arkansas Women's Project offers its Evangeline K. Brown Award to someone who has "made a difference in the local and global community."

Brown died on September 22, 2001.

Judge George Howard, Jr.

(1924–2007)

George Howard, Jr., was a trailblazing African-American attorney and judge in the second half of the twentieth century. After becoming one of the first black graduates of the University of Arkansas School of Law, he pursued a career dedicated to the expansion and guarantee of civil rights for all citizens. He became the first African American to be appointed to numerous Arkansas judicial posts, including the Supreme Court of Arkansas.

George Howard, Jr., was born on May 13, 1924, in Pine Bluff, Arkansas, to George Howard and Sara Howard, who was a public school teacher. He received his early education in Pine Bluff but left home to serve in the U.S. Navy during World War II. As an adult, he would often recall that the racism he experienced in the navy led to his choice of a career in law. After the war, Howard returned to Pine Bluff and graduated from high school. He married Vivian Smith on February 8, 1947; they had four children.

Howard entered Lincoln University in Missouri in 1948, where he undertook a joint degree program. After he had achieved sixty credits he could transfer to the university's law school, and upon completion of his legal studies he would receive both a Bachelor of Arts degree and his law degree. However, his plans changed when he learned that the University of Arkansas (U of A) at Fayetteville, which had a similar dual degree program, was accepting applications from black students. Howard entered the university in 1950 and graduated in 1954 with both a bachelor's degree and his Juris Doctorate. Not only was he one of the law school's first black graduates, he was also the first African American to live in university housing. Moreover, he became the university's first elected black office holder when he was elected president of the dormitory.

Following graduation, Howard returned to Pine Bluff and opened a private law practice. He made one unsuccessful bid for the city council but put politics aside to become one of the city's leaders in the developing civil rights movement. He pursued numerous discrimination suits. Following the Supreme Court's ruling in *Brown v. Board of Education of Topeka, Kansas,* he initiated suits aimed at desegregating the school systems in Fort Smith, El Dorado, West Memphis, and other Arkansas districts. He was also active in efforts to desegregate theaters and other public places while also seeking to address the inequalities related to jury composition and the use of the death penalty in the criminal justice system.

Howard was also active on the organizational side, and he served as president of the State Council of Branches for the National Association for the Advancement of Colored People (NAACP). He then embarked on a string of judicial appointments. In 1969, Governor Winthrop Rockefeller appointed him to the Arkansas State Claims Commission. In 1977, Governor David Pryor named him to the Arkansas Supreme Court, on which he served until 1979 when Governor Bill Clinton appointed him to the newly created Arkansas Court of Appeals. The following year, President Jimmy Carter named him a federal district court judge for the Eastern and Western Districts of Arkansas, a position he held until his death in 2007. These appointments made him the first African American to serve on the Arkansas Court of Appeals, on the Arkansas Supreme Court, and as a judge in an Arkansas federal court.

As a jurist, Howard was known for his thorough preparation and his fairness. He became the object of national attention when he presided over the Whitewater trials involving former governor Jim Guy Tucker, Jim McDougal, and Susan McDougal, one-time business partners of President Bill Clinton. He also directed Clinton to give a deposition for the trial.

Judge Howard was still performing his duties when he died on April 21, 2007. He is buried in Graceland Cemetery in Pine Bluff. Shortly after his death, Congress enacted legislation naming the federal building and courthouse in Pine Bluff the George Howard, Jr., Federal Building and U.S. Courthouse.

Ernest P. Joshua, Sr.

(1928–2005)

Ernest P. Joshua, Sr., was an entrepreneur and founder of J. M. Products, Incorporated, which grew to become the largest black-owned company in Arkansas. The multimillion-dollar manufacturer of ethnic haircare products was one of the largest in the country.

Ernest Parnell Joshua was born on November 3, 1928, in northern Pulaski County. He was the son of Morris "Mars" Joshua and Mable Byrd Joshua. His mother died during his early teen years, and he was reared by his father.

He enlisted in the U.S. Army in 1946 at Jefferson Barracks in Missouri and was discharged in 1949. He married Thelma Lee Ready, a childhood acquaintance, that same year. He was later called back into the army, served from 1953 to 1956, and spent time in Korea. Ernest and Thelma Joshua had four children: Ernest Jr., Sandra, Michael, and Christopher.

Joshua received a business degree from Cortez Peters Business College of Chicago, Illinois, and took chemistry courses at the University of Chicago so that he could learn to mix chemicals to make his own hair products. He later received an honorary doctorate from Shorter College in North Little Rock, Arkansas.

Joshua spent thirty years in Chicago learning the haircare industry. He worked miscellaneous jobs in his early days, including being a waiter, pest

exterminator, and taxi and bus driver. While driving a taxi, he met fellow Arkansan John H. Johnson, publisher of *Ebony* and *Jet* magazines. He also met George Johnson, founder of Johnson Products, which manufactured the Ultra Sheen haircare line, and Fred Luster, who founded Luster Products in 1957. Johnson Products, Luster Products, J. M. Products, and other black haircare companies would eventually become part of the American Health and Beauty Aids Institute (AHBAI), a trade association founded in Chicago.

In the 1960s, Joshua helped to start Ravel Products in Chicago but sold his share of the company to his business partner. He also worked as a chemist and plant manager for Luster Products. In 1972, Joshua moved his family to Los Angeles, California, started another company, and sold his Isodine (which later became Isoplus) product to black salons door-to-door.

Due to illness, he moved back to his home state of Arkansas in 1977. For almost ten years, he expanded his company to include two manufacturing facilities in Little Rock and North Little Rock. The Little Rock facility was located at 3117 Peyton Street (off Asher Avenue); the street was later renamed Joshua Street.

In the 1980s, Joshua purchased a building for the J. M. Products headquarters. By 1989, renovations were under way on the brick building that once housed the Economic Opportunity Agency (EOA), located at 2501 South State Street.

The company's four original brands were Isoplus, Isoplus for Kids, UpTurn, and Oil of K. It also began carrying Black Magic, which was purchased in 1994 from American Beauty Products of Oklahoma. The products were distributed to major retailers across the country. His business eventually included operations in Jamaica, South Africa, and the United Kingdom.

Thelma Joshua, who co-founded J. M. Products with her husband, also owned Thelma's Beauty Academy (a cosmetology school located on State Street across from the company headquarters) and AfraJaMex (one of the first shops to open in the River Market district), which sold authentic handcrafted items from Africa, Jamaica, and Mexico.

In the 1980s, Joshua began to gain recognition for his entrepreneurship. Governor Bill Clinton honored him for his contributions to the state, and in 1986, Joshua was chosen as the Arkansas Small Business Person of the Year. Joshua and his wife were honored at the White House by President Ronald Regan for their achievements in business. In 1987, the Greater Little Rock Chamber of Commerce presented Joshua with its first Pinnacle Award. That same year, he was runner-up for the U.S. Small Business Person of the Year. In 1994, President Bill Clinton invited him to participate in the first U.S. Trade Mission to South Africa.

By 2002, Joshua, who was chief executive officer, was semi-retired from the family-operated company, leaving his son Michael Joshua to run the day-to-day operations as president and general manager.

Ernest Joshua, Sr., died on September 22, 2005, and is buried in Arkansas State Veterans Cemetery in Sherwood. He was posthumously elected into the Arkansas Business Hall of Fame in 2007.

James McKissic

(1940–2013)

James McKissic was a world-renowned pianist from Pine Bluff, Arkansas, who spent much of his life in France but performed throughout the world, including more than two dozen events at Carnegie Hall in New York.

James Henry "Jimmy" McKissic was born on March 16, 1940, in Little Rock, Arkansas, to the Reverend James E. McKissic and Rosa Daniels McKissic; he had five brothers and five sisters, including one sister who was adopted. He grew up in Pine Bluff and could play the piano by the age of three. He played in his father's church and for other local congregations as a youth; his mother taught him until he was thirteen, when he began studying under a professional instructor. After graduating from Merrill High School in 1957, he attended Arkansas Agricultural, Mechanical, and Normal (AM&N) College—now the University of Arkansas at Pine Bluff (UAPB)—and graduated with a bachelor's degree in music in 1962.

He went on to graduate school and studied with noted concert pianist Marjorie Petray, who was then teaching at the University of California at Berkeley. After graduation, the chair of the music department offered him a job teaching chamber music. In 1969, he received the prestigious Hertz Scholarship to undertake additional study in Geneva, Switzerland. At the end of the scholarship, he moved to Paris, France, where he worked for two years doing youth programs at the American Church—a Protestant, English-speaking congregation serving expatriates. He established residency in the French city of Cannes and played at a piano bar there. From 1984 to 2007, he was the pianist for the Hotel Martinez in Cannes. The following year, he moved to Singapore, where he lived and worked at the Hotel Raffles. McKissic's talents made him a popular entertainer throughout the world, and he played in such places as Brazil, Kenya, and Thailand, in addition to various European locales. McKissic performed at Carnegie Hall in New York twenty-eight times (his first appearance was in 1986) and was the subject of the 1989 documentary *How Do You Get to Carnegie Hall?* In 2010, he released the album *Bless This House*, a collection of hymns.

McKissic was known for his wild dress, especially his trademark mismatched shoes, as well as for regularly giving free concerts. Many such concerts were held in Pine Bluff, where he often returned. He performed the works of Robert Schumann at Trinity United Methodist Church in Pine Bluff on September 12, 2010, and moved back to Pine Bluff the following year. He donated his extensive music collection to the Department of Music at UAPB.

McKissic died on February 13, 2013. A scholarship at UAPB was named in his honor.

Art Porter, Sr.

(1934–1993)

Art Porter, Sr., referred to as an "Arkansas treasure," was a pianist, composer, conductor, and music teacher. Though best known as a jazz musician, he also performed classical compositions and spirituals. Some of his more memorable performances include two gubernatorial inaugurations for Governor Bill Clinton. Joined by Art Porter, Jr., on saxophone, he performed at President Clinton's Inaugural Interfaith Prayer Service in January 1993 at one of the inaugural receptions in Washington, D.C. Porter was also responsible for entertaining many heads of state who visited Arkansas during the tenure of governors Dale Bumpers, David Pryor, and Jim Guy Tucker.

Arthur Lee "Art" Porter was born on February 8, 1934, in Little Rock, Arkansas, to Eugene Porter, Sr., a stonemason, and Lillie Mae Porter. He was the younger of two children. Porter began his music education at home with his mother. He played in church at age eight; played his first recital at twelve; and, by fourteen, hosted a half-hour classical music radio program on KLRA-AM. He earned a bachelor's degree in music from Arkansas Agricultural, Mechanical, and Normal (AM&N) College (now the University of Arkansas at Pine Bluff—UAPB) in May 1954. He married Thelma Pauline Minton on June 10, 1955. They spent their honeymoon in graduate study at the University of Illinois in Urbana in 1955. Porter continued his graduate study at the University of Texas at Austin in 1974 and earned a master's degree in music from Henderson State University (HSU) in Arkadelphia, Arkansas, in 1975.

Porter began his teaching career at Mississippi Valley State University in Itta Bena, Mississippi, in 1954 immediately after college graduation. After two years, he was drafted into the U.S. Army. His extraordinary musical talent on the organ and piano, along with his extensive repertoire of church music, was immediately recognized during his basic training. Consequently, he spent the next two years as a chaplain's assistant in Fort Niagara, New York.

Porter returned to Little Rock in the late 1950s and spent the next twelve years teaching vocal music at Horace Mann High School, Parkview High School, and Philander Smith College. Porter supplemented his income by playing piano jazz in the evenings, sometimes as a single but most of the time with his group, the Art Porter Trio. The trio was in great demand, especially for weddings, country club affairs, and city and state social affairs. Porter entertained all over the state and in surrounding states. He was once asked to play for the dedication of the ship *Arkansas* in Virginia Beach, Virginia. Singer Tony Bennett, during a two-week stay in Hot Springs, Arkansas, sat in with the Art Porter Trio and performed every night. Other entertainers, such as Liberace, Julius La Rosa, and Art Van Dam, often dropped by to join in and enjoy the trio's music.

By 1971, Porter's popularity was soaring. From 1971 to 1981, he hosted *The Minor Key*, a musical talent showcase on the Arkansas Educational Television Network (AETN), and *Porterhouse Cuts*, a syndicated series featuring the Art Porter Trio that was shown in a thirteen-state area in the South. Porter was approached many times to tour, but he declined. As he once said, "I don't like to travel, especially all the time." He made a couple of exceptions to travel in 1977 to the World Black and African Festival of Arts and Culture in Lagos, Nigeria, and in 1991 with his son, jazz saxophonist Art Porter, Jr., to jazz festivals in Germany, Belgium, and the Netherlands.

Despite Porter's popularity as a jazz pianist, he found time to pursue his interest in classical music. He was featured as a guest artist on piano as he performed with both the Arkansas Symphony Orchestra in Little Rock and the Northwestern Symphony Orchestra in Fort Smith, Arkansas. In 1976, Porter organized his former vocal music students as the Art Porter Singers to perform Handel's *Messiah* at his church, the Bethel African Methodist Episcopal (A.M.E.) Church in Little Rock. The Art Porter Singers remain together and are dedicated to continuing the legacy of Porter's service by performing throughout the years whenever they are invited to do so; they perform the *Messiah* each Christmas season.

Porter's music found continued expression in the performances of four of his children in their group Benkenartreg, Inc. The name is composed of the first three letters of each of the members' names: Benita, Kenneth, Art Jr., and Reginald. A fifth child, Sean Porter, also inherited his father's talent on organ and piano. Porter's musical legacy

was passed on to Art Porter, Jr., whose career, expressed in four albums, ended with his accidental death on November 23, 1996.

Though Porter received many honors and awards, he found particular satisfaction in the "Art Porter Bill" enacted by the state legislature, which allowed minors to perform in clubs while under adult supervision. Porter's children thus were able to perform with him throughout the state. Governor Bill Clinton, at the time a huge fan and friend of Porter, often joined Porter's group on his saxophone.

Porter died on July 22, 1993, of lung cancer. He was eulogized at Bethel, where he had been the organist for thirty-five years. He is buried at Little Rock National Cemetery. A newspaper article noted that Porter's "natural gifts" were "polished by intelligence, flawless phrasing, and good taste…with modesty."

Debbye Turner

(1965–)

Debbye Turner, who grew up in Jonesboro, Arkansas, was crowned Miss America 1990. After her reign as Miss America, she became a veterinarian. She has appeared on national television and is a motivational speaker on youth-related and Christian topics.

Debrah Lynn "Debbye" Turner was born on September 19, 1965, in Honolulu, Hawaii, to Gussie Turner and Frederick Turner, Jr., who was stationed there in the military. As a child, she set her goal to become a veterinarian but recognized the financial challenges ahead, especially after her parents' divorce. Living in Jonesboro with her sister, Suzette, and her mother, who became an academic counselor at Arkansas State University (ASU), Turner took a fast-food job at age sixteen and later became a department store clerk and grocery store cashier. She graduated from Jonesboro High School in 1983. In 1986, she graduated cum laude from ASU with a Bachelor of Science degree in agriculture. Still intent on becoming a veterinarian, she followed a path toward a scholarship which had begun several years earlier: beauty pageants.

Her first pageant had been Miss Black Teenage World in 1981, and she was first runner-up. She won the title of Northeast Arkansas Junior Miss that same year and was a semi-finalist in the 1982 Arkansas Junior Miss pageant. In 1983, she won the Jonesboro High School Valentines Sweetheart pageant, after which she was approached by the director of the Miss Jonesboro pageant, who encouraged her to enter that competition as her first pageant in the Miss America system. Turner was interested because the Miss America scholarship program was the largest source of scholarships in the world for young women. She placed as second- and first runner-up, respectively, in the Miss Jonesboro pageants of 1983 and 1984.

Turner then won three local pageants—Miss Arkansas State University (1985), Miss White River (1986), and Miss Northeast Arkansas (1987)—through which she went to the Miss Arkansas pageant three times and finished twice as first runner-up.

She entered graduate school in 1988 as a vet-erinary student at the University of Missouri at Columbia, thus becoming eligible for the Miss Missouri system. Turner won the Miss Columbia pageant in February 1989; won the Miss Missouri pageant that summer; and went in September to Atlantic City, New Jersey, where she was crowned Miss America 1990 and became the first delegate from Missouri to win the title.

After her reign as Miss America, she achieved her goal of becoming a veterinarian when she graduated from the University of Missouri in 1991 with a Doctorate of Veterinary Medicine. Since then, she has added other roles, including television host on the PBS series *The Gentle Doctor* (1995–98) and as a regular guest discussing animal issues on CBS's *The Early Show*. She received an Emmy nomination for her own regional program, *Show Me St. Louis* (1995–2001). She does not currently practice veterinary medicine; but as a motivational speaker, she continues to carry her message about responsible pet ownership, education, and personal achievement around the world.

In 1998, she was named a Distinguished Alumna of ASU, where she established the Debbye Turner Scholarship and the Gussie Turner Memorial Scholarship in memory of her mother. She has spoken to hundreds of thousands of people at hundreds of schools, youth organizations, and college commencement ceremonies, including Auburn, Cornell, and Notre Dame. She has hosted the Miss Missouri, Miss Florida, and Miss Georgia pageants and appeared as a guest on such television programs as *The Late Show with David Letterman*, *Oprah*, and the *Today* show.

She has served on local, state, and national boards, including the Children's Miracle Network, the National Council on Youth Leadership, and the National Advisory Child Health and Human Development Council (part of the National Institutes of Health). She resides in New York City and has completed both the New York Marathon and the Los Angeles Marathon. She married Gerald Bell in 2008; the couple has a daughter.

1995

Hubert "Geese" Ausbie

Lt. Col. Woodrow W. Crockett

Joycelyn Elders, MD

Ethel and James Kearney

Robert McFerrin, Sr.

William Grant Still

Hubert "Geese" Ausbie

(1938–)

Hubert "Geese" Ausbie joined the Harlem Globetrotters basketball team in 1961 following a standout college career at Philander Smith College in Little Rock, Arkansas. For the next twenty-four years, Ausbie played for the Globetrotters in more than 100 countries and became known as the "Clown Prince of Basketball" for his entertaining antics on the basketball court.

Hubert Ausbie was born in Crescent, Oklahoma, on April 25, 1938. He was one of eight children and the youngest son of Bishop and Nancy Ausbie. As a youth, Ausbie excelled in baseball, basketball, tennis, and track. He once scored seventy points in a basketball game for Crescent's Douglas High School and helped lead Douglas to four straight Oklahoma Basketball State Championships.

He graduated from high school in 1956 and had his choice of more than 200 athletic scholarship offers from major colleges. He accepted a basketball scholarship from Philander Smith College because of its religious affiliation and also because his brother Attaway was already a student there. During his senior year (1959–1960), he was named to the all-conference and several all-American basketball teams and finished the year as the third-leading scorer in the nation.

While at Philander Smith, Ausbie met Awilda Lee. They were later married and had four children.

Following his graduation from Philander Smith in 1960, Ausbie turned down a professional baseball contract with the Chicago Cubs and chose to travel to Chicago, Illinois, to try out for the Harlem Globetrotters basketball team, despite interest from the NBA's Cincinnati Royals and Los Angeles Lakers. The Globetrotters travel the world and have entertained millions with a combination of comic routines, basketball skill, and showmanship. In 1961, Ausbie was chosen from an open tryout of more than 500 players from around the country to join the Globetrotters.

Ausbie had been called "Goose" since childhood, but his nickname was changed to "Geese" when he joined the Globetrotters because they had been led for many years by another "Goose" from Arkansas, Reece "Goose" Tatum.

Because of his basketball skills and natural flair for visual humor, Ausbie was known as the "Clown Prince of Basketball" for his entire playing career with the Globetrotters, which continued until his retirement as a player in 1985. He shared center stage on the basketball court with two other popular Globetrotter players, Meadowlark Lemon and Curly Neal. In 1978, Lemon left the Globetrotters, and Ausbie became the lead entertainer of the team.

During Ausbie's career, the Harlem Globetrotters expanded into televised entertainment. They appeared frequently on *ABC's Wide World of Sports*, had their own Saturday morning cartoon show, starred in the live-action children's show *The Harlem Globetrotters Popcorn Machine*, and co-starred in the movie *The Harlem Globetrotters on Gilligan's Island*.

Ausbie was inducted into the Arkansas Sports Hall of Fame in 1990. In 1994, he received the Globetrotters' Legends Ring for his outstanding contributions.

He and his wife live in Little Rock, and he speaks to young people in Arkansas through the Drug-Free Youth Program. On January 31, 2017, the Globetrotters retired Ausbie's jersey, No. 35, in a halftime ceremony at Verizon Arena in North Little Rock, Arkansas.

Lt. Col. Woodrow W. Crockett

(1918–2012)

Miller County native Woodrow W. Crockett served as a combat pilot in both World War II and the Korean War. He entered the service as an artilleryman, transferred to Alabama's Tuskegee Institute as an aviation cadet, and became one of the pilots of the famous Tuskegee Airmen. Crockett remained in the service of his country for twenty-eight years.

Woodrow Wilson Crockett was born on August 31, 1918, in Homan, Arkansas. Nicknamed "Woody" as a child, he was the fifth of six children born to school teachers William Crockett and Lucindan Crockett. He grew up in Texarkana, Arkansas, and then lived with his sister in Little Rock in order to attend Dunbar High School. After he graduated from Dunbar High in 1939, he spent some time at Dunbar Junior College before he left in August 1940 to join the army. He became a soldier in the 349th Field Artillery Regiment, the first African-American field artillery unit in the regular army.

Crockett transferred to Tuskegee Institute in August 1942 and became an aviation cadet. After graduation, he was commissioned as a second lieu-

tenant on March 25, 1943, in class 43C, the twelfth class at Tuskegee Army Air Field. Crockett was the second Arkansas fighter pilot to graduate from the program for cadets. He served in the 100th Fighter Squadron and the 332nd Fighter Interceptor Group. While stationed in Italy between 1944 and 1945, he flew 149 combat missions in fifteen months. As a member of the Twenty-fifth Air Division, Crockett was stationed at various U.S. air force bases.

During the Korean conflict, Major Crockett completed forty-five missions, and he received numerous awards and accolades. During his military career, Crockett served at various times as a radiological safety officer, a flying safety officer, and a squadron commander. He was a member of a B-17 crew and was airborne during atomic bomb tests in the Marshall Islands.

In 1958, Crockett was the assistant test director for the F-106 Category II Test Program at Edwards Air Force Base in California. On June 2, 1959, Crockett gained some acclaim when he became a member of a select group of early pilots to fly at Mach 2 speeds. For a brief period, he was assigned to the North Atlantic Treaty Organization (NATO) in Oslo, Norway.

After nearly three decades of military service, Crockett retired in 1970 with more than 5,000 hours of flight time and 520 combat hours. Crockett was a graduate of the U.S. Air Force Command and Staff College. During his military service, he received many awards, including the Distinguished Flying Cross, the Presidential Unit Citation, and two soldier's medals for bravery for extricating pilots from their burning fighter aircraft in 1944 in Italy and in 1953 in Korea. Crockett also received the Air Medal with four oak leaf clusters, the Meritorious Service Medal, the Army Commendation Medal, and the Air Force Commendation Medal with one oak leaf cluster. He retired with the rank of lieutenant colonel.

In 1992, Crockett became the first African American elected to the Arkansas Aviation Hall of Fame. In 1994, he traveled to Europe with President Bill Clinton during events surrounding the fiftieth anniversary of the D-Day invasion during World War II, where he visited the Wall of Missing Airmen at the Cambridge American Cemetery and Memorial in England.

He was awarded an honorary doctorate degree from the University of Arkansas at Little Rock in 2001. He lived for many years in Annandale, Virginia, and became an avid tennis player after he retired. Crockett's wife, Daisy Juanita McMurray Crockett, with whom he had three daughters and a son, died in 2000. In his last years, he suffered from Alzheimer's disease. He died on August 16, 2012, at the Knollwood Military Retirement Community in Washington, D.C. He was buried with honors at Arlington National Cemetery. His World War II flight suit is a part of the collection of the National Museum of African American History and Culture in Washington, D.C.

✦ ✦ ✦

Joycelyn Elders, MD

(1933–)

Joycelyn Elders was director of the Arkansas Department of Health and the U.S. Surgeon General in the administration of President Bill Clinton. In Arkansas, she led the way in raising public awareness of the AIDS epidemic and promoting sex education for children. However, her controversial opinions led to her resignation after just over a year as U.S. Surgeon General.

Joycelyn Elders was born Minnie Lee Jones on August 13, 1933, in Schaal, Arkansas. She took the name Joycelyn while she was in college. The eldest of Curtis and Haller Jones's eight children, she spent much of her childhood working in cotton fields. From an early age, Jones showed considerable academic ability. In 1949, she earned a scholarship to Philander Smith College in Little Rock, Arkansas. She was the first in her family to attend college, and she initially intended to become a lab technician.

After attending a lecture by Edith Irby Jones, the first woman to attend the University of Arkansas Medical School (now the University of Arkansas for Medical Sciences), Jones decided to become a physician. Upon graduating from Philander Smith in 1952, she was briefly married to Cornelius Reynolds, whom she later divorced. The following year, she joined the U.S. Army's Medical Specialist Corps and served in Milwaukee, Wis-

consin. In 1956, she entered the University of Arkansas Medical School on the G.I. Bill. In 1960, she married Oliver Elders, whom she had met in Little Rock while performing physical exams for the Horace Mann High School basketball team he coached. The couple has two sons.

In 1961, after a brief internship at the University of Minnesota, Elders returned to Little Rock for her residency and was soon appointed chief pediatric resident. She specialized in pediatric endocrinology. She has also published dozens of scholarly papers, primarily on juvenile diabetes. In these years, Elders became an advocate for issues regarding adolescent sexuality, particularly teen pregnancy and contraception, topics that garnered her considerable acclaim, as well as scorn. By the 1980s, twenty percent of children born in Arkansas were the offspring of teenage mothers, a problem that Governor Bill Clinton considered a social and fiscal crisis. In 1987, he named Elders director of the Arkansas Department of Health.

As head of the health department, Elders instituted a controversial program to dispense contraceptives to public school students, a plan that drew fire from conservatives. As she began to establish public-school health clinics to distribute condoms and promote public awareness of AIDS and teen pregnancy, social conservatives increasingly attacked her as implicitly sanctioning abortion, a charge she denied. In 1989, largely at the behest of Elders, the legislature mandated a kindergarten-through-twelfth-grade sex education program that focused on personal responsibility, hygiene, and substance abuse prevention, issues she recognized as often being linked.

In January 1993, President-elect Clinton nominated Elders to the post of U.S. Surgeon General, tapping her as the second African American for a Cabinet-level position. Conservatives immediately mounted opposition to her nomination, particularly on the grounds that her views on abortion—especially her support for the controversial RU-486 abortion pill—were too radical for mainstream Americans. Despite considerable Republican opposition, Elders drew the support of former surgeon general C. Everett Koop and the endorsement of the American Medical Association. On September 7, 1993, after a heated confirmation process, the Senate confirmed her by a vote of sixty-five to thirty-four.

As surgeon general, Dr. Elders focused on several big health issues: tobacco-related disease, AIDS, and alcohol and drug abuse; she also continued her advocacy for sex education. In the fall of 1993, she drew fire for suggesting that the legalization of drugs such as cocaine and heroin should be studied; her opponents claimed that she supported the legalization of all drugs. Her views on drug policy drew increasing criticism in light of her son Kevin's public struggles with cocaine addiction. Moreover, her statements at the United Nations' 1994 World AIDS Day sparked widespread criticism and led to her resignation. During the conference, Elders said, "With regard to masturbation, I think it is something that is a part of human sexuality and a part of something that should perhaps be taught." Republicans had just regained a congressional majority on the strength of their Contract with America program. The political climate had changed considerably since her confirmation, and Clinton—facing stiff opposition to all of his policies—asked Elders to resign.

After 1994, Elders served as a faculty researcher at the University of Arkansas for Medical Sciences and lectured extensively on public health issues. In 1996, she published her autobiography, *Joycelyn El-*

ders, MD: From Sharecropper's Daughter to Surgeon General of the United States. She continues to promote sex education; and she views abstinence and "Just Say No" programs as myopic and unrealistic. After retiring from medicine in 1999, Elders returned to Little Rock, where she remains an outspoken proponent of public health education and has continued to speak on issues such as AIDS, adolescent sexuality, and national health care. She was inducted into the Arkansas Women's Hall of Fame in 2016.

James Kearney
(1906–2013)
Ethel Kearney
(1917–1982)

Thomas James (called James or "T. J.") Kearney and his wife, Ethel Virginia Curry Kearney, were cotton sharecroppers who were recognized for their contributions to childhood education and Christian service by the state of Arkansas; Johnson Publishing Company of Chicago, Illinois; President William J. Clinton; and the country of Israel. Of the couple's nineteen children, eighteen were college graduates, and a number of them served the state of Arkansas and the U.S. government in leadership roles.

T. J. Kearney, one of nine siblings, was born on June 25, 1906, to Thomas Clayton (T. C.) Kearney and Cynthia Davis Kearney in Lake Village, Arkansas. His parents were farmers. It is believed that both T. C. and Cynthia were the children of slaves. Cynthia is believed to have grown up in Lake Village and T. C. in Mississippi or Louisiana. They married on October 6, 1901, in Lake Village and began their lives as itinerant farmers, moving often throughout Chicot, Lincoln, and Jefferson counties.

T. C. Kearney died during the Flu Epidemic of 1918 at the age of forty-six. T. J. Kearney was only eleven at the time of his father's death. He began his life of "traveling the world" that same year—first, in nearby cities and towns and, later, to every region of

the country, working as an itinerant farmer in fruit orchards, as a chauffeur on a ranch, as a cook in a Greek restaurant in Chicago, and on the railroads throughout the country. He also hired himself out as a mercenary worker on ships that sailed as far away as Cuba and Liverpool, England. In 1926, T. J. married Temperance Watson of Plum Bayou, Arkansas; they were both about twenty-one. They had one child. The marriage ended in 1937.

Ethel Curry was born on February 4, 1917, in Magnolia, Arkansas, to the farming family of Luther Curry and Mattie Emma Russ Curry; Luther and Mattie, who was a native of rural Columbia County, had married in 1913. Luther's parents, Ned Curry and Priscilla Watson Curry, had been born into slavery—Ned in 1833 and Priscilla around 1847. They are believed to have married shortly before the Emancipation Proclamation set them free. Ned died in 1894 at the age of sixty-one. Priscilla died at eighty-three in 1926. The former slaves sought to rear their son Luther and his twelve siblings to fear God, to work hard, and to strive for an education. The couple had ten children who survived to adulthood—two died in infancy and one at the age of seventeen. Luther Curry died at the age of eighty-three in 1969. Mattie Emma Curry died at the age of ninety-nine in 1989.

Ethel's childhood was more traditional than her husband's. Each of her siblings graduated from grammar school in Union County and then attended high school in another town. Ethel was not allowed to attend high school. Her first child was born in 1934.

Thomas James Kearney and Ethel Virginia Curry met in December 1936 at a community "hog killing" in Pastoria, Arkansas. He was thirty years old, while she was nineteen. They married on March 17, 1937. The Kearney family resided for more than seventy-five years on Varner Road, eight miles north of the city of Gould, Arkansas. Ethel attained her GED certificate at the age of fifty at Gould High School, the school where most of her children received their high school diplomas.

T. J. and Ethel Kearney were recognized throughout the southeastern Arkansas region for their non-traditional roles of childhood educators, who taught their children the rudiments of education well before they set foot in their segregated and substandard schools. They were also religious leaders in their community and served in various roles—such as deacon, teacher, usher, women's missionary president, laymen president, and Sunday school superintendent—at Rankin Chapel Church during their decades-long membership. They also co-led the Parent Teacher Association at Fields High School, where their children attended school.

In spite of their poverty, the Kearney children were high achievers, who attended colleges and universities such as Harvard, Yale, Brown, Stanford, Syracuse, and Vanderbilt, as well as the University of Arkansas (U of A) at Fayetteville. Two served in the Clinton administration—Jude Kearney was deputy assistant director for international finance for the U.S. Secretary of Commerce, and Janis F. Kearney was the first person ever to be appointed as personal diarist to a U.S. president. Other Kearney siblings have served as federal and local judges, lawyers, city administrators, and educators.

In 1989, John H. Johnson of *Ebony* magazine recognized the family as outstanding based on the number of college graduates in the family. In 1999, President Clinton invited Thomas James Kearney to the White House to recognize his ninety-third birthday. Upon his death, the Jewish National Fund planted a tree in memory of Thomas James Kearney in the Coretta Scott King Forest in the Galilee region of northern Israel. The tree was planted "in memory of Thomas James 'T. J.' Kearney, family patriarch, bible scholar, and man of wisdom and peace."

Ethel Kearney died at the age of sixty-four on March 19, 1982. James Kearney died on December 29, 2013, at the age of 107. They are both buried in Union Cemetery in Gould.

Robert McFerrin, Sr.

(1921–2006)

Robert McFerrin, Sr., was an African-American baritone opera and concert singer. Fewer than three weeks after contralto Marian Anderson broke the color barrier there, McFerrin became the first black male to appear in an opera at the Metropolitan Opera House in New York City. However, McFerrin's career at the Met was brief, in that he was limited to ten performances in three seasons over three years. Although he sang in European opera houses and performed concerts extensively, he failed to attain major prominence. He is best remembered as the father of singer and conductor Bobby McFerrin, with whom he sometimes performed.

Robert McFerrin was born on March 19, 1921, in Marianna, Arkansas, to Melvin McFerrin, a minister, and Mary McKinney McFerrin. He had seven siblings. McFerrin showed musical talent at an early age. The family moved to Memphis, Tennessee, when he was two, and he completed eight grades there. A talented siffleur (whistler), he joined a family gospel-singing trio at age thirteen. His father arranged for him to attend Sumner High School in St. Louis, Missouri. McFerrin intended to become an English teacher but changed his career plans after he joined the high school choir and received his first formal music instruction under chorus director Wirt Walton.

After he graduated from high school in 1940, McFerrin was accepted at Fisk University in Nashville, Tennessee. He stayed only one year. In 1941, after he won a singing contest, he entered Chicago Musical College, where he studied under George Graham. In 1942, he won first prize in the Chicagoland Music Festival. After he was drafted and served in the army, he returned to college. In 1948, he moved to New York, where he became a student of Hall Johnson, a prominent figure in Afro-American music. He married Sara Copper in 1949; she was a Howard University graduate and singer who gave up her career to further his. She was also a polio victim and was in an iron lung while pregnant with their son Robert Jr. "Bobby," one of their two children.

McFerrin's New York career began in 1949 with a small part in Kurt Weill's *Lost in the Stars*. His performance attracted the attention of Boris Goldovsky, who gave him a scholarship to study at the Tanglewood Opera Theatre outside Boston. In 1949 he made his operatic debut in Giuseppe Verdi's *Rigoletto*. He then joined Goldovsky's touring company, where he added roles in Charles Gounod's *Faust* and Christoph Willibald Gluck's *Iphigenie en Tauride*. In addition, he sang with the National Negro Opera Company in Verdi's *Aida* and at the New York City Center Opera Company in the world premiere of William Grant Still's *Troubled Island*. Finally, he returned to Broadway for a revival of *Green Pastures* in 1951 and the following year for some performances in *My Darlin' Aida*, an updated version of the Verdi opera set in Memphis in 1861.

In 1953 urged on by his manager, he entered the Metropolitan Opera's "Auditions of the Air," which he won. Usually, the winner received a contract and six months of training. In McFerrin's case, he received no contract, and his training lasted for thirteen months. McFerrin did not object and later lauded the program for teaching him fencing, ballet, and other aspects of stage deportment.

The second African American and first black male to sing at the Metropolitan Opera, McFerrin debuted on January 27, 1955, when he was cast as Amonasro in *Aida*. Racial politics rather than sound musical values dictated his being cast as Amonasro. The black Ethiopian king (and father of Aida) has no love duets to sing with white women. At five foot seven inches tall and 140 pounds, the young McFerrin was hardly prepossessing on stage as an evil father-figure. His voice was not displayed to its best advantage. In addition, prior to the performance, he had never met the evening's female leads, Aida (Herva Nelli) or Amneris (Blanche Thebom).

McFerrin found that he preferred the audiences in Town Hall recitals. He eventually sang only ten performances at the Metropolitan Opera. He did, however, record excerpts from *Rigoletto* in 1956 for the Metropolitan Opera Club. In addition, there exists a 1956 recording taken from a live broadcast of *Aida* from Naples, Italy. In 1958, he went to Hollywood to supply the vocals for Sidney Poitier's Porgy in the motion picture version of George Gershwin's *Porgy and Bess*. McFerrin and his wife decided to remain in California, where they became music teachers. In 1973, following their divorce, McFerrin moved back to St. Louis, where he lived until his death. In 1989, he suffered a stroke that affected his speaking but not his singing. He occasionally performed with his son Bobby and his daughter Brenda. In 1994, he and William Warfield appeared in a Schiller Institute concert.

"I am not attempting to carry the load for all Negro singers," McFerrin had told the *New York Post* prior to his debut, but in reality the load he had to carry transcended vocal concerns. One major reason for his truncated career was management's fear of the reaction of audiences to seeing black males on stage as husbands or lovers of white females.

McFerrin died on November 24, 2006, in St. Louis. He is buried in Jefferson Barracks National Cemetery.

William Grant Still

(1895–1978)

William Grant Still grew up in Little Rock, Arkansas, and achieved national and international acclaim as a composer of symphonic and popular music. As an African American, he broke race barriers and opened opportunities for other minorities. He was a strong advocate for the performance of works by American composers.

William Grant Still was born on May 11, 1895, in Woodville, Mississippi, the only son of William Grant Still, Sr., and Carrie Lena Fambro Still. Still's mother moved to Little Rock with her infant son shortly after the death of her husband in 1895. Still and his mother lived with his grandmother, and his mother was a teacher. In 1904, his mother married a railway postal clerk, Charles Benjamin Shepperson, whose own interest in music influenced the young Still. With Shepperson's support, he studied violin in 1908 with American violinist William Price, who lived for a short time in Little Rock.

Still attended M. W. Gibbs High School in Little Rock and graduated in 1911 as class valedictorian. That fall, he enrolled at Wilberforce University in Ohio (which was supported by the African Methodist Episcopal Church), where his mother hoped he would pursue studies in medicine. His preference to pursue a career in music caused him to leave Wilberforce in 1915 to play in bands and orchestras in Ohio; he did not graduate.

On October 4, 1915, he married Grace Bundy. The couple had four children, but the marriage ended in divorce in 1939.

In 1916, Still was in Memphis, Tennessee, where he met blues musician W. C. Handy, who provided him with the opportunity to arrange and perform with his band. The next year, he entered the Oberlin Conservatory of Music in Ohio to pursue a formal education in music. Still's education was interrupted by World War I, when he served in the U.S. Navy. He served as a mess hall attendant and violinist for officers' meals. He returned to Oberlin after his discharge but did not receive a degree. Instead, in 1919, he moved to Harlem in New York City, where he worked for the Pace and Handy Music Publishing Company and performed with bands and orchestras. He also studied music with George Whitefield Chadwick, director of the New England Conservatory of Music, and Edgard Varese, the French modernist. These diverse experiences provided Still with professional contacts and valuable insight to performing, arranging, orchestrating, and composing popular and symphonic music.

From the Black Belt (1926), *From the Land of Dreams* (1924), *Darker America* (1924–1925), *From the Journal of a Wanderer* (1924), *La Guiablesse* (1926–1927), and *Levee Land* (1925) are among the noteworthy works Still composed during his developmental period. *The Afro-American Symphony*, completed in 1930 and first performed in 1931 by the Rochester Philharmonic Orchestra under conductor Howard Hanson, is Still's most well-known composition. It was the first symphony composed by an African American that was performed by a major orchestra, and it is still performed today. Hanson later conducted many of Still's compositions as part of Hanson's American Composers' Concerts in Rochester and also in Europe, where he conducted programs of American music.

While living in New York, Still met Paul Whiteman, who hired him to arrange music. When Whiteman took his orchestra to Hollywood, California, in May 1929, Still went, too. During the course of a year, he completed more than 100 arrangements for Whiteman. Whiteman later commissioned Still to create original compositions, including *A Deserted Plantation* (1933), *Beyond Tomorrow* (1936), *Land of Superstition* (1933), *Ebon Chronicle* (1934), *Down Yonder* (circa 1935), and *Blues from Lennox Avenue* (circa 1937). Still moved permanently to Los Angeles, California, in 1934.

The 1930s and 1940s proved to be quite successful for Still, as major orchestras increasingly performed his compositions. The Chicago Symphony Orchestra performed La Guiablesse, written for the ballet, on June 16, 1933. On November 20, 1935, the New York Philharmonic performed Still's *Afro-American Symphony* at Carnegie Hall. Leopold Stokowski and the Philadelphia Symphony premiered his *Symphony in G Minor* on December 10, 1937. Still wrote the theme music for the 1939–1940 New York World's Fair. *Song of a City*, once recorded, was played 31,857 times at the fair, according to *New Yorker* magazine. The New York Philharmonic first performed *And They Lynched Him on a Tree* on June 24, 1940, at Lewisohn Stadium. The New York Philharmonic also premiered *Plain-Chant for America* on October 23, 1941, and *The Colored Soldiers Who Died for Democracy* on January 5, 1944, both at Carnegie Hall. The Cleveland Orchestra premiered *Poem for Orchestra* on December 7, 1944, and the Cincinnati Symphony Orchestra premiered *Festive Overture* on January 19, 1945. The opera *Troubled Island*, with a libretto by poet Langston Hughes, was premiered by the New York City Opera Company on March 31, 1949.

Two days after his divorce from Grace Bundy on February 6, 1939, he married Verna Arvey in Mexico where interracial marriages were legal. Arvey was an accomplished pianist and excellent writer, talents that served her husband well for over forty years. They had two children.

Still's compositions include symphonies, ballets, operas, chamber music, and works for solo instruments. Together, they number almost 200 pieces. His lengthy list of honors and awards includes the William E. Harmon Award for Distinguished Achievement among Negroes in Music in 1928; the Guggenheim Fellowship in 1934, 1935, and 1938; the Julius Rosenwald Foundation Fellowship in 1939 and 1940; and a Freedoms Foundation Award in 1953. He received honorary degrees from the following institutions: Wilberforce University in 1936; Howard University in 1941; Oberlin College in 1947; Bates College in 1954; University of Arkansas in 1971; Pepperdine University in 1973; Peabody Conservatory of Music in 1974; and the University of Southern California in 1975.

Still's health began to decline in 1970. He spent his last years in a convalescent home and died in Los Angeles on December 3, 1978. His ashes were scattered over the Pacific Ocean.

1996

Lawrence A. Davis, Sr., PhD

Grover Evans

Scipio A. Jones

Herwald "Hal" Morton

Judge Andree Layton Roaf

O. C. Smith, Jr.

Lawrence A. Davis, Sr., PhD

(1914–2004)

Lawrence A. Davis, Sr., served as president of Arkansas Agricultural, Mechanical, and Normal College (AM&N) in Pine Bluff, Arkansas, from 1943 until his resignation in 1973. During his tenure, he oversaw the school's 1972 transition from college to university status as part of the University of Arkansas System. The merger entailed a name change to the University of Arkansas at Pine Bluff (UAPB). During his tenure, Davis, whom Pine Bluff residents and students at AM&N affectionately called "Prexy," was among the most prominent heads of a historically black college (HBC) in the country.

Lawrence Arnette Davis, an only child, was born on July 4, 1914, in McCrory, Arkansas, to Virgil Davis and Prawnee Davis. For most of his childhood, he lived with his maternal grandmother, Emma Janie Brown. He attended public schools in McCrory until eighth grade, when he went to Pine Bluff to attend Merrill High School. He graduated as valedictorian in 1933.

Davis attended AM&N and graduated magna cum laude in 1937 with a bachelor's degree in English. After his graduation, the college employed him as a teacher, registrar, and cashier until he left in 1939 to pursue graduate studies at the University of Kansas in Lawrence. After completing a Master of Arts in English, he returned to Pine Bluff and resumed his employment as registrar at AM&N. He advanced rapidly to become assistant to college president John Brown Watson and then to become dean of administration.

After Watson's death, Davis was a member of a three-person committee that headed the college until Davis was chosen as president in 1943. At only twenty-nine years of age, he became the youngest college president in the country. The U.S. was engaged in World War II at the time, and consequently student enrollment was low. After the war, Davis oversaw record growth; enrollment reached 2,200 by the 1948–49 term.

Davis married Rachel L. Johnson of Prescott, Arkansas; they had four children, including Lawrence A. Davis, Jr., who served as chancellor of UAPB from 1991 to 2012.

The national African-American press took notice of the elder Davis's rapid rise to the presidency at AM&N and of the school's achievements during his administration, including gaining accreditation from the North Central Association of Colleges and Secondary Schools as a four-year college in 1950 and a $1.5 million building program that expanded the campus's physical plant. Davis completed a doctorate in educational administration at the University of Arkansas (U of A) at Fayetteville in 1960.

The 1960s marked a difficult time for the heads of HBCs, who had to strategically navigate the civil rights movement and student activism without angering political leaders who ultimately set funding for their colleges. Davis's selection of Dr. Martin Luther King, Jr., as commencement speaker in 1958 upset a number of Arkansas legislators. The following year, legislators gave Davis a chilly reception when he lobbied for AM&N's funding, and they cut the college's appropriation. Perhaps because of that experience, when some students joined the Student Nonviolent Coordinating Committee (SNCC) in 1963 and participated in demonstrations, Davis expelled several of them.

Davis was chancellor when a merger was proposed for AM&N to join the University of Arkansas System. This period was a major ordeal, in that students, alumni, and African Americans statewide opposed the merger because they feared the merger meant the institution would lose its unique identity. Despite the fact that Davis was widely criticized by supporters and opponents of the action, the merger went forward and he remained as the first chancellor of UAPB.

After a year as chancellor, Davis resigned and took a position at the R. R. Moton Foundation in New York City for one year. He then returned to higher education as president of Laney College, a two-year institution in Oakland, California, from 1974 to 1982. He spent his retirement years in California.

Davis died on June 5, 2004, and is buried in Pine Bluff. His many awards and accolades included honorary doctorates from two HBCs: Lane College in 1948 and Morehouse College in 1950.

Grover Evans

(1952–)

Grover Evans is known throughout central and northeastern Arkansas for his political endeavors, sports accomplishments, and career as a motivational speaker. In 1978, he was in a single-car accident that left him paralyzed from the neck down. The road to recovery placed many challenges in his path, but he was able to meet those challenges and has since received much recognition, including being inducted into the Arkansas Swimming Hall of Fame.

Grover Evans was born on March 6, 1952, the first African American born at St. Bernards Hospital in Jonesboro, Arkansas; he was named after the delivering doctor, Dr. Grover Poole. His parents were William Evans and Georgia Lee Holiday, and he had five younger siblings.

After his car accident, Evans was told that he would likely live only three to five more years, and he was determined to make the best of that time. Two months after his accident, he began to regain some sensation in his right arm, followed by his left

arm. He spent six months in a hospital in Memphis, Tennessee, and then was moved to a hospital in Jonesboro for occupational and physical therapy. Working in the swimming pool allowed him to gain more mobility.

During his rehabilitation, Evans was exposed to several sports opportunities through the National Wheelchair Sports Association. He was an avid table-tennis player and participated in several track-and-field wheelchair competitions. His greatest accolades, however, came in swimming. His first swim competition, in 1989, was at an intramural event at Arkansas State University (ASU) in Jonesboro. At ASU, he teamed up with a university swimming instructor who helped to perfect his swimming technique and established a training program for him. Evans went on to set several national and world swimming records in the fifty-meter backstroke, fifty-meter freestyle, fifty-meter breaststroke, 100-meter backstroke, and 100-meter freestyle.

In Barcelona, Spain, in 1992, Evans became the first African American to swim on the U.S. Paralympic Team. He participated in several more Paralympics—as an alternate for the 1996 games in Atlanta, Georgia, and team member for the 2004 games in Athens, Greece, and the 2008 games in Beijing, China. He set five world records, one Paralympics record in Barcelona, sixty-one American records, and eight Pan-American records. He also won sixty-nine National Championships. In 1997, he was inducted into the Arkansas Swimming Hall of Fame.

During this time, Evans was also pursuing his education. He attended ASU, from which he received a bachelor's degree in music and health education. In 1989, he graduated from the ASU Leadership Program. He also holds a doctorate in nutrition counseling from LaSalle University in Philadelphia, Pennsylvania.

Evans's political endeavors began in 1984 when he became the first African American to be elected to the Jonesboro City Council; he served six terms and was vice-mayor from December 1984 to July 1996. On October 1, 1996, he was appointed by Governor Mike Huckabee as the director of Disability Determination for the Social Security Administration for the State of Arkansas. He served as the deputy director of the same agency. He also once served as the interim director for the Capital Zoning District Commission with State Building Services, a position that placed him in the governor's cabinet. Evans has also served as a member of the Strategic Planning Board of University of Arkansas-Pulaski Technical College, was a member of the City of Little Rock Workforce Investment Board, and worked on the Olmstead Steering Committee and as a member of the City of Little Rock Workforce Investment Board Youth Council. He is also a council member for the Arkansas Injury Prevention Coalition under the Arkansas Department of Health. Evans helped Congress pass the Brady Bill, named after former White House press secretary James Brady, who was shot and became permanently disabled in 1981 during an attempted assassination of President Ronald Reagan. He also helped with the passage of the 1990 Americans with Disability Act, having been involved with many legislative meetings in Washington, D.C. Evans was often referred to as the "Martin Luther King" of disabilities due to his breadth of knowledge and experiences. In December 1998, he received the Disability Leadership Award from the Social Security Administration.

Evans has traveled all over the country as a motivational/inspirational speaker to various groups about overcoming adversity; he also discusses faith, nutrition, and his own accomplishments. He is the founder and CEO of Evans and Associates Company of Arkansas, LLC, founded in February 2005. He has been featured through various media outlets, including ABC, CBS, NBC, BET, UPN 38, local and national FOX stations, *City and Town*, *Ebony*, *Jet*, the *Arkansas Times*, *Team Rehab*, and *Power Play*.

Evans has volunteered his time to hospitals, schools, rehabilitation centers, the Spinal Cord Commission, Easter Seals, and the Martin Luther King, Jr., Commission. He serves on the Advisory Council for Education of Children with Disabilities for the Arkansas Department of Education. He has served as special consultant for systems design for the Department of Career Education/Arkansas Rehabilitation Services. He was named client advocate for people with disabilities for the state in 2004.

Evans was one of two in the nation to be awarded the National Easter Seal Society's Johanna Cooke Plaut Community Leadership Award. He serves as a member on the Central Arkansas United Way Board; Little Rock's Housing Advisory Board; Pulaski County Advisory Board on People with Disabilities; Delta Airlines Advisory Board for People with Disabilities; and Coalition Board on Transportation Service Administration (TSA) of Homeland Security. Evans is also a member of the Christian Men's Club and of the Knights of Columbus in Little Rock.

After retiring, Evans began serving as head swim coach at Parkview Magnet High School in Little Rock. He currently resides in Little Rock with his wife, Helen Malchan Evans; they have two children.

Scipio A. Jones
(1863–1943)

Scipio A. Jones was a prominent Little Rock attorney and one of the city's leading African-American citizens at the end of the nineteenth century and during the first decades of the twentieth century. Jones is most significantly

Jones practiced law in Little Rock for the rest of his life. He frequently represented indigent citizens and worked to correct abuse and injustice in Arkansas's penal system; Jones twice served in a temporary capacity as a judge. He was elected a special judge to hear a case in the Little Rock Municipal Court when the regular judge disqualified himself. In 1924, Jones was elected a special chancellor in Pulaski County Chancery Court.

The most significant case in which Jones was involved, though, was the defense of twelve black men arrested during the Elaine Massacre. Between November 3 and 17, 1919, twelve men were tried, convicted, and sentenced to death for murder in their roles in a supposed black uprising; the trials were marked by weak evidence, a lack of cross-examination of witnesses, and short deliberations by the local juries. Jones was hired by African-American citizens of Little Rock on November 24, 1919, to work with the firm of George W. Murphy, an attorney hired by the National Association for the Advancement of Colored People (NAACP), to defend the twelve condemned men. By January 14, 1925, all twelve defendants had been released. In one legal brief, Jones described his case as "the greatest case against peonage and mob law ever fought in the land."

As a leader in the African-American community in Little Rock, Jones is also recognized as responsible for having prevented a repeat of the Elaine Massacre in the state's capital city. He and other community leaders persuaded their fellow African-American citizens to remain out of sight and avoid confrontation amidst the mob violence surrounding the lynching of John Carter on May 4, 1927.

Jones was often criticized for his non-confrontational approach to race relations. He counted many leading white citizens of Arkansas among his friends, including Governor George Donaghey, and Jones—like John Bush of the Mosaic Templars of America (MTA)—worked with Booker T. Washington in building a black middle- and upper-class society separate from white society. However, when the leaders of the Republican Party in Arkansas sought to exclude African Americans from the workings of the party, Jones resisted. In 1900 and 1902, he worked to present a slate of delegates to the Republican Convention that included African

remembered for his role defending twelve men sentenced to death following the Elaine Massacre of 1919. He is also remembered for his role in the Republican Party at a time when many Arkansas Republicans were trying to restrict membership in the party to whites only.

Scipio Africanus Jones was born to a slave, Jemmima Jones, in 1863 in the area of Tulip, Arkansas. His father was generally believed to have been Dr. Sanford Reamey, a prominent citizen of Tulip and the owner of Jemmima at the time of Jones's birth. Jones attended schools for African Americans in the Tulip area and later moved to Little Rock, where he attended Walden Seminary (now Philander Smith College) and where he completed the four-year college preparatory course in only three years. He then attended Bethel Institute (now Shorter College) in North Little Rock. He received a bachelor's degree in 1885. During the next four years, Jones taught public school while studying law on his own time. On June 15, 1889, Jones passed the bar. His credentials were accepted by the Supreme Court of Arkansas in 1900 and by the U.S. Supreme Court in 1905.

Americans from Pulaski County. In both cases, the slate was rejected by party leadership. Jones himself ran for the Little Rock School Board in 1902 but was defeated by a vote of 2,202 to 181 after the *Arkansas Gazette* published warnings about the danger of having a black man seated on the school board.

In 1920, Jones helped to organize a separate party convention for black voters after the Pulaski County convention was moved without advance notice having been given to African Americans, but both the state and national party conventions refused to seat the black delegates. In 1924, the Republican state committee did agree to hold party conventions in "places where all Republicans can attend" and expanded its committee to include two positions reserved for African Americans. On May 1, 1928, Jones was chosen as a delegate from Arkansas to the Republican National Convention. He also served in this position in 1940. In 1930, Jones was among a group of African-American lawyers who sued (unsuccessfully) the Democratic Party in Arkansas to reverse rules that prevented black citizens from voting in the Democratic state primary elections.

In addition to his legal and political careers, Jones attempted to gain income through investments, although he appears not to have been successful. Jones is said to have owned roughly ten houses in Little Rock around 1907, including a "splendid" house in which he and his family lived at 1808 Ringo Street. Jones was a major stockholder in the Arkansas Realty and Investment Company and was also elected president of the company. The corporation failed and was dissolved on June 19, 1911. Jones also heavily invested in the People's Ice and Fuel Company of Little Rock, which succeeded for a time but failed during the Depression.

Jones was married twice. His first wife, Carrie Edwards Jones, was twenty-five when they were married on March 14, 1896. They had a daughter, Hazel, who died as a young adult. After the death of Carrie, Jones married Lillie M. Jackson of Pine Bluff in 1917. The couple had no children.

Jones died at his home in Little Rock on March 28, 1943. His funeral at Bethel African Methodist Episcopal Church in Little Rock (where Jones had been a member for over fifty years) was attended by many government and political leaders, both black and white. Among the honors given to Jones are two significant buildings named for him. The junior and senior high school in North Little Rock bore his name from its construction in 1928 until its closing in 1970 (due to the end of segregation), and the U.S. Post Office at 1700 Main Street in Little Rock was named for him in 2007.

Herwald "Hal" Morton

(1931–)

Herwald "Hal" Morton was a member of the United States Foreign Service and spent most of his career working in the U.S. Information Agency (USIA). In a military career that spanned more than thirty years—and which culminated in his earning the rank of Career Minister—he lived in five different countries and visited more than 100 as a representative of the United States.

Herwald Morton was born on July 19, 1931, in Little Rock, Arkansas, the youngest of Rachel and James Morton's five children. He recalled the childhood memory of getting his first job as a ten-year-old, having lied about his age in order to be hired as a popcorn vendor in one of the city's African-American movie theaters. He grew up in Little

Rock and was the valedictorian in the Class of 1948 at Dunbar High School. Following graduation and having earned a scholarship from the Pepsi-Cola Company, he spent a year and a half at New York University before he entered the U.S. Air Force. He served in Alaska, Germany, and France from 1949 to 1954. By the time he was discharged and returned to civilian life, he had risen to the rank of first lieutenant.

After his stint in the military, he settled in Chicago, Illinois, and registered at Northwestern University, but he was put off by their racial quota. He switched to Roosevelt University, where he earned a Bachelor of Arts degree in political science in 1960.

He married Christine Hicks in Chicago on May 19, 1958. The couple had two sons.

After he graduated from Roosevelt, Morton continued his education, and earned a master's degree in international law and diplomacy from the University of Chicago in 1961. After considering positions with both the Defense and Commerce Departments, Morton ultimately accepted a job with the U.S. Information Agency, where he began as a management trainee in 1961.

Over the course of his expansive career, he served as a personnel officer, a management and budget officer, and an executive officer in multiple countries. He also served as the director of USIA programs in Kingston, Jamaica, and La Paz, Bolivia. As his career advanced, he assumed ever greater administrative responsibilities, and he was named Deputy Director of the Office of Personnel and Training in 1977. In that capacity, he oversaw a world-wide personnel and training system—one that served thousands of foreign national employees and foreign service officers in over 100 countries, as well as 3,000 civil servants in the United States. In 1980, he returned overseas and became Counselor of Public Affairs and Director of the United States Information Service, serving in Bangkok, Thailand, and Manila, Philippines. In that post, he was an advisor to the ambassador and other U.S. government agencies on public diplomacy activities, while he was also responsible for all public affairs activities for the embassy. From there, he became director of the Office of East Asia and Pacific Affairs in 1986. In that position, he supervised a number of offices and served as a senior management advisor to the

director of the USIA. By the time he retired from the USIA in October 1993, he had earned the rank of Career Minister, one of the highest ranks of the Foreign Service.

Morton was also an active contributor to numerous organizations, including the American Foreign Service Association, the Asia Society, the World Affairs Council, and the National Association for the Advancement of Colored People (NAACP). In recognition of his distinguished efforts, Morton was the recipient of numerous honors and awards. He was awarded the Diplomatic and Consular Officers Presidential Awards for Outstanding Service, and he was recognized with the Superior Honor awards in 1986 and 1988. Upon his retirement in 1993, he was recognized with the Distinguished Honor Award. In 1989, he was inducted into the Dunbar Alumni Hall of Fame.

Living in Silver Spring, Maryland, Morton has served as the president of the USIA Alumni Association, has taken classes at the local community college, and has traveled extensively throughout United States and abroad with his wife. Active in his church, he performs considerable volunteer work under its auspices.

Judge Andree Layton Roaf
(1941–2009)

Andree Yvonne Layton Roaf was an Arkansas attorney and jurist who distinguished herself in the fields of biology, law, and community service.

Andree Layton was born on March 31, 1941, in Nashville, Tennessee. The daughter of William W. Layton, a government official, and Phoebe A. Layton, an educator, she grew up in Columbus, Ohio, and in White Hall and Muskegon Heights, Michigan. She had two sisters. She graduated from high school in Muskegon in 1958. Originally intending to pursue a career in the biological sciences, she attended Michigan State University and received a Bachelor of Science degree in zoology in 1962. While an undergraduate, she met another student, Clifton George Roaf, who became a dentist in Pine Bluff, Arkansas. The two were married in July of

1963, and they had four children. From 1963 to 1965, she worked as a bacteriologist for the Michigan State Department of Health in Lansing, transferring in 1965 to become a research biologist for the Food and Drug Administration in Washington, D.C., where she stayed until 1969. She moved to Arkansas and was a staff assistant to the Pine Bluff Urban Renewal Agency from 1971 to 1975.

In 1975, she took a job as a biologist with the National Center for Toxicology Research in Jefferson, Arkansas. However, by that time, she had decided upon a career change. She entered the University of Arkansas at Little Rock William H. Bowen School of Law in 1975, where she served as member and articles editor on the law review from 1976 to 1978. She graduated with high honors in May 1978 with a Juris Doctorate degree. Roaf was second in a class of eighty-three.

After graduation she remained at the law school for the 1978–79 school year as an instructor teaching research, writing, and appellate advocacy. Thereafter, in 1979, Roaf went into private practice with the law firm of Walker, Roaf, Campbell, Ivory and Dunklin, where she handled a variety of legal matters, primarily bankruptcy, real estate, probate, wills and estates, and domestic relations.

On January 17, 1995, Roaf became the first African-American woman and only the second woman to ever serve on the Arkansas Supreme Court when she was appointed by then-Governor Jim Guy Tucker to succeed Justice Steele Hays, who had retired. Roaf served until 1996 and, not being eligible to run for the same position on the high court, was appointed by Governor Mike Huckabee to a judgeship on the Arkansas Court of Appeals. After four years of service, she was elected as a judge on the Court of Appeals. Roaf served until December 2006. On May 30, 2007, she undertook a new role when she was appointed as the director of the federal Office of Desegregation Monitoring to oversee the desegregation cases in Pulaski County.

Roaf participated in various professional and service organizations, including the Pulaski County, Jefferson County, and Arkansas bar associations and the W. Harold Flowers Law Society, and received the 1996 Gayle Pettus Pontz Outstanding Arkansas Woman Attorney Award. She was awarded an honorary Doctor of Laws degree from her undergraduate alma mater, Michigan State University.

Roaf died on July 1, 2009, in Little Rock.

O. C. Smith, Jr.
(1936–2001)

Ocie Lee "O. C." Smith, Jr., started out singing jazz before moving into the genres of country and rhythm & blues/soul. After replacing legendary jazz singer Joe Williams, he began touring with the Count Basie Orchestra in the early 1960s. He later became a solo artist. In the 1980s, he put aside his career as a recording artist to become a minister.

O. C. Smith was born in Mansfield, Louisiana, on June 21, 1936 (although some sources say 1932). His parents, Ocie Lee Smith, Sr., and Ruth Edwards Shorter Smith, who were both teachers, moved to Little Rock, Arkansas, when Smith was ten years old. Three years after the family had moved to Little Rock, Smith moved to Los Angeles, California, with his by-then-divorced mother.

Attending Jefferson High School, Smith learned music from the legendary teacher Samuel Brown. Smith said his early influences were bebop jazz

greats Dizzy Gillespie and Charlie Parker.

Smith attended East Los Angeles Junior College and then Southern University in Baton Rouge, Louisiana, majoring in psychology. After college, Smith joined the U.S. Air Force and toured the world with a special services band. He spent the next several years in New York, singing in small clubs in the winter months and in the Catskills in the summer. Next came his stint with the Count Basie Orchestra.

Leaving the orchestra after a few years, Smith eventually settled in Los Angeles and was soon signed with Columbia Records. Singing country music for a time and having a hit with Dallas Frazier's story-song "Son of Hickory Holler's Tramp," Smith later became a soul singer.

Among his many recordings, Smith's biggest hit was composer Bobby Russell's "Little Green Apples," which reached the number-two slot on both the pop and R&B charts in 1968. The hit song also won its composer Grammy awards for Song of the Year and Best Country Song that year. Smith's other big R&B single, "Daddy's Little Man," reached the number-nine spot on the charts in 1969. He remained with Columbia Records until 1974.

Smith married Robbie Gholson on February 14, 1976; they had two daughters and five sons.

In 1980, some friends invited him to attend a service for the religious movement Science of the Mind at the Wilshire Ebel Theater. Smith began studying for the ministry and became a reverend 1985. That same year, he and his wife founded the City of Angels Church of Religious Science.

Smith died suddenly of an apparent heart attack at his Ladera Heights, California, home on November 23, 2001. He had officiated at a Thanksgiving service at his church the day before his death. His book, co-written with James Shaw, titled *Little Green Apples: God Really Did Make Them!* was published posthumously in 2003.

1997

Barbara Higgins Bond

Gretha Boston

Lloyd C. Elam, MD

Keith Jackson

Samuel Lee Kountz, Jr., MD

Rodney E. Slater

Barbara Higgins Bond

(1951–)

merous art classes taught by Lee Anthony, who remained her mentor for many years; she also participated for three years in her school's Arts and Letters Club. Her mother encouraged her to study painting at the Arkansas Arts Center, and she graduated from historic Little Rock Central High School in 1969.

After high school, Higgins entered Phillips University, a private, co-educational institution in Enid, Oklahoma. By the end of the year, her confidence and skill as an artist had grown such that she began considering art as a career, and she decided to transfer to the Memphis College of Art in Memphis, Tennessee.

While in Memphis, she met Benny Hayes Bond, a New Jersey native and recent graduate of Tennessee State University, who was in town visiting relatives. They married on January 20, 1973.

Throughout art school, she had signed her paintings with simply "Higgins." After she was married, she added her new surname to her signature and became known professionally as Higgins Bond.

In 1973, she graduated with a Bachelor of Fine Arts degree in advertising design. She and her husband moved to Teaneck, New Jersey, where he worked as a recreational therapist and she accepted a job with Stanley Arnold and Associates, a Park Avenue advertising agency in nearby New York City. They had one child, Benjamin Garnett Bond. After the birth her son, she resigned her position with the agency and began practice as a freelance artist, which allowed her to stay at home with their son.

In the 1970s, Anheuser-Busch, Inc., began sponsoring "The Great Kings and Queens of Africa" program to advance black cultural understanding and to afford African-American artists the opportunity to display their art. Twenty-three artists were commissioned to create thirty paintings that depicted noteworthy African leaders. Higgins Bond was the only artist to have three pieces in the collection: Mansa Kankan Musa, a fourteenth-century king of Mali; Egyptian pharaoh Akhenaten and his wife, Queen Nefertiti; and Yaa Asantewaa, Queen of Ghana. To advertise "The Great Kings and Queens of Africa" series, Anheuser-Busch displayed her paintings in a television commercial for *Roots: The Second Generation*.

In 1980, Higgins Bond was commissioned by

Barbara Higgins Bond is a nationally recognized illustrator and commercial artist whose most important works have chronicled the history and struggles of African Americans. A pioneer freelance artist since the early 1970s, she has designed and illustrated cultural heritage stamps published by the U.S. Postal Service and the United Nations. Her art has been exhibited prominently in the U.S. and abroad.

Barbara Ann Higgins was born in Little Rock, Arkansas, on December 14, 1951, to Henry Drew Higgins and Edna Washington Higgins. She grew up in Little Rock in a home on South Park Street with three sisters and a brother. She also had three paternal half-siblings.

Influenced by her father, a creative and skilled artisan, Higgins was drawing and painting by age twelve. She was educated in the Little Rock School District, attending Carver elementary and Booker and Dunbar junior high schools. In junior high school, she won first place in a Black History art contest two years in a row. Higgins enrolled in nu-

Calhoun's Collectors Society to paint a series of collector plates titled *Windows on the World*. Motivated by a lifelong passion for nature and animals, she illustrated many plates featuring kittens, tropical fish, butterflies, and dogs for the Bradford Exchange, a source of limited-edition collectibles. Higgins Bond has since illustrated many plates for Hamilton Collection, a maker of limited-edition plates. Perhaps her best-known plate projects were the *Treasured Days* series and *Songs of the American Spirit* series.

Higgins Bond has exhibited at numerous museums and institutions in one-person shows and in group shows with other artists. Notable among these were exhibitions at New York's Metropolitan Museum of Art in 1974, Hunter College in 1975, and the DuSable Museum of African-American History (a Smithsonian affiliate in Chicago, Illinois) in 1977.

Higgins Bond has been acknowledged with numerous artistic awards, prizes, and honors. In 1979, she received the Certificate of Merit at the twenty-first Annual National Exhibition of the Society of Illustrators. She was recognized by the Communications Excellence to Black Audiences (CEBA) Award of Merit for her work with *Black Enterprise* magazine. In 2009, Higgins Bond won the Ashley Bryan Award, presented by the Atlanta-Fulton Public Library System, for outstanding contributions to children's literature. In 1986, Higgins Bond was recognized by Governor Bill Clinton during the Arkansas Sesquicentennial at a ceremony honoring distinguished Arkansans.

In 1991, Higgins Bond became the first African-American woman to design and illustrate a stamp for the U.S. Postal Service. The first of her three stamp illustrations was of Jan Matzeliger, the inventor of a shoe-lasting machine that revolutionized shoe manufacturing. The next year, Higgins Bond illustrated the W. E. B. DuBois stamp commemorating the life of the historian and civil rights activist and, in 1993, followed with a stamp honoring research chemist Percy L. Julian. This Black Heritage stamp series is the longest-running commemorative series in U.S. history. In 2001, Higgins Bond illustrated four stamps for the United Nations Postal Administration on endangered species.

Benny Bond died in November 1996. Two years later, Higgins Bond moved to Nashville to be near her son, who was then attending Tennessee State University, and also to be nearer to her husband's family.

Higgins Bond has illustrated more than forty books by authors such as Joan Banks, Mary Batten, Melvin and Gilda Berger, and Melissa Stewart. Many of the books won awards. In 1993, *When I Was Little* by Toyomi Igus won the Multicultural Exchange Book Award of Excellence, and 1998's *Song of La Selva: A Story of a Costa Rican Rain Forest* by Joan Banks received the Parents' Choice Approval Seal. Melissa Stewart's *A Place for Turtles* earned several awards, including in 2014 the Sigurd F. Olson Nature Writing Award and the Green Earth Book Award. In 2010, Higgins Bond illustrated the thirtieth-anniversary edition of Alex Haley's *Roots: The Saga of an American Family* for Easton Press.

During her long career, Higgins Bond has served as resident artist, teacher, and lecturer at numerous educational institutions, including the University of North Carolina at Charlotte and Nossi College of Art in Nashville. Her paintings and drawings can be found in Arkansas in public collections, such as at the Mosaic Templars Cultural Center, and in countless private collections throughout the United States. She is a member of the National Society of Illustrators and resides and works in Nashville.

Gretha Boston

(1959–)

Gretha Denise Boston is a celebrated mezzo-soprano and award-winning actress who has performed in some of the most prestigious venues in the United States and abroad, and she won the coveted Tony Award in 1995 for Best Featured Actress in a Musical for her role as Queenie in the Broadway revival of *Showboat*; she was the first Arkansan to receive that honor. The same role earned Boston the Theatre World Award as Outstanding Debut Artist. She was also nominated for the Helen Hayes Award for Outstanding Lead Actress in a Non-Resident Production for the 2000–01 season at the Kennedy Center in Washington, D.C., for her performance in *It Ain't*

Nothin' But the Blues.

Gretha Boston was born in Crossett, Arkansas, on April 18, 1959, the eldest of seven children of Delores Tucker Boston and Curtis Joe Boston, Sr. Her early musical training was in the Gates Chapel African Methodist Episcopal Church and in her high school choir, where she was encouraged by Bill Stroud, then head of the school's music department, and by C. T. Foster, her band director. She graduated from Crossett High School in 1977.

Boston attended North Texas State University (NTSU—now the University of North Texas) in Denton, Texas, earning her Bachelor of Arts degree in music and performance. As a member of the NTSU A Capella Choir, she recorded Mendelssohn's *Walpurgisnacht* with the Royal Philharmonic Orchestra in London. After graduation, she attended the University of Illinois at Urbana-Champaign, where she was a two-time winner in the D'Angelo International Young Artists Competition. She studied with Johnson Wustman at the University of Illinois, with Margaret Hoswell in New York City, and with Maestro Franco Iglesias, also of New York. Boston has also performed in concert in St. Louis, Missouri; Champaign, Illinois; and Santa Barbara, California.

She made her debut at Carnegie Hall in May 1991 in Mozart's *Coronation Mass* and returned later in Beethoven's Ninth Symphony. Her operatic roles include Amneris in *Aida* (at the University of Illinois; the Intiman Theater in Seattle, Washington; and the Denver Center in Denver, Colorado), Maddelena in *Rigoletto* (New York Grand Opera), and Maria in *Porgy and Bess* (Buffalo Philharmonic and Opera Delaware). Her choral works include *Messiah*, *Elijah*, and Verdi's *Requiem* (New York Grand Opera).

Boston has appeared on television in PBS's *An Enchanted Evening: A Salute to Oscar Hammerstein* and has also appeared on the *David Letterman Show* and the *Today* show, as well as the television dramas *Hope and Faith* (2004), *Law and Order* (2001), and *Law and Order: Criminal Intent* (2004).

In 2002, Boston played Bloody Mary in the national tour of *South Pacific*, starring Robert Goulet. In December 2002, she performed as the character Ethel in the musical *Let Me Sing* at the Charlotte Repertory Theater in North Carolina. Later that year, she acted the role of Lola in the play *Jar the Floor*, also in Charlotte. In the field of musical comedy, Boston has performed the role of Velma Crowns in *Portraits of Black Women in Church Hats* in Buffalo, New York (Studio Arena); Rochester, New York (GEVA Theater); and Washington, D.C. (Arena Stage).

Boston resides in New York City.

Lloyd C. Elam, MD
(1928–2008)

Lloyd C. Elam was a groundbreaking psychiatrist and college administrator who founded the Department of Psychiatry and Behavioral Sciences at Meharry Medical College in Nashville, Tennessee, and who later served as president of Meharry.

Lloyd Charles Elam was born on October 27, 1928, in Little Rock, Arkansas, to Harry Elam and Ruth Davis Elam. He was baptized at age seven at Christ Temple Church of Christ (Holiness) USA in Little Rock, where he was active in and eventually became superintendent of the Sunday school

at age seventeen. He attended Stephens Elementary School and then Paul Laurence Dunbar High School. He graduated at the age of fifteen in 1944. Elam attended Dunbar Junior College in Little Rock before moving to Harvey, Illinois.

While in Harvey, Elam worked for the Maremont Automobile Plant and traveled back and forth to Chicago, Illinois, to attend classes at Roosevelt University. He graduated with a Bachelor of Science degree in zoology with distinction in 1950. Elam then enlisted in the U.S. Army and after two years, he had earned his medical degree from the University of Washington School of Medicine in Seattle in 1957. During his senior year there, he married Clara Carpenter, whom he had dated throughout most of his years in medical school; they had two daughters.

Elam and his wife moved back to Chicago, where he completed his internship at the University of Illinois Hospital from 1957 to 1958. In 1961, he finished his residency in psychiatry at the University of Chicago Hospital and joined Chicago's Billings Hospital as a staff psychiatrist and instructor of psychiatry.

Later in 1961, Elam moved to Nashville, Tennessee, and became an assistant professor, the chairman of the Psychiatry Department, and a faculty member in the Department of Internal Medicine at Meharry Medical College. He became a full professor of psychiatry and founded the Department of Psychiatry and Behavioral Sciences both in 1963, started the inpatient psychiatry program in 1964, and originated the residency program in psychiatry in 1965. Also in 1965, Elam launched one of the first hospital day-programs in the city for psychiatric patients. From 1966 to 1968, he served as the interim dean of the college.

In 1968, Elam was nominated as president of Meharry Medical College, and he managed the school's development in that capacity until 1981. During his presidency, an $88 million capital campaign was completed, adding much-needed buildings and property to the campus, including the Russell Towers of what was then the George W. Hubbard Hospital (now called Nashville General Hospital at Meharry Medical College), the library (now called the S. S. Kresge Learning Resource Center), the Meharry Towers (apartments for students and faculty), the Elam Mental Health Center (previously the Community Mental Health Center), the Comprehensive Health Center (for outpatient care), the Robert Wood Johnson Center (previously called the Center for International Studies), the Harold D. West Basic Science Center, the Dental School, the Dr. Henry A. Moses Building (previously called Alumni Hall), the Dorothy Brown Residence Hall (for young women), and the Matthew Walker Community Health Center. Eleven buildings were erected during Elam's presidency. Master of Science and PhD degree programs were established, along with the School of Allied Health Sciences in conjunction with Tennessee State University.

From 1981 to 1982, Elam served as chancellor of Meharry Medical College. He then went on sabbatical for one year at Stanford University in Palo Alto, California, where he served as a fellow at the Center for Advanced Studies in the Behavioral Sciences. In 1982, Elam returned to Meharry and served as Distinguished Service Professor of Psychiatry until 1995. In 1996, he was made professor emeritus of the Department of Psychiatry and Behavioral Sciences, and he was made chairman emeritus in 1997. Elam officially retired 1995 but served as a volunteer lecturer for the Department of Psychiatry and remained active in the profession.

Dr. Elam was a member of several associations and numerous organizations as part of the greater Nashville community, such as the Omega Psi Phi Fraternity, Inc. He held honorary degrees from Harvard University, St. Lawrence University, Roosevelt University, and Meharry Medical College. He was on the board of directors for several religious, community, civic, and educational organizations, and has received numerous awards from these entities.

Elam died on October 4, 2008, and is buried at Greenwood Cemetery in Nashville.

Keith Jackson

(1965–)

Keith Jackson is a former college and professional football player and current radio broadcast color analyst for University of Arkansas (U of A) at Fayetteville football. Jackson began working with the Arkansas Razorback Sports Network in 2000. Jackson is the founder of P.A.R.K. (Positive Atmosphere Reaches Kids), a nonprofit recreational and educational program designed to provide "high-risk" students the opportunity to further their education by completing high school so they can attend college.

Keith Jerome Jackson was born on April 19, 1965, in Little Rock, Arkansas, and grew up in a single-parent home with his mother, Gladys Jackson. He went on to become a successful high school athlete, earning letters in football, basketball, and track at Little Rock Parkview High School.

A highly recruited football player, Jackson chose to play for head coach Barry Switzer at the University of Oklahoma in Norman. Due to his phenomenal blocking skills in Oklahoma's wishbone offense, he was named by consensus All-American as a tight end in 1986 and 1987. He was named to the Big Eight All-Conference team three times. Despite playing in the run-heavy offense, Jackson finished his collegiate career with sixty-two pass receptions for 1,470 yards and fourteen touchdowns, averaging 23.7 yards per catch. He helped the Sooners to a 42–5–1 record and the 1985 national championship. Jackson also was named a Big

Eight All-Academic four times, earning his bachelor's degree in communications in just three and a half years.

Jackson was selected by the Philadelphia Eagles with the thirteenth pick of the 1988 National Football League (NFL) draft as a 6'2", 250-pound tight end. Head coach Buddy Ryan named Jackson his starting tight end upon drafting the rookie, placing him ahead of two veteran players. Despite playing in a run-heavy offense in college, he set a new team receptions record for the Eagles in his first season and finished with eighty-one catches for 869 yards and six touchdowns. He was named *Sporting News* Rookie of the Year and National Football Conference (NFC) Rookie of the Year. He became the only rookie selected on the NFC Pro Bowl team. Jackson went on to be selected to play in six Pro Bowls (1988–90, 1992–93, 1996).

Jackson played nine seasons in the NFL with the Eagles, Miami Dolphins, and Green Bay Packers, winning Super Bowl XXXI with the Packers in January 1997. Considered to be one of greatest tight ends to play football, Jackson finished his career with 441 catches for 5,283 yards and forty-nine touchdowns.

Upon retirement, Jackson began working with the Arkansas Razorback Sports Network in 2000

after three years of television and radio experience. Jackson was inducted into the College Football Hall of Fame in 2001. He serves as an inspirational speaker at churches, civic groups, businesses, and schools.

In 1993, Jackson founded P.A.R.K. in his hometown of Little Rock. It is an after-school program for 8th-12th grade students with low grade-point averages who are at-risk of dropping out of school. P.A.R.K. offers five years of tutoring, recreation, community service, and summer programs for its participants to help boost their self-esteem, to teach them how to foster long-term relationships, and to direct their focus to attending and graduating from college.

Jackson has received numerous awards over the years, such as being named "Outstanding Young Arkansan" by the Jaycees in 1994 and receiving the National Conference for Community and Justice Humanitarian Award in 2005.

Jackson resides in Little Rock with his wife, Melanie. The couple married on February 5, 1994, and they have three children.

Samuel Lee Kountz, Jr., MD

(1930–1981)

Samuel Lee Kountz, Jr., was a physician and pioneer in organ transplantation, particularly in renal transplant research and surgery. An Arkansas success story, he overcame the limitations of his childhood as an African American in the Delta region of a racially segregated state to achieve national and world prominence in the medical field.

Sam Kountz, Jr., the eldest of three sons, was born on October 20, 1930, in Lexa, Arkansas, to the Reverend J. S. Kountz, Sr., a Baptist minister, and his wife, Emma. He lived in a small town with an inadequate school system in one of the most impoverished regions of the state. He attended a one-room school in Lexa until the age of fourteen, at which point he transferred to a Baptist boarding school in the same town; he later graduated from Morris Booker College High School in Dermott, Arkansas.

Kountz applied to Arkansas Agricultural, Me-

chanical, and Normal College (AM&N), now the University of Arkansas at Pine Bluff (UAPB), in 1948, but he failed the entrance examination. Undaunted, he applied directly to the college president, Lawrence A. Davis, Sr., who was so impressed by Kountz's ambition, his inquiring mind, and his determination to become a physician that he admitted him despite his scores. During Kountz's senior year, he conducted a tour of the campus for Senator J. William Fulbright, who encouraged him in his goal of becoming a physician. He earned a Bachelor of Science degree in chemistry in 1952, graduating third in his class.

Kountz went on to graduate school and earned a Master of Science degree in biochemistry from the University of Arkansas (U of A) at Fayetteville in 1956. His medical degree was conferred in 1958 from the University of Arkansas Medical Center's School of Medicine in Little Rock (now the University of Arkansas for Medical Sciences—UAMS). He married Grace Atkin, a teacher, on June 9, 1958, one day after his medical school graduation. They had three children. During the next two years, he interned at the prestigious Stanford Service, a San Francisco hospital. He completed a rigorous surgical residency there in 1965. Two significant experiences during these years shaped Kountz's future. The first was studying with Roy Cohn, one of the world's pioneers in organ transplantation. The second was receiving the Giannini Fellowship in surgery that supported his post-doctoral training at the San Francisco County Hospital and his post-graduate medical studies at Hammersmith Hospital in London, England, from 1962 to 1963, where he continued his surgical training.

The apex of his achievement as a resident physician at Stanford came in 1961 when he performed the first kidney transplant between a recipient and a donor who were not identical twins. This single achievement guaranteed his status as a pioneer in surgery. Throughout his career, he performed more than 500 kidney transplants. In 1965, he performed the first renal transplant in Egypt as a visiting Fulbright professor in the United Arab Republic.

After he returned from overseas, Kountz was made assistant professor of surgery at Stanford University in 1966 and became an associate professor in 1967. He was also director of the transplant service of the University of California at San Francisco until 1972. It was here that Kountz made the breakthrough observation that high doses of a steroid hormone, methylprednisolone, arrested the rejection of transplanted kidneys. This discovery led directly to the current drug regimens that make organ transplants using donations from unrelated donors routine. The years between 1967 and 1972 were his most productive. The above discovery and his advocacy of earlier re-implantation—that is, the implantation of a second kidney at the earliest signs of rejection—were his two greatest contributions to the field.

Kountz became professor of surgery and director of the transplant service at the University of California at San Francisco. The combination of an academic and a clinical appointment clearly showed the pathway he intended to follow. In 1972, Kountz moved to the East Coast and became professor of surgery and chairman of the Department of Surgery at the State University of New York Downstate Medical Center in Brooklyn, New York. He told friends that he wanted to improve healthcare for the black community there. Also in 1972, Kountz became chief of surgery at New York City's Kings County Hospital Medical Center.

On a temporary teaching visit to South Africa in 1977, Kountz contracted a neurological disease that remains undisclosed to this day. Its outcome, permanent brain damage, disabled him both physically and mentally. In February 1978, he was transferred to the Burke Rehabilitation Center in White Plains, New York. Kountz remained chronically ill thereafter until he died on December 23, 1981, at home in Kings Point, New York. A memorial service was held on December 29, 1981, at the Downstate Medical Center in New York and another at the Fine Arts Building at Arkansas AM&N College on January 19, 1982. He is buried near his home in Great Neck, New York.

Dr. Kountz wrote seventy-six professional papers and other scholarly articles. In 1964, the American College of Cardiology honored him with an Outstanding Investigator Award. In 1974, the U of A awarded him an honorary Juris Doctorate degree as a distinguished alumnus, honoring his pioneering achievements in the field of kidney transplant research, and he was elected president of the Society of University Surgeons as an expression of respect for his clinical and research achievements. In 1976, Kountz performed a live kidney transplant on NBC's *Today* show, resulting in 20,000 persons responding with offers to donate kidneys. In April 1985, the First International Symposium on Renal Failure and Transplantation in Blacks was held and dedicated to his memory. The National Association for the Advancement of Colored People (NAACP) gives a yearly award in his honor to an outstanding black student in the sciences.

Rodney E. Slater

(1955–)

Rodney E. Slater rose from poverty to become an Arkansas assistant attorney general and served in several positions under Arkansas Governor, and later U.S. President, Bill Clinton. He was chairman of the Arkansas Highway Commission, director of governmental affairs for Arkansas State University (ASU) in Jonesboro, the first African-American director of the Federal Highway Administration, and U.S. Secretary of Transportation.

Rodney Earl Slater was born on February 23, 1955, in Tallahatchie County, Mississippi. Soon after, Slater's mother married Earl Brewer, a mechanic and maintenance man about whom Slater has said, "My stepfather was my father." When Slater was a small child, the family moved across the Mississippi River to Marianna, Arkansas, where as a young boy he picked cotton in the fields with his mother. He picked cotton and peaches throughout his youth to supplement the family's income despite his father working five or six jobs to provide for the family.

Slater attended segregated schools in Marianna until the eleventh grade when he entered the newly integrated Lee High School, where he became a senior class officer. In 1972, city officials charged him with inciting a riot during a student demonstration on the birthday of Martin Luther King, Jr.; he and other students were taken to the police station, booked, and charged. John Walker, a civil rights attorney from Little Rock, helped to get the charges dropped, but Slater was prohibited from participating in extracurricular activities his senior year. This was significant because Slater was

a star halfback on the school football team and had hoped to attend college on an athletic scholarship.

Despite the setback, he was offered academic and athletic scholarships to Eastern Michigan University (EMU) in Ypsilanti, where he was a running back and was voted team co-captain. He was on the Dean's List each semester and graduated in 1977 with degrees in political science and speech communications.

Slater returned to Arkansas and entered law school at the University of Arkansas (U of A) at Fayetteville, where he became president of the U of A chapter of the Black American Law Students Association and the Student Bar. While he was in law school, his future father-in-law, Arkansas State Representative Henry Wilkins, III, introduced him to then-Governor Bill Clinton. Slater also met George Haley, brother of *Roots* author Alex Haley and the second African American to graduate from the U of A School of Law; Haley became a longtime mentor to Slater. In May 1980, he graduated with a Juris Doctorate degree and was admitted to the state bar in August.

From 1980 to 1982, Slater served as an assistant attorney general in the litigation division under Attorney General Steve Clark. In 1982, he left that office to join Gov. Clinton's staff and also served as his deputy campaign manager in 1984 and 1986. Clinton appointed Slater special assistant to the governor for community and minority affairs and then to the position of executive assistant to the governor for economic and community programs. In 1987, Clinton named him to the Arkansas Highway Commission. He was the youngest commissioner and the first African American to serve on that state board, to which he was elected chairman in December 1992.

From 1987 to 1992, Slater was also director of governmental relations for ASU in Jonesboro. He took a leave of absence from ASU to serve as deputy campaign manager and senior travel adviser for the 1992 Clinton–Gore presidential campaign. After Clinton's election, Slater served as an aide to the presidential transition director, Warren Christopher. In March 1993, President Clinton appointed Slater as director of the Federal Highway Administration, the agency's first African-American administrator in its century-long history. In that capacity, Slater developed an innovative financing program that resulted in the completion of hundreds of projects ahead of schedule with greater cost efficiency. His agency also provided major assistance in transportation infrastructure to California after the Northridge earthquake in 1994.

His wife, attorney Cassandra Wilkins-Slater, originally from Pine Bluff, was appointed senior adviser to the Social Security commissioner in 1994. Their daughter, Bridgette Josette, had been born earlier that year.

Slater was popular with both political parties. President Clinton said, "I had Republican congressmen calling me, saying, 'You ought to name Slater to be Secretary of Transportation.'" On February 14, 1997, Slater replaced Federico Pena as Transportation Secretary, to oversee the nation's highways, airways, railways, and waterways. He held that position until the end of the Clinton administration in 2001.

As Transportation Secretary, Slater's popularity continued with the legislative and executive branches of government, as well as with industry officials. Only activist Ralph Nader was critical, saying Slater's plans to improve national highways would allow people to go faster and thus increase fatalities. Slater secured bipartisan support in Congress for projects such as the Transportation Equity Act for the 21st Century (TEA-21), a record $200 billion investment in surface transportation; the Wendell H. Ford Aviation Investment Reform Act for the 21st Century (AIR-21), which provided a record $46 billion to provide for the safety and security of the nation's aviation system; and the negotiation of forty Open Skies Agreements with other countries, expanding U.S. reach in aviation and promoting U.S. carrier access to international markets. Secretary Slater held the first International Transportation Symposium, with representatives from more than ninety countries attending.

Slater, living with his wife and daughter in Washington, D.C., was a partner in the law firm Patton Boggs LLP, where he headed the transportation and infrastructure practice group. Along with fellow Arkansan Wesley Clark, Slater was a partner with James Lee Witt Associates, a Washington consulting firm specializing in emergency management. Slater is a public speaker on topics including global transportation, critical infrastructure, international transportation negotiations, and labor-management issues for aviation, rail, highways, and maritime and transit systems.

His honors and recognitions include the 1994 Black Alumni Achievement Award from Eastern Michigan University and an honorary doctorate from EMU in 1996. In 1998, *Ebony* magazine named him one of the 100 Most Influential Black Americans; the *Arkansas Times* named him an "Arkansas Hero"; and the National Bar Association gave him the President's Award. In 1999, he received an honorary doctorate from Howard University in Washington, D.C., and the Lamplighter Award for Public Service from the Black Leadership Forum. In April 2006, Slater was honored by the U of A as a recipient of the Silas Hunt Legacy Award, and at its May commencement, he received an honorary doctorate of laws. He has also served on the board of Philander Smith College in Little Rock, as well as on the boards of Northwest Airlines, the Smithsonian Institution, Kansas Southern Industries, the Urban League, and the United Way. He is part owner of the Washington Nationals baseball team (formerly the Montreal Expos).

At the time of Slater's confirmation by the U.S. Senate as Transportation Secretary, Ernest Green, one of the Little Rock Nine, said Slater's story offered a lesson for all young people regardless of race or class: "You, too, can make it and have an impact on this country."

1998

Daisy G. Anderson

Wiley A. Branton

Michael A. Conley

Danny K. Davis, PhD

Samuel Massie, Jr., PhD

Anita M. Pointer

Phyllis Yvonne Stickney

Daisy G. Anderson

(CA. 1900–1998)

Educator, author, and lecturer Daisy G. Anderson was best known for having been one of the last surviving widows of the American Civil War (1861–1865). She had been married to a former slave and U.S. Colored Regiment soldier and Union veteran.

Daisy Graham was born circa 1900 in Civil District 8, Hardin County, Tennessee, to John Wesley Graham and Alice Graham; she was the oldest of their eight children. Her father was a poor farmer, but he owned their home. Education was stressed to the children, in that both parents could read and write.

Graham, whose education ended with her eighth-grade graduation, sought to escape the hard labor and poor conditions of farming that she and her siblings engaged in as children. Around 1918, she moved to Arkansas, settled in Forrest City, and became a rural schoolteacher. Graham discovered that poverty and the racial injustice of Jim Crow laws were even more prominent in Arkansas than they had been in Tennessee. However, her meager salary still allowed her to send $10 per month home to help her family in Tennessee.

In 1922 while in her early twenties, Daisy met

and married seventy-nine-year-old Robert Ball Anderson, who was in the area on an extended visit with his older brother, William Anderson. She was candid about the fact that Anderson loved her and that she did not share the sentiment when they were first married.

Robert Anderson had been born in 1843 into slavery in Green County, Kentucky. In 1865, he enlisted in Company G of the 125th U.S. Colored Volunteer Infantry Regiment and served under the name Robert Ball, his master's surname. After his military service, he settled in Butler County, Nebraska. By the time he had made his way to Arkansas, Anderson had become the richest black man in Nebraska, and he owned more than 2,000 acres of farmland there.

In November 1930, Robert Anderson was killed in an automobile accident on a return trip to Nebraska after a visit to Forrest City.

Daisy Anderson wrote a personal account of her husband's life entitled *From Slavery to Affluence: Memoirs of Robert Anderson, Ex-Slave*; it was privately published in 1927 and reissued in 1988. She also took up one of Robert Anderson's favorite activities, which was to attend Grand Army of the Republic (GAR) reunions and other Civil War–related events. In 1997, Daisy Anderson (Union widow) and Alberta Martin (Confederate widow) extended their hands toward each other in friendship at the wall of "Pickett's Charge" in Gettysburg National Military Park 134 years after that bloody combat.

Daisy Graham Anderson died on September 19, 1998, in Denver, Colorado.

Wiley A. Branton

(1923–1988)

Wiley A. Branton was a civil rights leader in Arkansas who helped desegregate the University of Arkansas (U of A) School of Law and later filed suit against the Little Rock School Board in a case that went to the U.S. Supreme Court. His work to end legal segregation and inequality in Arkansas and the nation was well known.

Wiley Austin Branton was born on December 13, 1923, in Pine Bluff, Arkansas, the second child of Pauline Wiley and Leo Andrew Branton; he had three brothers and one sister. His father and paternal grandfather owned and operated a taxicab business. His mother had been a schoolteacher in segregated public schools prior to her marriage.

Branton was educated in the segregated schools of Pine Bluff, and he attended Arkansas Agricultural, Mechanical, and Normal College (AM&N) there (now the University of Arkansas at Pine Bluff—UAPB); he was drafted into the U.S. Army in 1943 during World War II. His wartime experience opened his eyes to the horror and madness of prejudice. Upon his return from military service, Branton became active in civil rights activities even while he operated the family business. He married Lucille Elnora McKee in January 1948, and they had six children.

At this time, he was also involved in integrating the U of A School of Law in Fayetteville. The university, similar to most other Southern colleges and universities, traditionally had refused to admit African Americans as full-time students. In 1948, U.S. Supreme Court opinions had required the state-supported graduate schools of several

other states to admit black students. Branton was a member of the National Association for the Advancement of Colored People (NAACP) Arkansas State Conference of Branches when Arkansas Governor Ben Laney held a statewide conference to promote his idea for a regional graduate school for black students. Branton was so disgusted with the discussion that he declared his intention to register in the undergraduate school of the university. He also persuaded a friend, Silas H. Hunt, to register for the university's School of Law. (Hunt had graduated from AM&N and had planned to attend the University of Indiana School of Law.) They traveled to Fayetteville accompanied by Pine Bluff attorney Harold Flowers and photographer Geleve Grice. Branton was refused admission, but Hunt was accepted.

Branton was admitted to the U of A School of Law in January 1950. He was the fifth black student admitted to the school and, in 1953, the third to graduate. After he was admitted to the Arkansas bar, Branton operated a general law practice in Pine Bluff from 1953 until 1962.

In early 1956, he filed suit against the Little Rock School Board for failing to integrate the public schools properly after the U.S. Supreme Court decision in *Brown v. Board of Education of Topeka, Kansas*. Branton's lawsuit precipitated the desegregation of Central High School, a case which was ultimately argued before the U.S. Supreme Court as *Cooper v. Aaron* in 1958. During the years he was involved in that case, Branton worked primarily with Thurgood Marshall, who presented the arguments to the Supreme Court as the director-counsel of the NAACP Legal Defense and Education Fund, Inc. They won the case, and the school board was ordered to proceed with desegregation. Branton and Marshall became fast friends during this time. The case brought Branton national recognition and led to his becoming the executive director of the Voter Education Project in 1962.

During a thirty-month period between 1962 and 1965, Branton worked with representatives of the major African-American civil rights organizations to register almost 700,000 new black voters in eleven Southern states, despite massive resistance from the white population of most of those states. This is also when Branton met and mentored a young Vernon E. Jordan, Jr., who succeeded him as executive director of the Voter Education Project. The two eventually became close friends.

Following this successful venture, Vice President Hubert H. Humphrey asked Branton to become executive director of the President's Council on Equal Opportunity and help coordinate implementation of the Civil Rights Act of 1964. After President Lyndon B. Johnson abolished the council in September of 1965, he asked Branton to move to the Department of Justice as his personal representative and to continue working to implement the Civil Rights Act and the Voting Rights Act of 1965.

In 1967 after two years with the Justice Department, Branton was appointed as executive director of the United Planning Organization (UPO), which provided social service programs to Washington, D.C., under grants through the Equal Opportunity Act of 1964. In this role, Branton helped the nation's capital recover from the effects of riots that followed the 1968 assassination of Dr. Martin Luther King, Jr. From the UPO, Branton moved to the Alliance for Labor Action in 1969, where he helped Walter Reuther, president of the United Auto Workers Union, to create social service programs across the country. Reuther's unexpected death in May 1970 thwarted the program's progress. Branton left the Alliance for Labor Action in August 1971 and returned to private law practice.

He joined with others to create the firm Dolphin, Branton, Stafford and Webber in Washington, D.C., where during one point in his practice he supervised the successful effort to obtain court-ordered protection of illegal FBI surveillance files on Dr. King. He also continued his active involvement in the many social organizations of which he was a member. The most prominent among those were the NAACP Legal Defense and Education Fund, Inc.; the NAACP; the National Bar Association; Sigma Pi Phi Fraternity; and the Masonic Order.

In December 1977, Wiley Branton became the new dean of Howard University School of Law. He took that post during a troubled period in the school's existence and was proud of his work in restoring some of its historical prominence of laying the foundations of a new battery of black civil rights lawyers. Branton left that post in September 1983 to join the Chicago law firm of Sidley and

Austin in its Washington, D.C., office. There, in a reprise of earlier years, he resisted Senator Jesse Helms's efforts to obtain access to the FBI's files on Dr. King.

Branton died of a heart attack on December 15, 1988, two days after his sixty-fifth birthday.

✦ ✦ ✦

Michael A. Conley
(1962–)

Michael A. Conley is a former basketball player and track and field athlete for the University of Arkansas (U of A) at Fayetteville. One of the most successful combination long and triple jumpers in history, he achieved career long jump bests of 8.46 meters outdoors (1996) and 8.31 meters indoors (1986), and triple jump bests of 17.87 meters outdoors (1987) and 17.76 meters indoors (1987). The latter stood as the world record until 1994. Ranked among the world's top ten triple jumpers from 1983 to 1996, Conley claimed number one in 1984, 1986, 1989, 1992, 1993, and 1994. He ranked second in the world in the long jump in 1985. In all, Conley won thirty-three national and international horizontal jump titles, most notably the 1989 World Indoor triple jump, the 1992 Olympic triple jump, and the 1993 World Outdoor triple jump.

Born in Chicago, Illinois, on October 5, 1962, Michael Alex Conley is the second of three children of Alex and Ora Conley. At Luther South High School, he played basketball and competed in track and field. Conley led the basketball team to the Illinois Class A State Championship in his junior year and was runner-up in his senior year. In track and field, he won state titles in the triple jump from 1979 to 1981, the long jump in 1980 and 1981, and the 100 and 200 meters in 1981. Also in 1981, he won the triple jump and placed second in the long jump at The Athletics Congress (TAC) Junior National Track and Field Championships.

After he graduated from high school in 1981, Conley earned an athletic scholarship to the U of A, where he could participate in both basketball and track and field. After his freshman year, basketball coach Eddie Sutton encouraged him to concentrate on track and field, where he recognized Conley's greatest potential. However, he maintained his basketball skills also and later won the Foot Locker Celebrity Slam Dunk contests in 1988, 1989, and 1992.

He won sixteen National Collegiate Athletic Association (NCAA) titles, including the indoor long jump in 1984 and 1985, the indoor triple jump from 1983 to 1985, the outdoor long jump in 1984 and 1985, and the outdoor triple jump in 1984 and 1985. As a Razorback, he also won four TAC national titles, including the outdoor triple jump in 1984, indoor long and triple jumps in 1985, and outdoor long jump in 1985. Conley's other notable performances include second in the triple jump at the 1982 World University Games, third in the long jump and fourth in the triple jump at the 1983 World Outdoor Championships, second in the triple jump at the 1984 Olympic Games (behind Arkansas State University's Al Joyner), and first in the long jump at the 1985 World Cup.

After completing his eligibility at the U of A, Conley continued to compete in the long and triple jumps. He captured thirteen TAC (USA Track & Field after 1992) national titles, including the long jump in 1986 and the triple jump indoors in 1986, 1987, and 1992 and the triple jump outdoors from 1987 to 1989 and 1993 to 1995. Internationally, Conley won the triple jump at the 1987 Pan-Amer-

ican Games, 1987 and 1989 World Indoor Championships, 1989 World Cup, 1992 Olympic Games, and 1993 World Outdoor Championships. His other significant triple jump performances include second in the 1987 World Championships, third in the 1991 World Championships, and fourth in the 1996 Olympic Games. Upon retirement in 1996, Conley ranked as the second-best triple jumper with the second-best performance of all time indoors, and as the ninth-best performer with the twelfth-best performance outdoors.

Conley is married and has four children. After retiring from competition, he served as the executive director of the Elite Athletes Division of USA Track and Field, where he established the Professional Athletics Association to protect the rights of professional track and field athletes. He earned a Bachelor of Science in business administration from Indiana Wesleyan University in 2004. Also in 2004, Conley was inducted into the USA Track and Field Hall of Fame. Later, as the executive director of the World Sports Chicago, he worked in an unsuccessful attempt to bring the 2016 Olympic Games to Chicago. He also served as the president/CEO of MMG Sports Management of Indianapolis, Indiana, facilitating college athletes making the transition to professional sports. He represented his son, Mike Jr., and his son's Ohio State teammate, Greg Oden, in contract negotiations with the National Basketball Association.

Danny K. Davis, PhD
(1941–)

Danny K. Davis is an Arkansas-born politician who has represented the Seventh District of Illinois in the U.S. House of Representatives for almost two decades. First elected in 1996 to the 105th Congress, he began his congressional service in 1997. In 2014, Davis was reelected to the 114th Congress, and he began his tenth term in January 2015.

Daniel K. Davis was born in Parkdale, Arkansas, on September 6, 1941, to Hezekiah Davis and Mazzie Davis. He received his early education in the local schools and graduated from Savage High

won his first election to the U.S. House of Representatives in 1996; he had run unsuccessfully in 1984 and 1986. In 1996, he won eighty-three percent of the vote; in subsequent elections, he never received less than eighty percent of the vote in the general election.

In the House, Davis has served on the Small Business Committee, the Oversight and Government Reform Committee, the Education and Labor Committee, the Homeland Security Committee, and the Ways and Means Committee. He has performed additional work on the subcommittees on Human Resources; Energy Policy; Health Care and Entitlements; and Economic Growth, Job Creation, and Regulatory Affairs. An advocate for improved health care, educational opportunities, and job creation, he is also known for his constituent services and communication.

Davis is a member of many caucuses that reflect the areas in which he has been most active. Those groups include the Congressional Black Caucus (for which he has served as secretary), the Congressional Postal Caucus (which he has chaired), the Congressional Children's Caucus, the Congressional Cancer Caucus, the Congressional Urban Caucus, and the Congressional Labor and Working Families Caucus. He is also a member of a number of health-oriented caucuses and is active civic organizations such as the Urban League, the Boy Scouts of America, the Congress of Racial Equality (CORE), and the National Association for the Advancement of Colored People (NAACP).

Congressman Davis is married to Vera G. Davis, and the couple has two children. During his congressional off-time, he lives in Chicago.

Samuel Massie, Jr., PhD
(1919–2005)

School in 1957. He earned his Bachelor of Arts degree in history from Arkansas Agricultural, Mechanical, and Normal College (AM&N—now the University of Arkansas at Pine Bluff) in 1961 and moved to Chicago, Illinois. He worked as a clerk in the Chicago Post Office from 1961 to 1965 and taught in the city's public schools from 1962 to 1968. Davis received a Master of Science degree in guidance from Chicago State University in 1968.

He left the classroom to work as the executive director of the Greater Lawndale Conservation Commission in 1969, before he became director of training at the Martin Luther King Neighborhood Health Center, a position he held until 1971. Davis served as executive director of the Westside Health Center from 1975 to 1981. He continued his formal education and earned a PhD in public administration from Union Institute in Cincinnati, Ohio, in 1977.

He soon entered politics and served as an alderman on the Chicago City Council from 1979 until 1990, when he gained a seat on the Cook County Board of Commissioners. While he made an unsuccessful attempt to secure the 1991 Democratic nomination for mayor of Chicago, Davis remained a member of the County Board of Commissioners. He resigned from the powerful body only after he

Samuel Massie, Jr., overcame racial barriers to become one of America's greatest chemists in research and teaching. As a doctoral candidate during World War II, he worked on the Manhattan Project with Henry Gilman at Iowa State University in the development of uranium isotopes for the atomic bomb. In 1966, the U.S. Naval Acade-

my appointed him as its first black faculty member. Massie's research over fifty years led to the development of drugs to treat mental illness, malaria, meningitis, gonorrhea, herpes, and cancer. *Chemical and Engineering News* in 1998 named him one of the top seventy-five chemists of all time, along with Marie Curie, Linus Pauling, George Washington Carver, and DNA pioneers James Watson and Francis Crick.

Samuel Proctor Massie, Jr., was born on July 3, 1919, to school teachers Samuel Proctor and Earlee Jacko Massie of North Little Rock, Arkansas; he had one younger brother. Massie quickly advanced to high school and graduated second in his class from Dunbar High School in Little Rock by age thirteen. Early on, his ambition was to become a chemist so he could discover a cure for his father's asthma.

After he had worked for a year at Horton's Grocery Store across the street from his home in North Little Rock, Massie had saved enough to afford the $15 per semester tuition at Dunbar Junior College. A year later in 1934, the University of Arkansas (U of A) at Fayetteville denied him admission because he was black. Instead, he enrolled at Arkansas Agricultural, Mechanical, and Normal College (AM&N—now the University of Arkansas at Pine Bluff). He earned a Bachelor of Science degree in chemistry with a minor in mathematics in 1937; with the aid of a federal National Youth Administration scholarship, he earned his Master of Science degree in chemistry in 1940 at Fisk University in Nashville, Tennessee. He returned to Arkansas and taught for a year at AM&N before enrolling in a doctoral program in chemistry at Iowa State University.

Racial discrimination did not make Massie's life any easier in Iowa. The closest housing available for African Americans was three miles from campus, requiring him to hitchhike to classes. He noted that he was assigned to a separate lab space "next to the rats in the basement" until he proved himself.

He almost did not get to complete the doctoral program because, according to his autobiography, when Massie returned to Arkansas in 1943 for his father's funeral and to renew his draft deferment, a member of the draft board in Pine Bluff decided that he had too much education for a black man and should be drafted into the military. He quickly contacted Dr. Gilman in Iowa, who assigned him to his research team working on the atomic bomb. In 1946, Massie received his PhD in organic chemistry at Iowa State and took a teaching position at Fisk. He went on to publish seven research papers with Gilman in the *Journal of the American Chemical Society*.

In 1947, Massie married Gloria Bell Thompkins, a fellow Fisk alum. She became a psychology professor, and the couple had three sons. Massie taught at Langston University in Langston, Oklahoma, from 1947 to 1953 and again at Fisk from 1953 to 1960. In 1954, he published "The Chemistry of Phenothiazine," an article in *Chemical Review* that led to a breakthrough by French chemists in the development of the anti-psychotic drug Thorazine. Work followed at the National Science Foundation and Howard University in Washington, D.C., in the early 1960s. The Manufacturing Chemists Association recognized Massie in 1961 as one of the six best chemistry teachers in America. He served as president of North Carolina College in Durham for four years prior to his appointment in 1966 as professor of chemistry at the U.S. Naval Academy in Annapolis, Maryland, where he was the first black faculty member. In 1970, the U of A awarded Massie an honorary Doctor of Laws degree.

He retired from the Naval Academy in 1993. During his tenure there, he served on the academy's equal employment opportunity committee and helped establish a black studies program. His portrait was hung in the National Academy of Sciences Gallery in 1995. In 1994, the U.S. Department of Energy created the Dr. Samuel P. Massie Chair of Excellence, a $14.7 million grant to nine historically black colleges and one for Hispanic students to further environmental research.

Massie died in Laurel, Maryland, on April 10, 2005, and is buried at St. Anne's Cemetery in Annapolis.

✦ ✦ ✦

Anita M. Pointer

(1948–)

Anita M. Pointer is an original member of the singing group the Pointer Sisters. She started singing gospel in her father's church in West Oakland, California, and went on to attain pop/R&B music stardom. The group's top-ten hits include the songs "Fire," "Slow Hand," "He's So Shy," "Jump (For My Love)," "Automatic," "Neutron Dance," and "I'm So Excited."

Anita Marie Pointer was born on January 23, 1948, in Oakland, California, the fourth of six children (four of them daughters) of Elton Pointer and Sarah Elizabeth Silas Pointer. Her parents were Arkansas natives, and Pointer's two older brothers, Fritz and Aaron, were born in Little Rock. Shortly thereafter, their parents moved the family to Oakland. They made almost annual road trips from California to Arkansas to visit Pointer's grandparents. Usually, the trip was related to her father's ministry.

As a child, Pointer loved Arkansas so much that she did not want to leave one year, so her mother allowed her to remain in Prescott with her grandparents to attend fifth grade. She came back to Arkansas again for her seventh- and tenth-grade school years. Pointer still owns the land where her grandfather had built a two-story house.

She noticed the differences between Oakland and racially segregated Prescott: "Going to school in the segregated South is an experience that will bring history to life. The 'colored only' and 'white only' signs, I never saw in Oakland, even though there were places we knew not to go just because. Only being allowed to sit in the balcony of the movie theatre, picking up food from the back door

of the restaurant because you can't go inside, picking cotton, I did all that and then some."

Pointer attended then-all-black McRae Elementary, McRae Junior High, and McRae High School. She was a member of the McRae High School Band and played the alto sax. She did not get to listen to much radio, but she was able to listen to broadcasts from the Grand Ole Opry and sneak out to juke joints occasionally.

Pointer and her sisters began singing gospel in their father's church, the West Oakland Church of God. Before long, their interest in music expanded and proved too strong for their parents to corral. Bonnie and June Pointer began performing as a duo in the Bay Area, calling themselves Pointers—A Pair. Shortly thereafter, Anita Pointer quit her job at a law office to join the fold, and the Pointer Sisters were officially born. The group started singing back-up in clubs and in studio sessions for such acts as Taj Mahal, Grace Slick, Boz Scaggs, Elvin Bishop, and others. Ruth Pointer later joined the group, and they released their debut album in 1973. Critics called the Pointer Sisters "the most exciting thing to hit show business in years." The Pointer Sisters were the first black female group ever to perform at the Grand Ole Opry. Their song "Fairytale," written by Anita and Bonnie Pointer, won the sisters their first Grammy Award in 1975 for Best Country Performance by a Duo or Group. Elvis Presley later did his own rendition and recording of "Fairytale."

With her sisters, Pointer has performed in front of millions around the world and recorded eighteen albums and one solo album. She has performed in diverse settings from Disneyland and the San Francisco Opera House to Roseland Ballroom, Carnegie Hall, and the White House. She has also performed on television shows such as *American Bandstand*, *Soul Train*, *The Flip Wilson Show*, *The Carol Burnett Show*, *The Tonight Show*, and *Arsenio Hall*. The Pointer Sisters were one of the first black acts to be played in heavy rotation on MTV. Pointer also participated in the recording of "We Are the World," the 1985 charity single that raised funds to help famine-relief efforts in Africa. Her acting roles have included the movie *Car Wash* (1976) with Richard Pryor, as well as *The Love Boat*, *Gimme a Break*, and the Pointer Sisters' NBC Special *Up All Night*.

The Pointer Sisters have been the recipients of many music awards, including three Grammys and three American Music Awards. They have five gold records, one platinum record, and one multi-platinum record. They were presented with a star on the Hollywood Walk of Fame in 1994. That same day, it was announced that Pointer and her sisters would embark on a national tour of the Tony-winning musical *Ain't Misbehavin'*.

Pointer, who had married at age seventeen, is divorced; she had one daughter, who was born in 1966 and died in 2003. She has said of Arkansas: "I do feel like home is where the heart is, and my heart feels at home in Arkansas. I love the South."

❖ ❖ ❖

Phyllis Yvonne Stickney

Phyllis Yvonne Stickney is an actress, comedian, poet, playwright, producer, and motivational speaker best known for her television and film roles in the late 1980s and 1990s. She was noted in the twenty-fifth anniversary issue of *Essence* magazine as one of 200 African-American women who have changed the world.

Phyllis Stickney was born in Little Rock, Arkansas, to Belle Stickney and Felix Stickney, Jr. She has publicly been vague about her age, and no available sources offer the year of her birth. Her father was an executive with the Young Men's Christian Association (YMCA), and the family moved frequently. She has two siblings, one of whom, Timothy, is also an actor and a director. Stickney studied at the University of California, Los Angeles (UCLA) and taught drama at the University of Delaware before relocating to New York City in 1979. She eventually settled in Harlem. In 1989, she married Rayford Galen Griffith, a jazz musician; the couple, who had no children, later divorced.

Stickney asserts that she naturally gravitated toward comedy as a way to get attention or to be "different." As an aspiring actress in New York, she honed her acting and comedic skills performing in predominately black theaters and on the streets of the city in public sites such as Washington Square Park. She also received theater training at the University of the Streets Theater and New Heritage Repertory Theatre (now the Heritage Theatre Group), working with her mentor, Robert Furman. Furman, a playwright and director, founded New Heritage in 1964 to provide training, exposure, and experience to artists of color; it is the oldest nonprofit black theater company in New York City.

Stickney soon gained recognition for her work with Furman. In 1983, she won an Audience Development Committee Recognition Award (AUDELCO), which rewards excellence in black theater and performing arts, for her performance in Furman's adaptation of Molière's *Tartuffe*, called *Monsieur Baptiste, the Con Man*.

It was, however, comedic performances that introduced Stickney to a wider audience. In 1986, she won first place at Amateur Night at the Apollo Theater. This led to engagements at comedy clubs throughout the city. Later that year, she was the opening act for singer Roberta Flack during her 1986 tour. She was also the warm-up announcer for NBC's *The Cosby Show* in 1986 and 1987.

In 1989, Stickney was cast as "Cora," a single mother of five children, in the ABC-TV miniseries *The Women of Brewster Place*, adapted from the Gloria Naylor novel of the same title. The miniseries depicts the lives of seven urban African-American women who live in the Brewster Place Housing Project and featured an ensemble cast that also starred Robin Givens, Lynn Whitfield, Cicely Tyson, and Oprah Winfrey.

In 1990, Stickney brought her comedic timing and Afro-centric flair to network weekly television. She co-starred in *New Attitude*, a short-lived mid-season replacement. The comedy featured Stickney and actress Sheryl Lee Ralph as sisters and co-owners of a beauty salon. The series lasted only eight episodes, but Stickney continued to have guest appearances on a variety of television programs, including *Law & Order, New York Undercover*, and *Linc's*. Her film credits include *New Jack City, Jungle Fever, Malcolm X, What's Love Got to Do with It, The Inkwell, Die Hard with a Vengeance*, and *How Stella Got Her Groove Back*.

Stickney continued to work in theater as an actress, director, and producer. In 1994, she appeared as Jesse in a stage version of the Gloria Naylor novel *Bailey's Café*. That same year, she earned her second AUDELCO for Outstanding One-Person Performance for *Big Momma 'n' 'Em*, which was written and performed by Stickney. She convincingly plays five different urban black women in crisis. The title character, Big Momma, was modeled after Stickney's own grandmother. The play highlighted Stickney's skill as a storyteller and contemporary African griot. *Big Momma 'n' 'Em* is also one of the plays featured in *Black Comedy: 9 Plays, A Critical Anthology with Interviews and Essays* (1997).

In 2001, Stickney made her directorial debut and also starred in *Been There, Done That*, a gospel stage play starring television personality Judge Greg Mathis and gospel singer Fred Hammond. She often returns to Arkansas, and she appeared in the Arkansas Repertory Theatre's adaptation of *A Raisin in the Sun* in 2011, playing Lena Younger.

Stickney is also an author. Her book *Loud Thoughts for Quiet Moments* (1988) is a compilation of her poetry, which she has been writing since the age of ten, and her personal perspectives. She gives back to the community in a variety of ways, including her program Alternative Careers in the Arts, which provides technical training for at-risk youth in various aspects of the entertainment business.

1999

Ernest James Harris, PhD

Gertrude Hadley Jeannette

Eliza Ann Miller

Vice Admiral Edward Moore, Jr.

Johnnie H. Taylor

John W. Walker

Ernest James Harris, PhD

(1928–)

Ernest James Harris is an accomplished entomologist known for his work on breeding *Biosteres arisanus*, a species of wasp that parasitizes fruit fly eggs. Thanks to the work done by Harris, *B. arisanus* has been bred on a large scale for the purposes of pest eradication. More than twenty nations have adopted use of the "Harris strain" of the wasp for fruit fly eradication.

Ernest J. Harris was born on May 24, 1928. His parents had a farm in North Little Rock where Harris's interest in insects first developed. After high school graduation, he attended Arkansas Agricultural, Mechanical, and Normal (AM&N) College (now the University of Arkansas at Pine Bluff—UAPB). There, he majored in chemistry with a minor in zoology, and graduated magna cum laude in 1951. However, despite his education, he could only find janitorial work. After a cross-country motorcycle ride, he eventually found employment in a Milwaukee, Wisconsin, laboratory. While in Wisconsin, he met a woman named Bettye Jo, and the couple married.

Harris later moved to Minnesota to take a position with the forest service. While there, he stud-

ied for his master's degree in entomology at the University of Minnesota, and he graduated in December 1959. He returned to Pine Bluff to teach science at AM&N but left in 1962 to take a job with the United States Department of Agriculture (USDA) in Hawaii. In 1975, he graduated from the University of Hawaii at Manoa with his PhD in entomology.

During more than forty years with the USDA, Harris served in a number of research capacities, including as research leader of the Biology and Ecology Research Unit of the Tropical Fruit and Vegetable Research Laboratory and research entomologist at the Pacific Basin Agriculture Research Center. However, he is most well known for his research on the control of fruit flies, a common pest that damaged and destroyed fruit crops. This prevented some nations from being able to export produce for fear of introducing the pest to other parts of the globe. Harris was able to develop a strain of *B. arisanus* wasps that could be used for fruit fly eradication without fear of introducing into the environment a population of the wasps themselves, in that the strain included sterile males. Thanks to his work, the nation of Chile, for example, has been free of fruit flies since 1975.

Harris received an official commendation from the Chilean government in 1996. He has been the recipient of several other honors, including induction into the Royal Entomological Society of London in 1989, and is a member of the Hawaiian Entomological Society, the Entomological Society of America, the International Organization of Biological Control, Sigma Xi Scientific Research Society, the Florida Entomological Society, and the African Association of Insect Scientists, among other organizations. He has published more than 100 peer-reviewed articles in a variety of scientific journals.

After retirement, Harris continued to serve as the Biological Science Collaborator at the Pacific Basin Agricultural Research Center in Honolulu. Alpha Phi Alpha Fraternity, Inc. offers a scholarship in his name. On January 14, 2012, Harris received the Lifetime Achievement Award for Distinguished Service from the National Association for the Advancement of Colored People (NAACP).

Gertrude Hadley Jeannette

(1914–)

Throughout her career, Gertrude Hadley Jeannette was a playwright, producer, director, and actress with roles on Broadway. She was involved in the civil rights movement, and she enjoyed a few unique firsts, including being the first woman to drive a cab in New York City. She retired after a seven-decade theater career and still remained active in the New York theater scene as long as her health permitted her to.

Gertrude Hadley was born in Urbana, Arkansas, on November 28, 1914, to Willis Lawrence Hadley and Salley Gertrude Crawford Hadley. She attended Dunbar High School in Little Rock and had plans to attend Fisk University. Instead, she eloped in 1934 to New York City with Joe Jeannette, II, a prizefighter and the president of the Harlem Dusters, a motorcycle club.

The couple became involved in the civil rights movement. When American singer, actor, and activist Paul Robeson came to New York City to deliver a speech, Joe Jeannette served as one of his bodyguards. In an interview, Gertrude Jeannette remembers Robeson's visit as the first time she saw the Ku Klux Klan: "They came out to lynch Paul Robeson; and I said, 'Oh my God.' I said, 'I lived in the South all my life and I never heard of this…Ku Klux Klan.' This is the first time I saw the robes and everything. So my husband said, 'Get to the motorcycle! Get to the motorcycle!' And then we rushed Robeson out of there. And all the motorcycles cranked up and…got him out of there."

In 1935, Jeannette learned to drive and became the first woman to get a license to drive a motorcycle in New York City. In 1942, she responded to a taxicab shortage by becoming the first woman to drive a cab in New York City. Her male coworkers did not respond to her employment favorably. In one instance, she said a driver in a green checker cab cut in front of her on the road. "I rammed my fender under his fender, swung it over to the right and ripped it!" she said. When the driver became angry, she yelled from her car, "You tried to cut in front of me! I couldn't stop." Surprised by her feminine voice, the angry cabbie yelled, "A woman driver! A woman driver!"

During this time, Jeannette also took bookkeeping classes at Abyssinian Baptist Church and speech classes at the American Negro Theatre.

In 1945, Jeannette began pursuing an acting career, first through her lead role in the play *Our Town*. Five years later, she performed in *This Way Forward*, which was the first play Jeannette wrote. The autobiographical play shows the life of sharecropping families in the South. She replaced Pearl Bailey in *God's Trombones*, in which she appeared alongside Fred O'Neil.

Jeannette continued to work in the theater as well as in film and television. Her experience driving a cab inspired her creatively, especially as a playwright. She went on to hold roles in Broadway plays such as *Lost in the Stars*, *Amen Corner*, and *The Great White Hope*. Some of Jeannette's film credits included *Shaft*, *Black Girl*, and *Cotton Comes to Harlem*. Jeannette directed, produced, and wrote her own plays, as well as producing the works of other playwrights.

In 1979, Jeannette founded the Harlem Artists Development League Especially for You (H.A.D.L.E.Y.) Players. The mission of the H.A.D.L.E.Y. Players was to give artists a chance to develop their talents and skills in the theater, and to enrich Harlem's cultural life.

Jeannette has received numerous accolades. She received the Outstanding Pioneer Award from

Audelco in 1984, the AT&T and Black American Newspaper's 1987 Personality of the Year Award, and the 1992 Harlem Business Recognition Award from the Manhattan Section of the National Council of Negro Women. In 1991, Jeannette was honored as a living legend at the National Black Theatre Festival in Winston-Salem, North Carolina. Seven years later, she was honored with the Lionel Hampton Legacy Award. In 2002, she received the prestigious Paul Robeson Award from the Actors' Equity Association. While celebrating her 100th birthday in November 2014, she invited her guests back for her 110th.

Jeannette had a seventy-year career in television, movies, and the theater, and remains a celebrated figure in the New York theater world. She is affectionately known as Ms. "J" or Ms. "G."

Eliza Ann Miller

(1869–1938)

Eliza Ann Miller was an African-American businesswoman and educator, as well as the first woman to build and operate a movie theater in Arkansas. She was the wife of prosperous Helena, Arkansas, businessman, state legislator, and church leader Abraham Hugo Miller. After her husband's death, she continued his business operations while also providing leadership in the Helena school system.

Eliza Ann Ross was born in Arkadelphia, Arkansas, on September 6, 1869, to George and Sarah Ross. On June 15, 1887, she married Abraham H. Miller in Arkadelphia. The couple had eight children, five of whom survived into adulthood. Abraham Miller, who had been successful in real estate and other ventures, noted that his wife was a "fair and handsome" woman, but what he valued most about her was her business sense. He praised her abilities as a "collector, supervisor secretary, bookkeeper and general manager for the past seven years. Instead of business failing or dropping back under her administration, it has gone steadily forward."

After Abraham's death in 1913, Eliza Miller built the Plaza Theatre, which opened around 1917 at 116 Walnut Street in downtown Helena. By 1918, audiences at the Plaza could view silent films by Charlie Chaplin, Norma Talmadge, and Jackie Saunders, which Miller obtained from distributors in Dallas, Texas, and Memphis, Tennessee. In 1921, the Plaza showed a film starring black actor Sidney P. Dones with an "all Colored Star cast." By the 1920s, Miller's son Lucian, a graduate of Fisk University and Arkansas Baptist College, was living with her and running the Plaza. By the 1930s, Eliza Miller was again in charge of the theater, which she operated until her death.

In addition to running the family's businesses, Miller was also active in education. With her husband, she served on the board of trustees at Arkansas Baptist College in Little Rock. In the mid-1920s, she bought land that belonged to Sacred Heart Academy, which was run by the Sisters of Charity. In 1926, Eliza Miller High School, the first African-American high school in the area, was established at the site. In later years, the Eliza Miller Award was given to the best teachers at the school.

Eliza Miller died on August 28, 1938. She is buried in Magnolia Cemetery in Helena.

In 1970, Eliza Miller High School was desegregated and renamed Eliza Miller Junior High School. Over the years, in addition to instructing Helena children, the school hosted such musical acts as the Staple Sisters and B. B. King. In 1978,

Eliza Miller Park was established in Helena. Three schools in the area now bear her name: Eliza Miller Junior High School, Eliza Miller Elementary School, and Eliza Miller Primary School. Combined, the schools number roughly 1,000 students, more than ninety percent of whom are African American. The schools are located at 106 Miller Loop in Helena-West Helena.

In 2003, the Arkansas General Assembly recognized Eliza Miller and the Miller family for their accomplishments in its House Concurrent Resolution 1028: "Recognizing and Commending the Miller Family." The resolution, sponsored by Helena's state representative, Barbara King, noted: "Eliza Miller's legacy to her family and today's black youth is the value of an education, determination, and respect." That same year, New York Institute of Technology student and filmmaker Dana Bingham completed a short documentary film, *Eliza Ross Miller: Ye Shall Know Thee by Thy Fruits*, which was funded by the Arkansas Humanities Council. According to Bingham, whose parents and grandparents attended Eliza Miller High School, the film examined how the school "went against every stereotype of education in the segregated South."

Miller's descendants have gone on to become successful lawyers and business owners. Her grandson George Miller, Jr., opened a movie theater in Memphis in 1974 and founded Miller Memphis, Inc., which had large holdings on Beale Street. Another grandson, Dr. Robert Dan Miller, became the first black board president of the Arkansas Board of Health, the first black doctor at Helena Hospital, and the first black mayor of Helena. Dr. Miller's son, Brian Miller, was appointed a federal judge.

Vice Admiral Edward Moore, Jr.
(1945–)

Edward Moore, Jr., is a retired vice admiral who served in the U.S. Navy. At the time of his retirement, he was the highest-ranking African American in the navy.

Edward Moore, Jr., was born on February 18, 1945, in New York City. He is the eldest child of Edward Moore, Sr., and Freddie Mardell Hayes Moore. He has two brothers and a sister. The family eventually moved to Little Rock, Arkansas, where Moore graduated from Horace Mann High School in 1963.

On April 2, two months before his high school graduation, Moore enlisted in the U.S. Navy Reserve. The day after his high school graduation, he departed Little Rock for recruit training in San Diego, California. While in training, Moore was accepted into the Reserve Officer Candidate program. As part of this program, he began college at Southern Illinois University after completing his training in August 1963. A full-time student, Moore was required to maintain satisfactory reserve status while in school, including regular drills and annual active duty periods; during these periods, Moore served on the USS *Hyman* and USS *Woodson*. He graduated with a degree in psychology and received his commission as an ensign in 1968.

Moore was immediately assigned to a ship, the fleet oiler USS *Severn*, in June 1968. On the ship, he attended Legal School, Registered Publications

School, and a navigation refresher course. He spent a total of eighteen months on the *Severn* with time spent as the administrative officer, gunnery officer, communications officer, classified material officer, and navigator. In June 1969, Moore was promoted to lieutenant, junior grade. In December 1969, Moore was assigned to the pre-commissioning unit for the USS *Lang*, a frigate. He initially served as communications officer and later served as operations officer, with two deployments to the Tonkin Gulf during the Vietnam War. He married Deborah Cooper in Champaign, Illinois, on December 24, 1969. Moore was promoted to lieutenant in December 1970.

In August 1974, Moore became a junior officer, assignment officer, and shore assignments coordinator for the Surface Warfare Community in the Bureau of Naval Personnel. The same month, he earned a graduate degree in business administration from the U.S. Naval Postgraduate School. In December 1974, he was promoted to lieutenant commander. He attended the Department Head Course at the Surface Warfare Officer's School Command in 1976 and 1977 before joining the USS *Sterett*, a cruiser. Moore served as the executive officer of the USS *Buchanan*, a destroyer, from 1978 to 1979. He was promoted to commander in December 1979.

Next serving as the Current Navy Operations Analyst on the staff of the commander of the U.S. Pacific Command from 1980 to 1984, Moore received his first command after that assignment. He commanded the USS *Lewis B. Puller* from 1984 to 1986. The guided missile frigate was deployed to the western Pacific in 1986. Moore was promoted to captain in August 1986. He served as the assistant chief of staff for manpower and personnel on the staff of the commander of the U.S. Pacific Fleet from 1986 to 1989, and he was selected to become the first commanding officer of the USS *Cowpens*, then under construction in Bath, Maine. The ship was commissioned on March 9, 1991. Moore led the *Cowpens* and three other ships in a missile attack on an Iraqi nuclear weapons site near Baghdad on January 17, 1993. In June 1993, Moore was promoted to rear admiral (lower half).

From 1993 to 1995, Moore served as the commandant, Naval District, Washington, D.C. He returned to sea in 1995 as the commander of the USS *Carl Vinson* Task Group and commander of Cruiser Destroyer Group Three. This force consisted of eight surface ships, two submarines, and one aircraft wing. It was tasked with enforcing the no-fly zone over southern Iraq and also launched missile strikes against military sites in the country in September 1996. In July 1996, Moore was promoted to rear admiral (upper half).

In 1997, Moore returned to Washington, where he served as the assistant deputy chief of Naval Operations, Plans, Policy, and Operations, and as director of the Strategy and Policy Division, Chief of Naval Operations Staff. During this period, he was also the Naval Operations deputy representative to the Joint Chiefs of Staff. In August 1998, Moore was promoted to vice admiral and became the commander of the Naval Surface Force, U.S. Pacific Fleet. He held this position until May 2001, and he retired from the navy in July 2001.

After retiring from active service, Moore served as a vice president at the Anteon International Corporation, a defense contractor, until 2006. That year, the company was bought by General Dynamics, and Moore served as its vice president of navy services until January 2012.

Moore and his wife have four adult children: three daughters and a son. They reside in California.

Johnnie H. Taylor

(1934–2000)

Johnnie H. Taylor was a popular gospel and rhythm and blues singer, known as the "Philosopher of Soul," whose recording career spanned forty-six years. His single "Disco Lady" was the first single ever to be certified platinum.

Johnnie Harrison Taylor was born in Crawfordsville, Arkansas, on May 5, 1934. The official date of his birth was not revealed until after his death; he had long claimed to be four years younger. The youngest of three siblings, he was reared by his grandmother in West Memphis, Arkansas. She was religious and made sure he attended church regularly. He made his church singing debut at age six. Inspired by both gospel and the blues, he de-

cided at a young age that he wanted to become a professional singer.

Taylor moved to Kansas City, Missouri, at age ten with his grandmother. During his teen years, he sang with a gospel quartet, the Melody Kings. They occasionally opened for the famous, highly influential gospel group the Soul Stirrers, whose young lead singer, Sam Cooke, befriended Taylor.

By 1953, Taylor had moved to Chicago, Illinois, and was singing with the doo-wop group the Five Echoes, with whom he made his first recordings on the VeeJay label. Shortly afterward, he also began singing with the Highway QCs, a long-running, popular gospel quartet of which Cooke and Lou Rawls had previously been members. The QCs made their recording debut in 1955 with Taylor singing lead on "Somewhere to Lay My Head," which made the group a nationwide gospel attraction.

When Cooke left the Soul Stirrers, Taylor was chosen to be his replacement in 1957. While a member of the group, he became an ordained minister and preached his first sermon at Fellowship Baptist Church in Chicago.

After a wreck in which he ran over a little girl in 1960, Taylor was booted from the Soul Stirrers. He went to Los Angeles, California, where he intended to preach full time. However, in 1963, Cooke signed him as the first artist on his new SAR label, and Taylor, still stinging from being kicked out of the Soul Stirrers and determined to find his place in the music marketplace, began recording secular music. His first solo single was "A Whole Lot of Woman" in 1961. Other notable early R&B recordings were "Rome (Wasn't Built in a Day)" (1962) and "Baby We've Got Love" (1963), which was his first song to appear on *Billboard* magazine's Top 100 chart. The label folded after Cooke's death in 1964.

In 1966, Taylor signed with Stax Records in Memphis, Tennessee, where Arkansas native and Stax executive Al Bell of North Little Rock dubbed him the "Philosopher of Soul." At Stax, Taylor polished his musical style, which combined gospel, R&B, and blues, as well as his flamboyant appearance, and he proceeded to become one of the label's top-selling performers, outselling such big stars as Otis Redding and Carla Thomas. He had a prolific run on the R&B charts, beginning with "I Had a Dream" (1966). His first song on the Stax label to break the pop Top 100 was "Somebody's Sleeping in My Bed" (1967).

In 1968, Taylor had his first major crossover pop and R&B hit in "Who's Making Love," a funk/soul song that went to number one on the R&B charts and hit number five on the pop charts. The success of "Who's Making Love" enabled Taylor to hire a superb, permanent touring band for the first time in his career, and he became a major performer on the "Chitlin' Circuit" all across the South. Subsequent hits included "Take Care of Your Homework" (1969), "Jody's Got Your Girl and Gone" (1971), "I Believe in You (You Believe in Me)" (1972), and "Cheaper to Keep Her" (1973). By this time, he had perfected his style of smooth, soulful crooning, which incorporated gospel, blues, and soul.

When Stax Records went bankrupt in 1975, Taylor signed with CBS/Columbia. In 1976, he released his first CBS album, titled *Eargasm*, which contained his biggest hit, "Disco Lady," which went to number one on both the R&B and pop charts and became the first single ever to be certified platinum, selling more than two million copies. CBS pushed him to record more tunes in the disco genre, not taking advantage of the full range of his talent. His record sales slipped, and he began to look for another label.

In 1982, Taylor signed with Beverly Glen Records and got back on the R&B charts with "What About My Love." In 1984, he signed with Malaco Records and became one of its most popular artists. He released a succession of hit R&B albums for the label, beginning with *This Is Your Night*. His 1996 album, *Good Love*, topped *Billboard*'s blues charts on the strength of the single "Last Two Dollars," and the album became the biggest seller in Malaco history. Taylor released his final album, *Gotta Get the Groove Back*, in 1999. In that same year, he was given a Pioneer Award by the Rhythm and Blues Foundation.

While living in Duncanville, Texas, a suburb of Dallas, Taylor suffered a heart attack, and on May 31, 2000, he died at Charlton Methodist Hospital in Dallas.

He is buried at Forest Hill Cemetery in Kansas City.

John W. Walker

(1937–)

John W. Walker is a nationally known civil rights lawyer and a Democratic member of the Arkansas General Assembly.

John Winfield Walker was born in Hope, Arkansas, on June 3, 1937. He graduated from Jack Yates High School in Houston, Texas, in 1954 and was subsequently admitted to the University of Texas, where he planned to become a petroleum engineer. He was one of six students who would be the university's first African Americans admitted, but the planned desegregation of the school was scuttled by officials after one of the six announced his plans to try out for the Longhorn football team. All six students were immediately unenrolled. (The university did not open its athletic programs to African-American students until 1963 and did not have a black football player until 1970.) Walker filed suit against the University of Texas, and en-

rolled at Arkansas Agricultural, Mechanical, and Normal College (AM&N) in Pine Bluff (now the University of Arkansas at Pine Bluff—UAPB), where he received a degree in sociology in 1958.

That same year, he got married and took a position as the assistant director of the Arkansas Council on Human Relations in Little Rock. It was during this time that he came to know Little Rock civil rights pioneers Daisy and L. C. Bates, who were still fighting the state regarding the desegregation of Central High School. Having received the John Hay Whitney Fellowship, Walker later entered graduate school at New York University. He graduated with a master's degree in education in 1961. He then entered Yale University Law School and earned a Juris Doctorate degree in 1964. From there, he interned with the National Association for the Advancement of Colored People (NAACP) Legal Defense Fund before moving back to Little Rock to open his own law practice.

Throughout his years of practice, Walker has represented thousands of clients across the greater

Little Rock region. One of the more well-known cases in which he was involved was *Little Rock School District et al. v. Pulaski County Special School District et al.*, a case that lasted from 1982 to 2014. The case was an outgrowth of the original desegregation of Central High School. In 1998, Walker was able to get the Little Rock School District to agree on a new desegregation and education plan. However, by the time a federal judge gave final approval to the settlement in 2014, Walker lamented that many of the original problems still persisted. He also won a class-action lawsuit against Walmart in 2009 after he successfully argued that the world's largest corporation had discriminated against African Americans in hiring for truck driver positions.

In 2010, Walker successfully ran for the Arkansas House of Representatives on the Democratic Party ticket. Running unopposed, he was subsequently re-elected in 2012, 2014, and 2016. He has served on the House Education Committee; the House Aging, Children and Youth Committee; the Legislative and Military Affairs Committee; and the Legislative Joint Auditing Committee.

Walker and a colleague, Omavi Kushukuru, received national attention following their September 26, 2016, arrest for "obstruction of governmental operations" after they filmed a traffic stop being carried out by the Little Rock Police Department.

Dashboard camera footage of their own arrest was circulated widely, and national media outlets noted the irony of Walker's arrest, given the fact that he had written the law allowing civilians to film police operations. After reviewing the records of the arrest, Kenton Buckner, Little Rock's chief of police, formally dropped the charges and issued an apology to Walker, which Walker rejected, citing "the issue of racial bias that is pervasive in some quarters of the police department."

During his time in office, Walker has opposed the state takeover of the Little Rock School District, attempted to increase worker protections, and sought to expand voting rights through automatic voter registration.

In 2017, during the wave of anti-immigrant sentiment unleashed following the previous year's presidential election, Walker pushed a bill to require that all members of the Arkansas General Assembly pass the civics portion of the immigrant naturalization test before they could be permitted to vote on laws, though this bill died in committee.

Walker is a member of the Alpha Phi Alpha Fraternity, Inc. He has received the War Horse Award from the Southern Trial Lawyers Association and the Lawyer of the Year Award from the Arkansas Bar Association. He has five children and lives in Little Rock.

2000

Floyd Brown

Lela Rochon Fuqua

E. Lynn Harris

Theressa Hoover

Wilbert C. Jordan, MD

Roy Roberts

Floyd Brown

(1891–1961)

Floyd Brown founded the Fargo Agricultural School in Monroe County, Arkansas, in 1919 to provide the equivalent of elementary and secondary vocational education for African-American students. The school was for both day and residential students and was modeled after Tuskegee Institute, which Brown attended, where students learned practical skills intended to help them achieve success and economic security.

Floyd B. Brown was born on April 27, 1891, in Stampley, Mississippi, the second of ten children and the son of black tenant farmers Charles and Janie Brown. As a youth, Brown worked with his father in the cotton fields of Mississippi and the cane fields of Louisiana. His mother, who had heard of the work of Booker T. Washington, encouraged him to enter Tuskegee, where he received a high school certificate in 1917. Washington had died in 1915, but his influence at Tuskegee and in the United States was immense, and his legacy lived on for several generations. In 1918, Brown was ordained as a Baptist minister after studies at Phelps Hall Bible School on the Tuskegee campus.

During the summer of 1915, Brown had visited Fargo, Arkansas, while selling books by Booker T. Washington, probably *Up from Slavery*, in eastern Arkansas. Fargo and nearby Zent were primarily black communities that lacked school facilities. He decided to return and start a school there patterned after Tuskegee. As he famously stated in his later autobiography, "I returned…with $2.85 with faith in God and the people to start my mission work."

Brown borrowed money as an initial payment for twenty acres of land a short distance southeast of Fargo. On January 1, 1920, the school opened with one teacher, Ruth Mahon, and fifteen students in a one-room school; at the same time, Brown developed a board of trustees composed of both African Americans and whites. He married Lillian Epps on March 5, 1921, and she also taught classes as head of the home economics department. The couple had no children.

The ideology that Brown learned from Booker T. Washington at Tuskegee particularly equipped him to face the racial conflicts of the Arkansas Delta in the early 1920s. Although Brown was never known to make direct references to racial violence, he must have been aware of the Elaine Massacre of 1919, which occurred just sixty miles south of Fargo. Moreover, the indignities of Jim Crow and the horror of lynching were daily reminders of racial conflict for African Americans. Brown accommodated himself to segregation and to "liberal" whites in return for their support of the school. To his students, Brown argued that they must earn greater rights based on accomplishment not confrontation, and he emphasized that they should not be ashamed to start at the bottom of the economic ladder nor to work with their hands. Brown stressed, as had Washington, what *could* be done rather than what *should* be done.

The Great Depression years compounded the school's challenges, but it was able to survive because of its farm. By 1945, the Fargo Agricultural School owned 550 acres of land, had twelve buildings constructed by faculty and students, and had an enrollment of 180 day and residential students. The school's products were sold for basic support, but Brown traveled extensively to raise additional funds from private individuals and businesses. One of the many aphorisms that Brown used, "Work Will Win," became the title of a documentary about the school made in 1994. In addition to his

...

other activities, Brown had a community service mission. He organized an annual Negro Farmers Conference for continuing education and groups to conduct annual maintenance of local cemeteries.

In 1949, when the need for the school had diminished, Brown sold the campus to the state of Arkansas. The state used the campus for a new school, the Fargo Training School for Negro Girls. Brown served as principal until his permanent retirement in 1954. None of the original campus buildings survive.

In the 1990s, alumni created the Fargo Agricultural School Museum at the School for Negro Girls site to honor Brown. The museum subsequently moved to Brinkley, Arkansas.

In 1955, the Browns moved to Pine Bluff, Arkansas, to live in a new home at 1401 Georgia Street. Brown died there six years later, on September 11, 1961, and he is buried at P. K. Miller Cemetery in Pine Bluff.

Lela Rochon Fuqua

(1964–)

Lela Rochon Fuqua, known professionally as Lela Rochon, has appeared in nearly fifty movies and television shows, starring alongside some of Hollywood's elite actors and actresses.

She was born Lela Rochon Staples in Torrance, California, on April 17, 1964, to Samuel Staples and Zelma Staples of Camden, Arkansas. Both of her parents are alumni of Lincoln High School and both attended Arkansas Agricultural, Mechanical, and Normal College (AM&N), now the University of Arkansas at Pine Bluff (UAPB). Her father graduated from Arkansas AM&N and went on to own and operate Aladdin Enterprises, a graphic-arts business in California, from 1968 until his retirement in 2002. Her mother became a nurse practitioner at the University of Southern California Medical Center and retired in 2000. Although she grew up in a single-child household, Rochon has an older half-brother named Kenneth. Her parents are of Haitian descent, and she was named for her paternal grandmother.

During her formative years, she spent time in Arkansas with her parents' families in Camden and at Arkansas AM&N for various alumni functions. She once stated, "Had I not had the upbringing, the morals, and the values that my parents placed within me, I would be lost in Hollywood." Rochon attended Cerritos High School in California and graduated in 1982. She excelled at competitive sports, particularly track and basketball. She also performed in school productions.

Rochon graduated from California State University, Dominguez Hills, in 1986; she majored in broadcast journalism with minors in sociology and theater. She modeled as a way to help pay for tuition and books, and she landed steady work appearing as a "Spudette" in Budweiser/Bud Light Spuds MacKenzie television commercials. After her college graduation, Rochon had contemplated law school but pursued acting instead.

She appeared in several sitcoms, including *The Cosby Show*, *21 Jump Street*, *227*, and *The Fresh Prince of Bel-Air*, as well as dancing in music videos for Lionel Richie and Luther Vandross. Her major film debut was in the small role of "Sunshine" in 1989's *Harlem Nights* with Eddie Murphy. She had a steady role during the first season of *The Wayans Bros.* cable show. Rochon's breakthrough came when she played the role of Robin Stokes in the 1995 box office hit *Waiting to Exhale* alongside Angela Bassett and Whitney Houston. In seeking the part, Rochon had wrangled a meeting with director Forest Whitaker, who had already cast another actress. The movie made her a household name. *People* magazine named her one of the fifty most beautiful people in the world in 1996. She went on to star as Mildred Loving in *Mr. and Mrs. Loving*, as attorney Nora Stark in John Grisham's *The Chamber*, and in *Brooklyn's Finest* and *Let the Church Say Amen*.

Rochon was married to dancer Adolfo Quinines from 1982 to 1987. She married Antoine Fuqua in 1999 and became stepmother to Fuqua's son, Zachary. Their daughter, Asia, was born in 2002, and their son, Brando, in 2004.

She has received numerous accolades throughout her career, including a Cable/ACE Award nomination, an Image nomination, and an MTC Movie nomination. Rochon returns to Camden often for special events. In June 2015, she served as the keynote speaker for the Dream Girls conference at Connection International Camden Church, where her aunt and uncle are co-pastors.

E. Lynn Harris

(1955–2009)

Everette Lynn Harris was a bestselling author of novels about African-American men in gay and bisexual relationships. In his nine novels, which have sold more than three million copies, the gay characters are "on the down low" or have not publicized their sexuality. Harris endured years of abuse at the hands of his stepfather and for years denied his own homosexuality.

E. Lynn Harris was born on June 20, 1955, in Flint, Michigan, to Etta Mae Williams and James Jeter, who were unmarried. When Harris was three, he moved with his mother to Little Rock, Arkansas, where she worked as a housekeeper. She married Ben Odis Harris, who helped rear Harris until he was thirteen, when the couple divorced. Harris had three younger sisters. The summer before his junior year of high school, when Harris was fifteen, he learned about his biological father and visited him several times while staying with relatives in Michigan. Jeter died in an automobile accident the next spring.

In his youth, Harris frequented the public library in Little Rock and fell in love with the writings of James Baldwin and Maya Angelou. He also worked at the Little Rock Zoo, Baskin-Robbins, Arkansas Paper Co., and M. M. Cohn; he used the income to buy clothes and school supplies.

Harris graduated from Hall High School in Little Rock in 1973 and attended the University of Arkansas (U of A) at Fayetteville in the mid-1970s. He was the school's first black male cheerleader and first black yearbook editor. He served as president of Alpha Phi Alpha Fraternity, Inc. He graduated with honors in 1977, with a Bachelor of Arts degree in journalism.

He sold computers for IBM and other companies for thirteen years; during this time, he lived in Dallas, Texas; New York City; Washington, D.C.; and Atlanta, Georgia. For years, he kept his sexual orientation hidden, and this led to depression and heavy drinking. In August 1990 while he lived in Washington, D.C., he attempted suicide by ingesting a mixture of champagne, vodka, and sleeping pills. He soon got sober and managed his depression with medication and therapy. He bought a computer and started writing his first book, which proved to be therapeutic.

While Harris lived in Atlanta, he self-published his novel *Invisible Life* in 1991 and personally hand-delivered it to black-owned bookstores and beauty salons. In this coming-of-age tale, the book's protagonist, Raymond Tyler, discovers his bisexuality and struggles to accept his true desires. *Invisible Life* caught the eye of a Doubleday sales representative, who bought a copy and sent it to the publishing house. Eventually, Harris made a presentation to company officials, who signed him to a three-book deal. Anchor Books, an imprint of Doubleday, published the book in trade paperback in 1994.

Among his other novels are *Just As I Am* (1994), *And This Too Shall Pass* (1996), *If This World Were Mine* (1997), *Abide with Me* (1999), *Not a Day Goes By* (2000), *Any Way the Wind Blows* (2001), *A Love of My Own* (2002), and *I Say a Little Prayer* (2006). His books tell ultimately optimistic stories that explore friendship, careers, romance, sexuality, and race. Harris wrote with an ear for black dialect, with descriptions, slang terms, and dialogue. *Just As I Am*, *Any Way the Wind Blows*, and *A Love of My Own* all won Novel of the Year designations by the Blackboard African American Bestsellers, Inc. In 1997, *If This World Were Mine* won the James Baldwin Award for Literary Excellence. His memoir, *What Becomes of the Brokenhearted*, which he wrote over a period of seven years, was published in 2003.

In 1999, Harris's college alma mater honored him with a Citation of Distinguished Alumni for outstanding professional achievement. Other honors include the Sprague Todes Literary Award, the Harvey Milk Honorary Diploma, and the Silas Hunt Legacy Award for Outstanding Achievement from the U of A.

Harris returned to the U of A in the fall of 2003 to teach literature and writing in the Department of English, and he served as cheer coach for the Arkansas Razorbacks cheerleading squad. For his class on contemporary black authors, he brought in authors as guest speakers. He also taught a class focused on black female writers. He lived in Fayetteville while he taught at the university, but he also had homes in Houston, Texas, and Atlanta at the time.

A musical based on *Not a Day Goes By* toured nationally in 2004. As a lecturer, Harris spoke at colleges across the country. He wrote articles for *Sports Illustrated*, *Essence*, *The Washington Post Sun-* *day Magazine*, *The New York Times Book Review*, *The Atlanta Journal-Constitution*, and *The Advocate*.

Harris's novel *I Say a Little Prayer* was released in May 2006. It was written while he was at the U of A and during the time spent at his Houston home. It debuted at number three on *The New York Times Book Review*'s bestseller list. He subsequently published *Just Too Good to Be True* (2008) and *Basketball Jones* (2009).

Harris died on July 24, 2009, in Los Angeles, Calibornia, while he was there on a business trip.

Theressa Hoover

(1925–2013)

Theressa Hoover worked for human rights and unity through the United Methodist Church for nearly fifty years. An Arkansas native, she represented those who, in the words of her 1974 monograph, were in "triple jeopardy": female, African American, and Christian. Hoover worked for justice and empowerment for women and children around the globe. She provided inspiration for others through her words and actions, and her influence has been far-reaching.

Theressa Hoover was born in Fayetteville, Arkansas, on September 7, 1925. She was one of five children of James C. Hoover and Rissie Vaughn. Her mother died when Hoover was a small child. She was reared by her father, who worked for many years at City Hospital in Fayetteville. Hoover attended elementary school in Fayetteville but could not attend the segregated high school. Instead, she went to live with an aunt in Atlanta, Texas, until she graduated. She returned to Arkansas to study at Philander Smith College in Little Rock, where she received a Bachelor of Science degree in business administration in 1946.

Hoover worked for the Little Rock Methodist Council as associate director. Her work in this position included a project that offered outdoor recreation opportunities for African Americans in Little Rock. This project brought her to the attention of the Methodist Church's governing body. In 1948, she was hired by the Women's Division of the United Methodist Church as a field worker to

assist in the integration of Methodist churches in Little Rock and then throughout the nation. She moved to New York during the decade she spent in this position and received her Master of Arts degree in human relations and social policy from the Steinhardt School of New York University in 1962.

Hoover rose through the ranks of the church government to become head of staff of the Women's Division of the General Board of Global Ministries of the United Methodist Church in New York City. *Time* magazine described her as "a highly influential Methodist bureaucrat." Asked about this description, Hoover said, "If you're going to be a bureaucrat, you ought to be a good one. I was a good one." She was known for her support of women, in particular women of color, using her strong communication skills to smooth integration and inclusion for those who had been excluded in the past.

Hoover worked in all fifty states at one time or another, as well as in both Pakistan and India. She wrote "Black Women and the Churches: Triple Jeopardy," anthologized in *Sexist Religion and Women in the Church: No More Silence* in 1974, and *With Unveiled Face: Centennial Reflections on Women and Men in the Community of the Church* in 1983, as well as regular columns in *Response* magazine. All these publications, and most of Hoover's speeches, focused on power and equality for women and for people of color in the church and in society.

Hoover also served on the Commission on the Churches' Participation in Development of the World Council of Churches, the Methodist Church's Joint Commission on Church Union, the executive board of the National Council of Negro Women, the National Board of the Young Women's Christian Association (YWCA), the National Council of Negro Women, and the board of the Bossey Ecumenical Institute in Celigny, Switzerland. She retired in 1990 and spent the next ten years traveling and speaking before retiring to Fayetteville.

On October 6, 1990, the Women's Division of the United Methodist Church established the $100,000 Theressa Hoover Community Service and Global Citizenship fund in her honor. This fund provided grants for young women to travel and study. In 2004, Hoover was on *Ebony* magazine's list of the 100 most influential African-American women. The Theressa Hoover United Methodist Church in Little Rock was named for her. In May 2008, a scholarship was established in Hoover's honor at the University of Arkansas (U of A) at Fayetteville, to support students from Fayetteville High School.

Hoover never married. She has a grandniece who was named after her. She said that she felt as if she had served as a mother and a grandmother to dozens of young women.

Hoover died in Fayetteville on December 21, 2013, and is buried in Oak Cemetery there.

Wilbert C. Jordan, MD
(1943–)

Wilbert C. Jordan is a Los Angeles, California, native who became an Arkansas transplant; he still owns eleven acres of land in Wheatley. He attended high school at Marian Anderson High School in Brinkley, Arkansas, through the eleventh grade before he entered Little Rock's Horace Mann High School. He graduated in 1961. He graduated from Harvard College in 1966 and received his MD in 1971 from Case Western Reserve University School of Medicine in Cleveland, Ohio. Jordan completed an intern-

next twenty-one years, Dr. Jordan treated 3,000 clinically diagnosed HIV/AIDS patients.

The first group of those patients was made up of four of the five people brought to him by the addict he had met. Jordan learned in his encounter with those men that patients who are often overlooked or ignored in the fight against HIV/AIDS are key figures in winning this battle, because the patients know who is at risk. This observation led to the development of a program that has amazed many with its unexpected success and, more importantly, its simplicity. Dr. Jordan has found more than 300 patients by inviting people to bring someone they know to the clinic for HIV testing. Nearly half (48 percent) of those patients were found to be HIV positive.

With more than half of the new cases of HIV in the United States reported to be African Americans, Jordan says the reason African Americans need to get involved in the fight against HIV is just as simple. "It's called self-preservation," he says. As the number of African Americans who are being diagnosed with HIV/AIDS continues to climb, Jordan believes that black people's approach to dealing with the HIV/AIDS pandemic cannot be the same as that for gay white men.

Jordan's genuinely cares for and is concerned about the welfare of his people and says that his patients do not have to have money to receive proper treatment. He says his work has taught him much about himself and his community over the years. He has seen the power of giving patients a more prominent role in their own recovery, as well as their friends' recovery.

"For patients, this is a chance to help give others information," explains Jordan. "When it is someone you know who is talking to you, the trust factor is higher. It brings down the stigma of getting tested, and it makes people more comfortable with the idea of going to the clinic to get treated." He has also found that those people who bring others in become more compliant with their own medication regimens. Some of his most non-adherent patients are now taking their medicine reliably.

Dr. Jordan is inspired by a personal experience, the passing of a close friend who succumbed to AIDS early in the epidemic, when people were ostracized due to ignorance of the disease. Few doctors were reaching out to African Americans at the

ship and junior residency in internal medicine at Beth Israel Hospital in Boston, Massachusetts, in 1973. As a Robert Wood Johnson Clinical Scholar, he received his Master in Public Health degree in 1976 at the University of California, Los Angeles (UCLA) and completed rotations in internal medicine and infectious diseases. HIV (human immunodeficiency virus) outreach has been a primary pursuit of Dr. Jordan's career.

As he left his office one evening, Dr. Jordan was approached by an addict who needed money. The conversation evolved into a discussion about HIV and AIDS (acquired immune deficiency syndrome). Across the street there was a mobile health unit. The addict told Dr. Jordan that the health unit's workers were looking for drug users to test for HIV infection but did not know where to find them. The addict revealed that he could find them. The two struck a deal. Dr. Jordan assured the man that if he brought him a person who was at risk for HIV infection, he would give him some money. Both men honored that agreement.

The result was the creation of the Oasis Clinic, of which Dr. Jordan is the director. The clinic started in 1979 when Dr. Jordan treated his first AIDS patient without knowing at the time that the symptoms were related to the disease. Over the time. Dr. Jordan's friend was abandoned by his wife and denied interaction with his children. All of his friends abandoned him, except Jordan, who continues to treat his own patients with the love and support his friend never received.

In addition to his directorship at his Oasis Clinic, he is also the director at the Los Angeles County Martin Luther King, Jr., Outpatient Center and an associate professor of internal medicine at Charles Drew University (CDU).

In 2000, he received the Surgeon General's Award for his work with HIV, which had included his involvement with the NIH-sponsored DATRI Study on low-dose oral alpha interferon, his chairing of the Los Angeles County Commission on HIV & AIDS from 1993 to 1995, and his service on the Los Angeles County HIV Planning Council and the Prevention and Planning Committee since their inceptions. Dr. Jordan has been honored by the *Los Angeles Sentinel*; by the Student National Medical Association when it renamed its research forum the Dr. Wilbert C. Jordan Research Forum; and by being named "Doctor of the Year" three times by the Charles R. Drew Medical Society. In 2002, he was the first recipient of the B.E.T. Community Service Pioneers Award. He has served as medical director for the Minority AIDS Project since its creation and has been chairman of the Black Los Angeles AIDS Consortium for more than twelve years. In 2015, Better Brothers Los Angeles and the D.I.V.A. Foundation (Divinely Inspired Victoriously Aware founded by Sheryl Lee Ralph in 1990) presented Dr. Jordan with the inaugural Advocate Truth Award, and he was honored by the National Medical Association. In 2017, he was presented with the Legacy Award by CDU.

✦ ✦ ✦

Roy Roberts

(1939–)

R oy Roberts, a native of Magnolia, Arkansas, rose through the ranks of the automotive industry from management trainee to vice president of General Motors Corporation (GM). He was a pioneer in the field, and by the end of his over twenty-year leadership career with GM, he was one of the most powerful executives in the automotive industry.

Roy Stewart Roberts was born in Magnolia on March 26, 1939, one of ten children of Turner Ray Roberts and Erma Lee Livingston Roberts. His father worked at several jobs, and his mother was the head chef at a local hotel. His mother died before he was three years old, and shortly afterward his father moved the family to Muskegon, Michigan. About six months after his mother's death, his father married Ethel Thomas.

After graduating from Muskegon High School in 1958, Roberts took an assembly line job at Lear Siegler Corporation, an aerospace parts manufacturer. He worked there for approximately seventeen years. He attended college classes after work and earned a Bachelor of Arts degree in business administration from Western Michigan University (WMU) in 1970. He also took graduate classes at WMU and Wayne State University, and he completed the Executive Development Program at Harvard Business School.

Roberts began his career at General Motors Corporation in 1977 when he became a manager-in-training in the diesel equipment division in Grand Rapids, Michigan. By 1981, he was promoted to manager of a local plant; he held the same position in several plants until 1988 when he was chosen to be the vice president in charge of personnel administration and became the second African-American vice president in the history of the company. In June 1988, he left GM, partly because he thought his ideas for the operation of the company were being poorly received. He then became vice president and general manager of truck operations at Navistar International Corporation in Chicago, Illinois.

Roberts returned to GM in 1990 as manufacturing and engineering manager for Cadillac Motor Car Division. In 1991, he was named general manager of Pontiac-GM, directing the merger of the two companies. His promotion of the light pickup truck and sports utility vehicle (SUV) helped inspire the rise of the popularity of those types of vehicles across the United States, which resulted in breaking several long-standing sales records over the next few years. As the general manager of the new division, he was the highest-ranking African-American executive in the American automotive industry. Many described him as a visionary in the industry.

In 1998, Roberts was promoted to group vice president for North American vehicle sales, service, and marketing. When he announced his retirement in the spring of 2000, he was the most senior African-American executive employed by the corporation.

Roberts remained active in his retirement. In 2000, he helped launch M-Xchange.com, an Internet trade exchange. The next year, he co-founded the private equity firm Reliant Equity Investors. Perhaps his most important post-retirement success was the role he played in the Detroit Public Schools. In 2011, the governor of Michigan appointed Roberts as the emergency manager of the Detroit Public Schools. The problems faced by the school system were many, but by the time Roberts left the position in 2013, the situation had improved. The schools were on a more sound financial footing, and academic achievement was on the rise by some measures, although some argue that these improvements, which focused on closing public schools in favor of charter schools, created hardships for local communities and further harmed the struggling public school system.

Roberts served on a number of corporate boards, including Burlington Northern Santa Fe Corporation, Enova Systems Corporation, and Abbott Laboratories. He was named a trustee emeritus at Western Michigan University, served as president of the Grand Rapids chapter of the National Association for the Advancement of Colored People (NAACP), and was a board member for the Boy Scouts of America. He also chaired Aspen Institute and National Urban League national conventions.

He was given the American Success Award in 1989, was made Executive of the Year by *Black Enterprise* magazine in 1996, and was awarded the Distinguished Service Citation from the Automotive Hall of Fame in 1998.

Roberts has been married twice. His 1958 marriage to Ruby West ended in divorce in 1971. He married Maureen Robinson in 1974. He has two sons and two daughters. In 2011, Roberts and his wife donated $1.1 million to create the Maureen and Roy S. Roberts Gallery of Contemporary African Art at the Detroit Institute of Arts. In 2015, he published his autobiography, titled *My American Success Story: Always the First, Never the Last.*

2001

Granville Coggs, MD

Henri Linton

Mahlon Martin

Sidney Moncrief

Amina Claudine Myers

Ozell Sutton

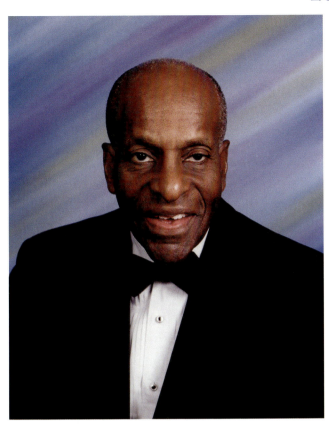

Granville Coggs, MD

(1925–)

Granville Coggs was a pilot in the United States Army Air Corps and was one of the Original Tuskegee Airmen. He later attended Harvard Medical School and became the first African American to serve as staff physician at the Kaiser Hospital in San Francisco, California.

Granville Coleridge Coggs was born on July 30, 1925, in Pine Bluff, Arkansas, to Dr. Tandy Washington Coggs and Nannie Hinkle Coggs. The family later moved to Little Rock, Arkansas. His father was an educator who served as the president of Arkansas Baptist College from 1937 to 1955.

Coggs attended Dunbar High School and graduated in 1942. He took classes at Arkansas Baptist College but had transferred to Howard University by the fall of 1943 before he enlisted in the U.S. Army and volunteered for the Black Army Air Corps. After he had trained at Tuskegee Institute in Alabama and at Tyndall Field in Florida, he served in the United States Army Air Corps from 1943 to 1946 as an aerial gunner, aerial bombardier, multi-engine pilot, and B-25 pilot trainee who was scheduled for the 477th Bombardment group but never made it to combat, in that the war ended in 1945 before he finished training.

Coggs earned his commission as lieutenant, second-class, in January 1945. He was commissioned on October 16, 1945, as a second lieutenant bombardier pilot, having received his bombardier training at Midland Army Airfield in Midland, Texas, and was a weather observer at Tuskegee Institute until the fall of 1946, when he was discharged.

He left Tuskegee Institute to attend the University of Nebraska at Lincoln. He graduated in 1949 with a bachelor's degree in science. He subsequently applied to Harvard Medical School and was the only African American in his freshman class there. The G.I. bill from his military service granted him $500 toward the cost of Harvard Medical School, and the school provided him a scholarship for $330, the remainder of his tuition. He graduated from Harvard Medical School in June 1953 with a medical degree. Coggs was also suitemates for a time with Dr. Martin Luther King, Jr., in the Boston, Massachusetts, area.

Coggs met Maud Currie in college. They married on August 20, 1946, in Arkansas. They had a son, Granville Currie Coggs, and two daughters, Anita and Carolyn Coggs.

Coggs became a physician; and in 1959, he became the first black staff physician at the Kaiser Hospital in San Francisco. In 1972, he became the first African American to lead the Ultrasound Radiology Division at the University of California at San Francisco.

Coggs also achieved renown as a runner. He began running in his early seventies after being diagnosed with narcolepsy. His wife, having been a track star in her youth, coached him. A friend recommended that he train for the National Senior Games. In 1999, he won eighteen gold medals in the 1500 meter at the national competition. He began to focus more on the 400-meter and continued to run both events at state senior races. He won gold in the 400-meter dash in the Senior Olympics on March 22, 2009, in San Antonio, Texas.

Dr. Coggs retired in San Antonio as a radiologist and breast cancer specialist. He lives there with his wife.

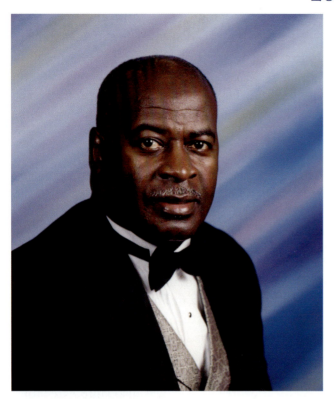

Henri Linton

(1944–)

Henri Linton has been recognized as one of the most talented artists working in the state of Arkansas. He has also served as chairman of the art department at the University of Arkansas at Pine Bluff (UAPB).

Henri Linton was born in Tuscaloosa, Alabama, in 1944. After discovering his artistic talents early, he soon began to paint and visit museums. To buy art supplies, he took odd jobs such as painting signs and shining shoes. After he entered a national art contest as a teenager, he won a four-year scholarship to the Columbus College of Art and Design in Ohio. Linton earned a Bachelor of Fine Arts degree from Boston University and a master's degree in art from the University of Cincinnati Graduate School of Fine Arts.

In 1969, John Howard, chairman of Arkansas Agricultural, Mechanical, and Normal (AM&N) College (now the University of Arkansas at Pine Bluff—UAPB) art department, offered Linton a position on the faculty. With Howard as his mentor, Linton began a career teaching aspiring artists. When Howard retired as chairman in 1980, Linton took the position.

Linton has also thrived as an artist. With scores of renderings, his work is noted for its examination of Arkansas Delta aerial landscapes. His paintings received critical praise from solo shows at the Arkansas Arts Center in 1996 and 2000. He was the first regional artist to exhibit at the Strauss Gallery after the expansion of the Arkansas Arts Center in 2000. His work is displayed throughout the state, including in public collections at the University of Arkansas for Medical Sciences (UAMS), the Winthrop Rockefeller Foundation, and the Arkansas Arts Center. He has highlighted some of his works in a book he co-authored, *The Art of Henri Linton: Sequences in Time and Space* (2003).

Linton's passion for African-American history and culture manifests itself in his work. He has organized and coordinated photographic exhibitions such as *And So Shall She Reap: The Seeds of Beulah Flowers*, the story of Maya Angelou's mentor and the mother of a family of influential professionals; *Honoring Our Roots: The Lives and Times of Isaac Scott Hathaway and John M. Howard*; and *Those Who Dare to Dream: The Works of Arkansas Photographer Geleve Grice*.

Linton also developed UAPB's University Museum and Cultural Center. He gathered historical photographs, papers, annuals, books, newspaper clippings, tokens, mementos, and a variety of other artifacts and organized, designed, and helped construct all the displays at the museum, which houses *Keepers of the Spirit: The L. A. Davis, Sr., Historical Collection*, which documents the history of UAPB.

Linton is married to Dr. Hazel Linton, a member of the School of Education at UAPB.

Mahlon Martin

(1945–1995)

Mahlon Martin was the first African-American city manager in Arkansas. He was later the chief fiscal administrator for Governor Bill Clinton and president of the Winthrop Rockefeller Foundation. As director of the Arkansas Department of Finance and Administration in Clinton's second administration,

Martin held the highest state government office ever achieved in Arkansas by an African American.

Mahlon Adrian Martin was born on July 19, 1945, the son of George Weldon Martin, a postal worker, and Georgietta Rowan Martin, who worked for many years at a Little Rock, Arkansas, department store. He had two brothers and a sister. He graduated in 1963 from the all-black Horace Mann High School.

Martin wanted to be a professional baseball player and received an athletic scholarship to Grambling College (now Grambling State University) in Louisiana, an all-black school. However, when his grandmother became ill, he enrolled instead in nearby Philander Smith College, also a historically black school, and received a degree in business administration in 1967. His first job was selling insurance for American National Life Insurance Company. He completed graduate courses in public administration and executive management at Harvard University in Cambridge, Massachusetts, and Cornell University in Ithaca, New York. Mar-

tin married Sheryl Macon of Little Rock, and they had a son and a daughter.

When Little Rock hired John T. "Jack" Meriwether as its city manager during labor strife in 1969, he obtained a Model Cities designation for Little Rock from the U.S. Department of Housing and Urban Development. Meriwether started a program called "New Careers," which gave on-the-job training to young African Americans to prepare them for professional jobs in a city government that was almost all white. Martin was one of his first recruits. He started as a community organizer and soon moved up to be the city's recruiting officer.

In 1972, Meriwether promoted him to director of training and operations and then to director of the Central Arkansas Manpower Program, a four-county, $7 million program to train public-service workers. Meriwether left as city manager in 1975, and Martin became an assistant to Meriwether's successor and gained the title assistant city manager in 1976. He left the government in 1979 to become an administrator at Systematics, Inc., which was based in Little Rock and was one of the world's largest data-processing firms.

The city hired him as city manager a year later. At thirty-four, he was one of the youngest chief administrators of a major city in the country and the first black city manager of Little Rock. He administered a $32.5 million budget and directed 1,350 employees. Like Meriwether, Martin won a reputation for working productively with disparate factions, including the rancorous board that governed the city.

Clinton, who had been defeated in 1980 after two years as governor, was re-elected in 1982. He persuaded Martin to leave the city government, where he was immensely popular, to become director of the Department of Finance and Administration, the fiscal administrator of the state government. It was the most sensitive position in the government because the director and his division heads regulated the purchasing, spending, and accounting for all government agencies; and he was the governor's chief liaison with the legislature, which had to approve the budgets of all state agencies and institutions.

When he dedicated the Mahlon A. Martin Apartments, built with federal housing assistance, in 1995, Clinton recalled that the state was in "an illegal financial condition" when he took office in 1983; and Martin's immediate task was to cut one percent from every state budget. A couple of years later, a deep recession forced Martin to cut spending across the state's operations six times in one fiscal year.

"I used to tell everybody that when I was governor," Clinton said, "Mahlon Martin was the government and I made the speeches. I never saw a fellow who could tell people 'no' and make them like it better than he did."

In 1989, the Winthrop Rockefeller Foundation appointed him its president. He was the second president of the foundation, which was formed in 1974 from the trust of Governor Winthrop Rockefeller, who had died the previous year. The foundation was dedicated to promoting social justice and encouraging balanced economic growth in the state. Martin was responsible for awarding $3 million a year to people and organizations working in education, economic development, and civic affairs to achieve social and economic justice and sustainable growth.

Martin developed cancer, and he died on August 31, 1995. He is buried in Haven of Rest Cemetery in Little Rock.

In 2004, the next African-American city manager of Little Rock, Bruce Moore, named the city's Employee of the Year Award for Martin. In 2011, the Butler Center for Arkansas Studies, a department of the Central Arkansas Library System, created a fellowship in memory of Martin to support research and programming on public policy in Arkansas.

Sidney Moncrief

(1957–)

Sidney Moncrief is one of the greatest basketball players ever to come out of Arkansas. While playing guard for the University of Arkansas (U of A) at Fayetteville basketball team from 1975 to 1979, Moncrief was named Southwest Conference Most Valuable Player and went on to help lead the Razorbacks to the National

Collegiate Athletic Association (NCAA) tournament and ultimately to the NCAA Final Four in 1978. After college, Moncrief was picked by the Milwaukee Bucks in the first round of the National Basketball Association (NBA) draft. He was a five-time NBA All-Star with the team and earned the praise and respect of such NBA luminaries as Magic Johnson, Larry Bird, and Michael Jordan.

Sidney Alvin Moncrief was born on September 21, 1957, in Little Rock, Arkansas. His mother, Bernice Perkins, and father divorced when Moncrief was five. He was supported by his mother on her modest salary as a cleaning woman at Howard Johnson Motel. Sidney was the second-to-youngest child in a family of seven children.

Although he was born in the same month as the federally mandated desegregation of Little Rock Central High School in 1957, Moncrief grew up in a housing project in an area of Little Rock that was still quite racially segregated. However, membership in a Boy Scout troop and hard work in his family's garden helped him dodge the crime and drugs of his rough neighborhood. Moncrief began playing on the basketball teams as a student at Dunbar Junior High School in the seventh and eighth grades, but he did not make the varsity team until ninth grade at Booker Junior High. Once he enrolled in Hall High in Little Rock, Moncrief made the varsity team and was named to several high school All-American teams as a senior.

As he prepared to graduate from high school, Moncrief was heavily recruited by Louisiana State University (LSU), Arkansas State University (ASU), and the U of A Razorbacks. Although it was then known primarily as a football school, Moncrief eventually chose U of A because it had a new coach, Eddie Sutton, who was ushering in a new, exciting brand of basketball. The 6'4" Moncrief ended up a team member of Ron Brewer and Marvin Delph, and the three players were known nationally as "The Triplets" for their play together. In his autobiography, however, Moncrief notes that the Triplets label was largely media hype and that the three players at the time never really thought of themselves as a special group. In 1977, Moncrief and his teammates won the Southwest Conference Championship. The next year the team made it to the NCAA Final Four. Before his senior year, Moncrief married his girlfriend, Debra, whom he had known since third grade. Eventually they had four sons. In 1979, the Razorbacks again went on to the NCAA tournament, only to lose by one point to Larry Bird and Indiana State University. Bird later praised Moncrief, saying that he had strength, perfect form, and a great understanding of the game.

After he graduated in 1979 with a Bachelor of Science degree in physical education, Moncrief entered the NBA draft and he was the fifth player chosen overall by the Bucks in the first round. At Milwaukee, Moncrief played under Coach Don Nelson and later under Del Harris. In his ten years with the Bucks, Moncrief averaged 16.7 points per game and over fifty percent in field goal percentage. His tight play also twice earned him the NBA Defensive Player of the Year award. Moncrief came out of a brief retirement to play one season for the Atlanta Hawks. A Milwaukee newspaper poll overwhelmingly ranked Moncrief as the favorite Bucks player of all time, beating out the likes of Kareem Abdul-Jabbar and Oscar Robertson.

After retiring from pro basketball, Moncrief owned Buick dealerships for several years in North Little Rock and in Pine Bluff, Arkansas. He was also an assistant coach for the Dallas Mavericks from 2000 to 2003. He operated the Back 2 Basics All-Star Basketball Academy for youth, coaches, and wellness-training and was also the head coach

of the Fort Worth Flyers of the National Basketball Developmental League. In 2007, Moncrief was hired as the shooting coach of the Golden State Warriors. In 2011, he was hired as an assistant coach of the Milwaukee Bucks, and two years later he became part of the broadcast team for the Bucks for Fox Sports Network Wisconsin.

◆ ◆ ◆

Amina Claudine Myers

(1942–)

Arkansas native Amina Claudine Myers is a noted pianist, singer, educator, recording artist, and composer who gained prominence in Chicago, Illinois, and New York City beginning in the 1970s. She has had a long career in jazz, choral/orchestral music, and theater. She was inducted into the Arkansas Jazz Hall of Fame in 2010.

Amina Claudine Myers was born on March 21, 1942, in Blackwell, Arkansas. She was reared by her great-aunt, Emma Thomas, and by her uncle, who gave her music lessons early in her life. She studied classical piano at Sacred Heart Catholic School in Morrilton, Arkansas. Myers moved to Dallas, Texas, in 1949 and kept studying piano. She played for a local church, co-led a gospel group, and performed in plays at school. She moved back to Blackwell in 1957 and graduated from Sullivan High School, Morrilton's African-American high school. In high school, she helped form a gospel/rhythm and blues (R&B) group. Myers received a scholarship to Philander Smith College in Little Rock, Arkansas, where she majored in music education and played in the jazz band. She continued to study classical piano and became student director for the choir. She also learned to play the pipe organ.

During her sophomore year, Myers began performing at the Safari Room, a jazz club in Little Rock's African-American Ninth Street business and recreational district. She also took a job playing church organ and later played the organ in an R&B club for three summers when she stayed with her mother in Louisville, Kentucky. During summer vacations from college, she directed and played for

church choirs in and around Louisville.

After she graduated from Philander Smith with a Bachelor of Arts degree in music education, Myers moved to Chicago to teach music at George T. Donoghue Elementary School, where she taught for six years. She played with the Gerald Donovan (Ajaramu) Trio as organist for several years. During this time, she became a member of the Association for the Advancement of Creative Musicians (AACM). Myers began composing for big band and various ensembles. In 1975, she wrote and directed the musical *I Dream*.

In 1976, Myers moved to New York City and soon began composing music for off-Broadway productions. In 1978, she served as choral director at the State University of New York at Old Westbury for one year. She began touring Europe with the Lester Bowie Quintet and the New York Organ Ensemble around the same time. Among other appearances around the world, Myers performed in Cape Town, South Africa, at the North Sea Jazz Festival with saxophonist/composer Archie Shepp and in West Africa with composer/vibraphonist Cecilia Smith.

Myers has released nearly a dozen recordings, including *Sama Rou (Songs from My Soul)* and *Augmented Variations* on her label, Amina C Records;

Amina Claudine Myers Live in Bremen, Germany, on Tradition and Modern Records; *Amina* and *In Touch* on RCA Novus; *Jumping in the Sugar Bowl* and *Country Girl* on Minor Music; *The Circle of Time* on Black Saint; *Amina Claudine Myers Salutes Bessie Smith* and *Song for Mother Earth* on Leo Records; and *Poems for Piano, the Piano Music of Marion Brown*, on Sweet Earth Records.

Her larger works include *Interiors*, a composition for chamber orchestra conducted by Peter Kotik and produced by the AACM and performed by the S.E.M. Ensemble at the New York Society for Ethical Culture; *The Improvisational Suite for Chorus, Pipe Organ and Percussion*; *When the Berries Fell*, for eight voices, piano, Hammond B3, and percussion; and *A View from the Inside*, a staged piece showing the workings of the mind. This work included original artwork by Myers as well as a chef from New Orleans, Louisiana, and his assistant; a dancer; a trumpeter; a weaver; and a pianist. *Focus*, a mixed-media piece written for piano, voice, and bass, included photographic images from Myers's hometown of Blackwell.

Her work *How Long Brethren*, based on African-American protest songs, was originally created by Helen Tamiris and was re-created by choreographer Diane McIntyre. The original orchestral score was discovered with instrumentation only, so Myers re-created and re-edited parts that were found in pieces from the archives of George Mason University. She conducted the symphony orchestras with choruses: the Wesley Boyd Singers of Washington, D.C., at George Mason University and the Western University Chorus from Western University.

In 2010, Myers was commissioned by the Chicago Jazz Institute to compose and direct *Sweet Mary Lou*, a composition for jazz orchestra in honor of what would have been the 100th birthday of the late composer, arranger, and pianist Mary Lou Williams. She also composed *I Will Not Fear the Unknown* for baritonist Thomas Buckner. Throughout her career, Myers has recorded with or performed with many notable musicians and groups, including Charlie Haden's Liberation Orchestra, Rahsaan Roland Kirk, and Anthony Braxton. Concerts with Sola Liu combining Chinese and African-American musical traditions are among Myers's many collaborations.

Myers has performed at Lincoln Center, Carnegie Hall, Town Hall, the Brooklyn Academy of Music, the Iridium Club, and Birdland. She has received many honors, including grants and awards from the National Endowment for the Arts, Meet the Composer, and the New York Foundation for the Arts.

Myers lives in New York City and is a private instructor in music theory, composition, voice, piano, organ, classical piano, and stagecraft.

Ozell Sutton

(1925–2015)

One of the most important Arkansas political activists at the height of the civil rights struggle during the 1950s and 1960s, Ozell Sutton was a key player at many of the movement's most critical moments—both in the state and throughout the South. He was present at watershed events that have impacted our nation's history, including having been with Dr. Martin Luther King, Jr., when King was murdered on the balcony of the Lorraine Motel in Memphis, Tennessee. He was also a trailblazer in Arkansas race relations and became the first black newspaper reporter to work for a white-owned newspaper when he went to work in 1950 as a staff writer for the *Arkansas Democrat*.

Ozell Sutton was born in 1925 just outside the town of Gould, Arkansas. His mother, Lula Belle, was a widow who raised the family on her own. As a sharecropper, she grew cotton to provide for her six sons and two daughters. Sutton's family eventually moved to Little Rock, Arkansas, where he attended Dunbar High School. In 1950, he graduated from Philander Smith College in Little Rock with a degree in political science and took a job with the *Democrat*.

It was at the *Democrat* that he began to focus his energies on achieving racial justice. He also quarreled with his editors over how to address African Americans in the newspaper's articles. Sutton wanted black men and women to be referred as "Mr." and "Mrs."—just as whites were. Eventually, Sutton's editors relented.

Sutton was at Central High School when the Little Rock Nine entered during the school desegregation crisis that gripped the city in 1957. In 1962, he received an honorary doctorate from Philander Smith in recognition of his political activism in the civil rights movement. The following year, he marched with Martin Luther King, Jr., and thousands of others in a historic march on Washington, D.C., that helped influence the federal government to play a larger role in race relations at the local level. In 1965, he was with Dr. King for the march in Selma, Alabama. During these years, he was also relocation and rehabilitation supervisor for the Little Rock Housing Authority.

From 1961 to 1966, Sutton served as assistant director of the Arkansas Council on Human Relations (ACHR), an organization that helped peacefully integrate businesses and public facilities across the state. Under Sutton's leadership, the ACHR acted as an important liaison between Arkansans and civil rights activists from outside the state. Most notably, Sutton forged a partnership with the Student Nonviolent Coordinating Committee (SNCC), whose idealistic young organizers worked in some of the state's most racially divided areas to help register black Arkansans to vote.

Following the assassination of King in 1968, Sutton served as special assistant to Republican governor Winthrop Rockefeller, a position he held until 1970. Under Gov. Rockefeller, Sutton advised on racial matters and sought to ease racial tensions between black Arkansans and local police. In the early 1970s, Sutton left Arkansas for Atlanta, Georgia, where he began working as a field representative for the U.S. Department of Justice Community Relations Service. In 1972, he was appointed director of the Community Relations Service in the southeast region, a position he held until his retirement in 2003. At the Justice Department, Sutton acted as a mediator in some of the country's most violent racial conflicts, including the riots that erupted in Los Angeles, California, following the verdicts in the Rodney King beating case. Through this work, he gained acclaim within the black community for his ability to handle high-pressure situations calmly, and he was awarded the Distinguished Service Award by the Department of Justice in 1994.

Sutton repeatedly made *Ebony* magazine's annual list of the "100 Most Influential African Americans." He also was awarded the Medallion of Freedom by the National Association for the Advancement of Colored People (NAACP). Sutton served as the national president of several organizations, such as the National Assault on Illiteracy and the Alpha Phi Alpha Fraternity, Inc., and was a founding member of the executive board of the National Center for Missing and Exploited Children and a co-chairperson of the Atlanta Black-Jewish Coalition. After his retirement, Sutton—who resided in Atlanta—spent much of his time lecturing around the country, relating his experiences from the frontlines of the civil rights movement. In 2009, he published *"From Yonder to Here": A Memoir of Dr. Ozell Sutton.*

Sutton died on December 19, 2015, in Atlanta.

2002

Al Bell

Faye Clarke

President Bill Clinton (Honorary)

Edith Irby Jones, MD

Haki R. Madhubuti, PhD

Bishop Charles H. Mason

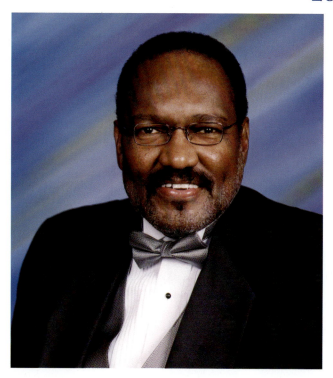

Al Bell

(1940–)

Al Bell (born Alvertis Isbell in Brinkley, Arkansas) is the former Chairman and Owner of Stax Records, where he was responsible for the careers of numerous music icons and the overall direction of American soul music and subsequently served as President of Motown Records Group. Today, Bell is the Chairman and Chief Executive Officer of Al Bell Presents, LLC, presenting a unique new paradigm of business innovation within the greater music industry.

Something happened inside of him one evening in Little Rock in 1971. Al Bell was sitting on the hood of an old school bus that his father kept in the backyard. He had just been to the funeral of his murdered brother. He didn't feel comfortable, even in that familiar place. Thinking about his brother, he began to hear music. Specifically, a bass line. Then words. *I know a place / Ain't nobody crying / Ain't nobody worried / Ain't no smilin' faces / Lying to the races.* That became "I'll Take You There." Recorded by the Staple Singers and released by Stax Records, the single written and produced by Bell was number one on the *Billboard* R&B Singles chart for four weeks.

Throughout his career, Bell has been consid-

ered a visionary, a seer, an icon, a music mogul, a communications and entertainment maverick, and a legend, which is how most people throughout the industry view him today. But he is not finished writing new chapters for his legend. He currently serves as Chairman and Chief Executive Officer of Al Bell Presents LLC, a new "rare performing artist" career and business development paradigm.

In 2011, Bell received the highest honor the music industry bestows, the Grammy Trustees Award, putting him in the company of an elite group that includes Steve Jobs, Walt Disney, Ira Gershwin, Frank Sinatra, the Beatles, and others who have received the award for making industry-changing contributions in music in their lifetimes. Bell has always been ahead of his time. Because of his ability to see things that others cannot and the guts to act on what he sees, he has always been miles ahead of his competitors.

In the 1970s, two of the largest African-American-owned businesses in America were Motown Records and Stax Records. Bell, who owned Stax, introduced marketing and promotional innovations that changed the music industry. It was believed impossible, but Stax produced gold and platinum hits with artists such as Isaac Hayes, the Staple Singers, Johnny Taylor, Sam and Dave, Booker T and the MGs, the Bar Kays, Otis Redding, the Emotions, Carla Thomas, Rufus Thomas, Richard Pryor, Billy Eckstine, Albert King, the Dramatics, and others.

Stax Records worked with Melvin Van Peebles on the release of his revolutionary film, *Sweet Sweetback's Baadasssss Song*, and with MGM Studios on the release of the film *Shaft*. In both cases, Bell employed marketing and promotional techniques that woke the film industry to the potential in the black marketplace and led to the black film renaissance of the 1970s. He successfully marketed the "Theme from Shaft" performed by Isaac Hayes, which won an Oscar for Best Original Song. As a result, he became the first African American to win that honor—or any other Academy Award—in a non-acting category. Bell added to the roster of box office hits with the landmark 1973 film *Wattstax*, a documentary based on a Stax Records concert that entertained 112,000 people in the Los Angeles Coliseum.

In *Soulsville USA: The Stax Records Story*, a book by Rob Bowman chronicling the history of Stax

Records, the Rev. Jesse Jackson says, "Stax was not just a record company. It was a sound. It was a piece of culture. It was a moment of conscience and experience of mankind….At the right time, it meant a lot to us. People still heavily borrow upon the tradition of Stax and the lineage laid down by the very special genius of Al Bell."

In the 1980s, Al Bell became President of the Motown Records Group (Motown had relocated to Los Angeles from Detroit) and worked with Berry Gordy in the sale of Motown to the MCA/Boston Ventures Group. After that, Bell discovered the music group Tag Team and released "Whoomp! (There It Is)," which sold over five million copies and remains one of the biggest-selling singles in history. Then, Prince asked Al Bell to release a single record, after Warner Bros. Records turned Prince down. Bell released "The Most Beautiful Girl in the World" and gave Prince his biggest-selling single ever.

Bell has received many honors and awards, including the National Award of Achievement from the U.S. Department of Commerce. He has been listed in Who's Who in Black America and was honored by *Black Enterprise* magazine in 1972 and 1973 as No. 2 in the Top 100 Black-Owned Businesses. *Ebony* magazine honored him in 1972 as one of the Top 100 Most Influential Black Men and in 1973 as one of the Top 1000 Most Successful Black Men in the World. He received an Achievement Award from the Boy Scouts of America in 1975, the Alex Haley Roots Award from the Greater Washington, D.C., Business Center in 1977, and the W. C. Handy Lifetime Achievement Award in 2002.

Bell received the Arthur A. Fletcher Lifetime Achievement Award from the National Black Chamber of Commerce in 2008, and he received honorary doctorate degrees from Philander Smith College in 1972 and 2011. He also received the Lifetime Achievement Award from National Association of Blacks in Higher Education in 2012 and was awarded the Lifetime Achievement Award from the National Association of Black Accountants in 2012. Also in 2012, he was recognized and honored during "An Evening with Al Bell" at the University of Arkansas in Fayetteville.

In May 2014, Arkansas's Maumelle High School honored Bell by creating the Al Bell Award

of Excellence, presented annually to a deserving Maumelle High School band student. This joins the school's John Philip Sousa, Louis Armstrong, and Semper Fidelis Awards.

On February 13, 2015, Bell was inducted into the prestigious Arkansas Business Hall of Fame. Through this honor, Bell joins an exceptional list of inductees who have been recognized to be among the best in Arkansas business for their outstanding achievements and their impact on the future business leaders in Arkansas and around the world. Also in 2015, on June 6, Bell was inducted into the Official Rhythm & Blues Music Hall of Fame in Clarksdale, Mississippi, with a subsequent induction ceremony held in October in Detroit, Michigan.

On September 29, 2015, Bell was honored with an induction into the Arkansas Entertainers Hall of Fame, which showcases the careers of the Natural State's sons and daughters who have made their marks on the entertainment world.

Faye Clarke

(1931–)

Faye Clarke co-founded the Educate the Children Foundation, which was created to support rural and impoverished school districts with donations of books and other educational materials.

Faye Wilma Robinson was born on August 6, 1931, in Pine Bluff, Arkansas, to Jerimah and Earnest (or Eariest) Robinson. In high school, she was an Arkansas National Merit Scholar, and she went on to attend Harvard Business School. She began working at Aramark, a company that provides food, facility, and uniform service, and she eventually became a regional vice president in the company. While at Aramark, she helped to organize services for the 1984 Olympic Games in Los Angeles, California.

She married Frank Clarke in 1982, and they had eight children.

In her work for Aramark and often accompanied by her husband after his retirement, Clarke frequently traveled throughout the South, where

they witnessed the many educational inequalities facing children in lower-income school districts. In particular, the Clarkes happened to meet the Superintendent of Public Instruction for Mississippi at an administrators' conference (Faye Clarke had the responsibility of securing food service contracts with school districts) and were invited to tour the schools of the Mississippi Delta region, where poverty is endemic.

Shocked at the conditions they observed, the Clarkes returned home to Long Beach, California, and began donating books and calculators to needy school districts in the South. After Faye Clarke retired in 1991, the couple used most of her $300,000 retirement fund to establish the Alabama-Mississippi Education Improvement Project, with Clarke as executive director. This was renamed the Educate the Children Foundation in 1993. The goal of the foundation was to locate books and other materials for school districts deprived of the means to secure those items themselves. To that end, the foundation worked to obtain surplus materials from educational publishers and discarded furniture from wealthier school districts. The foundation opened warehouses in Montgomery, Alabama; New Orleans, Louisiana; Atlanta, Georgia; and Greenville, Mississippi.

By 1999, more than $20 million worth of books

and other equipment had been distributed to schools in nine states and Washington, D.C., as well as in the U.S. Virgin Islands, Haiti, and Ghana. The Clarkes also worked to establish computer labs in various schools, including on Native American reservations in the American West. They also opened a computer-oriented summer camp for children in Compton, California, in 1997.

Faye and Frank Clarke received the President's Service Award from President Bill Clinton in 1996. They received the National Caring Award the following year.

President Bill Clinton (Honorary)
(1946–)

William Jefferson Clinton, a native of Hope, Arkansas, was the fortieth and forty-second governor of Arkansas and the forty-second president of the United States. Clinton was the second-youngest governor in the state's history, after John Selden Roane, and the third-youngest person to become president.

Bill Clinton was born William Jefferson Blythe IV on August 19, 1946, in Hope, the son of William Jefferson Blythe, III, and Virginia Cassidy Blythe. His father, a traveling salesman, was killed in an automobile accident before Clinton was born. He changed his name to Clinton after his mother married Roger Clinton, a car dealer. The family moved to Hot Springs, where he graduated from high school.

Clinton graduated from Georgetown University in Washington, D.C.; attended Oxford University in Oxford, England, on a Rhodes Scholarship; and, in 1973, received a Juris Doctorate degree from Yale University in New Haven, Connecticut, where he met his future wife, Hillary Rodham of Park Ridge, Illinois. He then returned to Arkansas to teach law at the University of Arkansas at Fayetteville (U of A). Rodham joined him on the faculty in 1974, and they were married on October 11, 1975.

In 1974 shortly after he joined the U of A faculty, Clinton ran for United States representative in the state's Third Congressional District. He won the Democratic nomination but lost in the general

make major strides in education, including a large investment of public money. The regular legislative session of 1985 was devoted to economic development. The legislature approved almost all of Clinton's program, which included changes in banking laws, start-up money for technology-oriented businesses, and large tax incentives for Arkansas industries that expanded their production and jobs.

He set his sights on the presidency. On October 3, 1991, Clinton announced that he would run for president in 1992. His education reforms and leadership of several national organizations, including the National Governors' Conference and the Democratic Leadership Council, strengthened his national stature and gave him important connections. He deflected several controversies during the primary election and easily won the Democratic nomination. Clinton chose Senator Albert Gore of Tennessee as his vice-presidential running mate.

President George H. W. Bush was high in poll ratings when the campaign began, but a sluggish economy and high unemployment damaged his chances. Clinton received forty-three percent of the popular vote to Bush's thirty-eight percent. He earned an even more decisive victory in the Electoral College with 370 votes to Bush's 168.

Although he had been battered by controversy during his first term and his party had lost control of both houses of Congress in 1994, Clinton had an easier election for a second term in 1996 when he defeated Senator Robert Dole of Kansas, the Republican nominee. Clinton was re-elected with forty-nine percent of the popular vote to Dole's forty-one percent. This time, Clinton won the electoral vote with 379 votes to Dole's 159.

Bitter controversy dogged Clinton from his election until he left office. However, in his first two years, he succeeded in passing a law that required companies with more than fifty employees to give them up to twelve weeks of unpaid leave each year to cope with family problems, in addition to another law that established a national service program called AmeriCorps which allowed young people to perform public service work for a period of time. His budget package, which passed both houses of Congress without a single Republican vote, reduced government spending and increased taxes mainly on high incomes. The legislation also expanded the Earned Income Tax Credit, which

election. Clinton made an easy and successful run for attorney general in 1976. In 1978, he easily defeated four candidates again for the Democratic nomination for governor and was elected.

In his first term, Clinton proposed modest reforms in education and commercial regulation, particularly to control pollution. However, his biggest initiative, a highway program, was expensive fiscally and politically. He persuaded the legislature to increase taxes on motor fuels and to raise other fees on vehicles. These increases were met with public opposition. Clinton was further hurt politically by the presence of Cuban refugees at Fort Chaffee sent there by his friend, President Jimmy Carter. Frank D. White, a former banker and state industrial-development official, switched parties to run for governor in 1980. He blamed Clinton for the threat to public safety that the Cubans represented (several had broken out of Fort Chaffee in May 1980 and rioted) and for higher vehicle license fees. He defeated Clinton in the election with almost fifty-two percent of the vote.

In the meantime, Clinton practiced law in Little Rock and prepared for the 1982 governor's race. He easily defeated White to regain the office and was subsequently re-elected in 1984, 1986, and 1990. During the campaign of 1982, Clinton promised to provided extra income for millions of low-income families. The deficit declined sharply over the next two years and disappeared in 1998. After Republicans regained control of Congress, Clinton spent the next six years battling conservatives over the federal budget and social issues. The Republican majority sought to cut federal spending on education, environmental protection, Medicare, and Medicaid.

In the field of foreign affairs, Clinton tried to arrange peace between religious and ethnic rivals in the Middle East and in Northern Ireland. He successfully brought an end to religious strife in Northern Ireland, a declaration of peace between Israel and the Palestinian Liberation Organization, and an agreement between Israel and Jordan to end their state of war. When the Mexican peso collapsed in 1995, Clinton devised a loan package to restore world confidence in Mexico. Mexico rallied and paid off the loans with interest three years ahead of schedule.

The major instrument of Clinton's foreign policy was trade and economic leverage. Late in 1993 in the face of opposition of even many Democrats, he completed negotiations and won ratification of the North American Free Trade Agreement (NAFTA), which reduced tariffs and created a free-trading bloc among the United States, Canada, and Mexico. He also finished work on a comprehensive world trade agreement called the General Agreement on Tariffs and Trade (GATT), which Congress ratified in 1994.

For his entire presidency, Clinton, his wife, and members of his administration were hounded by accusations of wrongdoing. After 1994 when Republicans regained control of both houses of Congress, congressional committees conducted investigations and lengthy hearings on accusations of misconduct, none of which produced evidence of illegal activities.

The most troublesome, damaging, and expensive investigation involved a real estate deal the Clintons and another couple undertook in 1978, while Clinton was attorney general. The investigation known as "Whitewater," the name of the land development company Whitewater Development Corp., accused the group and their real estate project of having benefited from the operations of a local savings and loan association that eventually

went bankrupt. Neither the Clintons nor any others in his administration were ever implicated in any wrongdoing in the Whitewater-related activities. However, the special prosecutor appointed to the case accused Clinton of "high crimes and misdemeanors" (the grounds for the impeachment and removal of a president) and brought four articles of impeachment against him. On December 19, 1998, in a vote along party lines, the House adopted two of the articles—perjury before the grand jury and obstruction of justice—for an inappropriate sexual relationship with a White House intern. Democrats charged that the impeachment proceedings were a Republican vendetta to destroy a popular president. On February 12, 1999, after a lengthy hearing, the Senate defeated the articles of impeachment. Clinton remained in office.

Since his presidency, the Clintons have bought a house in Chappaqua, New York, to establish residency in the state. Hillary ran for and was elected twice to the U.S. Senate from New York. She also ran twice unsuccessfully for the presidency (in 2008 and 2016) and served as U.S. Secretary of State under the forty-fourth president Barack Obama (her 2008 opponent). She is the first woman to have become the Democratic Party's presidential nominee. Bill Clinton retired to Chappaqua and opened an office in the nearby Harlem, New York, neighborhood and began to write his autobiography. The book, *My Life*, was published in 2004 and became a bestseller. Clinton's presidential library opened in November 2004 on the Little Rock riverfront. He has traveled extensively throughout the world, particularly in Africa and Asia, where he instituted efforts to import medicine to combat the AIDS epidemic. In 2005, President George W. Bush appointed Clinton and the elder President Bush to direct humanitarian relief efforts. Both Clintons have also been involved in the relief efforts for the victims of natural disasters nationally and worldwide. In 2013, he was awarded the Presidential Medal of Freedom by President Barack Obama. The Clintons and their daughter, Chelsea, are heavily involved the operations of the Clinton Foundation. They are proud grandparents to Chelsea's two children, Charlotte and Aidan.

Edith Irby Jones, MD

(1927–)

Edith Irby Jones was the first African American to attend and to graduate from the University of Arkansas Medical School, now the University of Arkansas for Medical Sciences (UAMS), in Little Rock. Not only was she a pioneer in the desegregation of higher education in Arkansas and the South, but she also has served as a highly successful doctor, educator, and philanthropist in Arkansas, Texas, and overseas.

Edith Irby was born on December 23, 1927, near Conway, Arkansas, to Robert Irby, a sharecropper, and Mattie Buice Irby, a maid. Her father died when she was eight, and the family moved to Hot Springs, Arkansas. Irby's older sister died of typhoid fever at the age of twelve, largely due to her impoverished family's lack of access to medical attention. Irby suffered from rheumatic fever when she was seven, which made her joints so painful that she was unable to walk or attend school for a year. These experiences prompted Irby to seek a career in medicine, with a goal to help those who could not afford standard medical care.

Irby graduated from Langston Secondary School in Hot Springs in 1944 and earned a scholarship to Knoxville College in Knoxville, Tennessee. She majored in chemistry, biology, and physics. Upon graduation, she applied to three medical schools: Northwestern University in Evanston, Illinois; the University of Chicago; and UAMS. She chose to remain in Arkansas largely because the tuition at UAMS was considerably less than at the other two schools. Earlier the same year, Silas Hunt had been accepted at the University of Arkansas School of Law. Now, Irby became the first African American accepted at UAMS—as well as the first accepted at any medical school in the South. This accomplishment was reported nationally in many publications, including *Life*, *Time*, *Ebony*, and the *Washington Post*.

Although she had been accepted to attend classes, she was not allowed to use the same dining, lodging, or bathroom facilities as other students at UAMS. Resisting the segregationist rules, many of her classmates chose to eat with her and to study with her at her apartment. During her second

year at the medical school, she married Dr. James B. Jones; they had three children. In 1952, she received her medical degree to become the first African-American graduate from UAMS. She then opened a general practice in Hot Springs.

Dr. Jones and her family moved to Houston, Texas, in 1959, where she became the first black woman intern at Baylor College of Medicine Affiliated Hospital. The hospital segregated her and limited her patient rosters. She completed the last three months of her residency at Freedman's Hospital in Washington, D.C. She was among several other black physicians who founded Mercy Hospital and one of twelve doctors who owned and developed Park Plaza Hospital. During her career, she accumulated staff privileges at nine Houston-area hospitals, including the Houston Hospital, which was renamed the Edith Irby Jones M.D. Health Care Center in her honor. However, she has always maintained her practice in Houston's "third ward" to serve those who could not afford to go anywhere else for medical care.

In 1985, she was elected the first female president of the National Medical Association (NMA). She is also the only female founding member of the Association of Black Cardiologists (ABC). Jones has taught, consulted, and/or provided healthcare in not only in the United States but also in Haiti, Mexico, Cuba, China, Russia, and throughout Africa. She provides support for two international healthcare locations that bear her name: the Dr. Edith Irby Jones Clinic in Vaudreuil, Haiti (which she helped to build), and the Dr. Edith Irby Jones Emergency Clinic in Veracruz, Mexico. Jones was a charter member of Physicians for Human Rights, which won the Nobel Peace Prize in 1997. In 2014, she began to divest herself of her professional obligations as a teacher and physician at the University of Texas Medical School and Baylor College of Medicine.

Haki R. Madhubuti, PhD

(1942–)

Haki R. Madhubuti is a renowned African-American writer, poet, and educator. The author of twenty-four books, he became a major contributor to the black literary tradition beginning in the mid-1960s. He has received the National Endowment for the Arts and National Endowment for the Humanities fellowships, as well as an American Book Award, and his books have sold over three million copies. A proponent of independent black institutions, Madhubuti is the founder, publisher, and chairman of the board of Third World Press, the oldest continually operating independent black publisher in the United States.

Haki Madhubuti was born Donald Luther Lee on February 23, 1942, in Little Rock, Arkansas, and grew up in Detroit, Michigan; he has one sister. His father, James Lee, deserted the family when Lee was very young. His mother, Maxine (Graves) Lee, was an alcoholic and died when Lee was sixteen. Lee attended Dunbar Vocational High School in Chicago, Illinois. He received his associate's degree from Chicago City College in 1966. He also attended Roosevelt University in Chicago (1966–1967) and the University of Iowa, where he earned a Master of Fine Arts degree.

After the publication of his first two collections, *Think Black* (1967) and *Black Pride* (1968), which both contained autobiographical as well as activist elements, Lee devoted himself full time to teaching, publishing, and writing. In his early work especially, he is known for capturing African-American speech patterns and playing with aural effects by using extra vowels or consonants, phonetic spellings, and elisions. Lee was married briefly in 1963 to Johari Aminia, and they had one son. In 1967, Lee founded Third World Press. Later collections saw Lee gradually shift to more political subject matter and the use of standardized English. Carol Easton, a teacher, invited him to read to her students, and they eventually married. They co-founded the Institute of Positive Education New Concept School in 1969.

In 1973, after traveling in Africa, Lee changed his name to Haki Madhubuti. "Haki" means "just," while "Madhubuti" means "precise, accurate, and dependable." Both names derive from the Swahili language. Madhubuti said that he wanted to arrive at a new definition of self. *Book of Life* (1973) was his first work to be published under his new name. Madhubuti continued to focus on political writing and activism while he developed a more technically controlled style to make political statements.

As an activist, Madhubuti has expressed the belief that it is the responsibility of the artist to expose injustice and the plight of the downtrodden. In 1998, Madhubuti co-founded the Betty Shabazz International Charter School in Chicago. He is also a founder and chairman of the board of the International Literary Hall of Fame for Writers of African Descent and founder and director of the National Black Writers Retreat.

Madhubuti was the founder and Distinguished University Professor of the Gwendolyn Brooks Center for Black Literature and Creative Writing and director of the Master of Fine Arts in creative writing program at Chicago State University. In 2006, he published the autobiographical novel *Yellow Black: The First Twenty-One Years of a Poet's Life*. He retired from teaching in 2011 but has continued to publish, including the 2016 book *Taking Bullets: Black Boys and Men in Twenty-First Century America, Fighting Terrorism, Stopping Violence and Seeking Healing*.

Bishop Charles H. Mason

(1866–1961)

An outstanding preacher and the founder of the Church of God in Christ (COGIC), the largest African-American Pentecostal denomination of the twentieth century, Charles Harrison "Bishop" Mason ordained both black and white clergy in the early 1900s, when few did so. Mason was baptized, licensed, and ordained in Arkansas.

Charles Mason was born on September 8, 1866, on the Prior Farm near Bartlett, Tennessee. His parents, tenant farmers Jeremiah "Jerry" Mason and Eliza Mason, had been converted to Christianity while they were slaves and attended the Missionary Baptist Church. Mason had two brothers and one sister. When he was twelve, a yellow fever epidemic forced his family to move from Tennessee to John Watson's plantation in Plumerville, Arkansas. The following year, Mason's father died from yellow fever, and Mason himself was sickened with tuberculosis in 1880. On Sunday, September 5, 1880, Mason experienced a vision of God and walked outside unaided. His half-brother, the Reverend Israel S. Nelson, baptized him at the local Mount Olive Missionary Baptist Church. Mason then entered the ministry as a lay preacher.

Mason married Alice Sexton on January 15, 1890, in Faulkner County. In 1891 after formally being licensed to minister by the Mount Gale Missionary Baptist Church in Preston, Arkansas, he began his preaching career. Mason soon learned that

his wife did not want to be married to a preacher. The couple divorced within two years, and Mason became depressed and suicidal. He entered Arkansas Baptist College on November 1, 1893, but he left within two months because he was unhappy with their teaching methods and presentation of the biblical message.

Mason preached his first official sermon, on holiness, in 1894 in Preston. In his doctrine, Mason was inspired by Amanda Smith, another African-American holiness evangelist, and by John Wesley, among others. While most Baptist groups, along with many other Christian denominations, emphasize the forgiveness of sins as a central teaching, holiness preaching places a much higher regard on sanctification—that is, on living a life fully obedient to God's commands as written in the Bible. This difference in doctrine caused Mason's congregations to reject his ministry, but expulsion from the Baptist pulpit in 1897 did not change Mason. He kept preaching holiness in various places, including an abandoned cotton gin in Lexington, Mississippi. The "gin house" became the birthplace of the Church of God in Christ. The name, which Mason said had been given to him by God as he walked down a street in Little Rock, was drawn from 1 Thessalonians 2:14. Mason's many preaching forays brought him into contact with other preachers who preached sanctification, such as Charles Price Jones, John E. Jeter, and W. S. Pleasant. These men collaborated in organizing the new denomination; Jones was the general overseer, Mason was over Tennessee, and Jeter was over Arkansas.

As Mason worked at organizing the new denomination, he heard the news that his former wife had died. Consistent with his holiness doctrine, Mason had remained convinced that he could not remarry while his former wife still lived, even though they were legally divorced. After her death, though, Mason married Lelia Washington in 1905. By 1920, they had six children. She died in 1936. In 1943—when he was seventy-seven years old and she was thirty-five—Mason married his third wife, Elsie Louise Washington, a Memphis, Tennessee, schoolteacher. She became very active in the administration of the Church of God in Christ, both as an office secretary and as editor-in-chief of the church's journal, *The Whole Truth Newspaper*.

When he learned of the Azusa Street Revival in California, Mason felt called to go to Los Angeles; he considered himself to have received Jesus in the form of the Holy Ghost in March 1907. He returned to Tennessee and began preaching the baptism of the Holy Ghost with the evidence of speaking in tongues. This theology of free and exuberant worship was not well-received by his former compatriots; and his associations with Jones, Jeter, and Pleasant were soon over. Mason called for like-minded men to join with him in organizing the first Pentecostal General Assembly of the Church of God in Christ, and twelve men responded. When the meeting was over, Mason had been named the General Overseer and Chief Apostle of the denomination with the authority to formulate doctrine, set up the organization, and assign responsibility. He went on to win a court battle to reclaim the name of "Church of God in Christ."

From 1909 to 1914, roughly equal numbers of African Americans and whites came to him for ordination (in 1910 alone, Mason ordained 300 white Pentecostal preachers). He wanted to see the denomination adopt the same vibrant and emotionally moving mannerisms that he had seen among former slaves, which were considered controversial—holy dances, ecstatic worship, and falling under the power of God.

Mason is credited with establishing the Young People's Willing Workers program in 1914, a Sunday school program in 1924, a foreign mission board in 1926, and numerous women's auxiliaries.

Mason's interracial work and his pacifism (although he preached allegiance to the United States and condemned the Kaiser during World War I) brought him to the attention of the Bureau of Investigation, the forerunner of the Federal Bureau of Investigation (FBI), which kept a file on him during the war. In 1918, he was arrested and jailed in Lexington, Mississippi, because he had a German aide, Pastor William B. Holt.

Mason died on November 17, 1961, in Harper's Hospital in Detroit, Michigan. His body was interred in the Mason Temple, headquarters of the Church of God in Christ in Memphis.

2003

James Hal Cone, PhD

Gladys McFadden and the Loving Sisters

Lawrence Hamilton

Deborah Mathis

J. Donald Rice

Judge Lavenski R. Smith

James Hal Cone, PhD

(1938–)

James Cone is known as the father of black liberation theology, which he describes as a "theological identity that was accountable to the life, history, and culture of African-American people." Cone often discusses the impact that growing up in Bearden, Arkansas, and attending the Macedonia African Methodist Episcopal (A.M.E.) Church had on his life. Both of these powerfully influenced his thinking: Bearden for the pain and suffering inflicted on African Americans and Macedonia as a place where he encountered Jesus. Cone has published numerous books on black liberation theology and has lectured at more than 1,000 universities and community organizations throughout the United States, Europe, Africa, Asia, Latin America, and the Caribbean.

Born to Charles and Lucy Cone in Fordyce, Arkansas, on August 5, 1938, James Hal Cone was reared in the "colored" section of Bearden. After he graduated from Ouachita County Training School,

he attended Shorter College in North Little Rock and later received a Bachelor of Arts degree from Philander Smith College in Little Rock in 1958. He earned his Master of Divinity from Garrett Theological Seminary in 1961, prior to earning a master's degree (1963) and doctorate (1965) from Northwestern University.

Cone was a young man during the 1957 desegregation crisis at Central High School, and he later became actively involved in the black freedom movement that became widespread throughout America. As he became increasingly frustrated with racism and injustice, he sought a means to create a Christian theology out of the black experience of slavery, segregation, and the struggle for a just society. He began writing from a theological perspective and formulated black liberation theology as the necessary tool to confront the suffering of poor African Americans; major publications of his early career include *Black Theology and Black Power* (1969, reprinted multiple times) and *God of the Oppressed* (1975). His theological perspectives are influenced by Martin Luther King, Jr., whom he referred to as the "most important Christian theologian," and Malcolm X, on whom he bestows the title of "America's most trenchant race critic." In 2011, Cone published *The Cross and the Lynching Tree*, in which he demonstrates black suffering through the birth, death, and resurrection of Jesus in an effort to integrate black and Christian identities.

An ordained minister, Cone has served as the Charles A. Briggs Distinguished Professor of Systematic Theology at Union Theological Seminary in New York City since 1987. He is an active member of numerous professional societies; has published twelve books and written more than 150 articles; and has earned countless awards and recognitions, including the Paul Robeson Award from Mother A.M.E. Zion Church, the American Black Achievement Award, the Theological Scholarship and Research Award from the Association of Theological Schools, the Fund for Theological Education Award for contributions to theological education and scholarship, and the Julius C. Hope Champion of Social Justice Award. He and his late wife, Rose, had two sons.

Gladys McFadden and the Loving Sisters

Gladys McFadden and the Loving Sisters were an African-American gospel group based in Little Rock, Arkansas. At its artistic peak in the 1970s, the group's adventurous, contemporary style put its sound outside the realm of traditional gospel music. The group included McFadden as well as Jo Dumas, Ann James, and Lorraine Leeks.

Gladys McFadden was born on September 10, 1934, in Little Rock. Her father, Aaron Williams, was a pastor, and her mother coached their church choir. McFadden sang in that choir until age nine, when she founded a group she christened the Loving Sisters, since the group included one of McFadden's sisters as well as a friend who brought her own sister along.

The Loving Sisters performed regionally and had a weekly stint singing on a local Sunday morning radio program. One Sunday when the Pilgrim Jubilee quartet was passing through town, the group heard the sisters' broadcast and invited them to audition for Peacock Records, where the quartet recorded. McFadden sent label owner Don Robey a demo, and he signed the group to the label. Its first radio single was "Who Can Ask for More?" This was followed by "Jesus Is Enough for Me." The group was marketed alongside Peacock's big R&B acts such as Joe Hinton, Junior Parker, and Jackie Verdell.

From the start, the Loving Sisters were ahead of their time musically. They entered the scene during an era when gospel music instrumentation was generally sparse—usually just a piano (like Mahalia Jackson) or a guitar (like Sister Rosetta Tharpe). Many in the gospel community thought that the more stripped-down the sound, the more sacred the music. The sisters fronted a full band, which earned them a bit of controversy. In one instance, they performed in September 1964 on a bill with the Staple Singers and the Mighty Clouds of Joy at Regale Theater in Chicago, Illinois. The *Chicago Defender*'s music critic Earl Calloway disparaged the "so-called gospel music" of the program in a scathing review. A reader wrote in to the newspa-

per with further disapproval for the show. "I was so ashamed of the entire program," she wrote. "I never expected to hear rock-and-roll at a religious service. We must be real and stop playing with God."

The group's debut album, *Trying Times*, was released in spring 1965 and earned a three-star review in *Billboard* magazine. McFadden wrote or arranged nine of the twelve tunes. The selections included traditional numbers such as the rollicking "An Unfailing God," which featured an intense, cracking vocal from McFadden's father, as well as a gospel blues, "Don't Let My Running Be in Vain." The set also included rhythms with a sock-hop flavor such as in "Get Thee behind Me Satan" and "Glory Hallelujah," which boasted the British Invasion musical styling that was popular in the American musical mainstream at the time.

The group was active in the cause of social justice, and they often performed at various protest events before civil rights leader Dr. Martin Luther King, Jr., spoke. As McFadden observed, "We were in every state with him and Klansman were trying to run us off the road and that's what we were sing-

ing about. You write from your own experiences. I wrote 'Trying Time' when we were marching in Tupelo, Mississippi. People were marching in front of the hotel and we were behind the barricade in the hotel and the hotel didn't want us to come out, so I was locked in there. I wrote that song because those were trying times." Following King's assassination in April 1968, the group recorded the album *A Tribute to Dr. Martin L. King*, which included songs such as "Precious Lord."

In the 1970s, the Loving Sisters continued to break new musical ground with McFadden as the producer. The 1973 album *Sounds of a New Era* included songs such as "Love in Action," with a then-futuristic sound akin to the soundtracks of *Shaft* or *Super Fly*. The following year, the album *The Sisters and Their Sons* continued their move into mainstream musical messaging; the sisters' three sons—George Williams, Larry James, and Leonard Givens—became their back-up band, Love Act, and contributed to the album.

Perhaps the group's finest musical moment is 1977's *Running Short of Love, Today* album, which included one of McFadden's most demanding vocals on "Anyhow," where she, at times, exhibited shades of Clara Ward's graceful blending, Tina Turner's rusty wailing, and Aretha Franklin's church-influenced belting.

The Loving Sisters' final album was 1978's *Gospel Soul*, which included spiritual remakes of Roberta Flack's ethereal "The First Time Ever I Saw Your Face," Debby Boone's "You Light up My Life," and the hymn "Amazing Grace"; the hymn won the group a Grammy Award nomination for Best Soul Gospel Performance, Traditional.

After the Loving Sisters' Peacock Records contract expired around 1979, the group retired from the national scene. "They were very attractive and they were real showmen," gospel music historian Anthony Heilbut said of the group. "I saw them at the Apollo Theater where they stole the show. They really knew how to work a house. [Gladys McFadden] was so scrappy. Such a nice little fighter on the floor. She would sing; she would preach; she would croon. She'd go up and down the aisles. She's very graceful."

Lawrence Hamilton
(1954–2014)

Lawrence Hamilton was a Broadway star who appeared in such shows as *Porgy and Bess*, *The Wiz*, and *Jelly's Last Jam*. He was inducted into the Arkansas Entertainers Hall of Fame in 2005.

Lawrence Oliver Hamilton was born on September 14, 1954, in Ashdown, Arkansas, one of six children of Oscar Hamilton and Mae Dell Neal-Hamilton. He later lived in Foreman, where he attended Foreman Public Schools and took piano lessons from a woman who had been a friend of ragtime composer Scott Joplin.

He studied music education, as well as piano and voice, at Henderson State University in Arkadelphia, receiving a Bachelor of Arts degree. In a 2002 interview, he said that he used to spend his high school summers working at a southwest Arkansas poultry plant while he dreamed of making it on Broadway. After college, Hamilton moved to Florida to perform at Disney World. There, he met talent manager Tommy Molinaro, who invited Hamilton to come to New York to audition for the actor/director Geoffrey Holder.

Starting out on Broadway, Hamilton played parts in many of the significant African-American-oriented musicals of the late twentieth century. After debuting in 1979 in *Timbuktu*, he appeared in the 1983 revival of *Porgy and Bess*. He joined the cast of a 1984 revival of *The Wiz*, first playing a Munchkin, then a Kalidah, then a field mouse, then an Emerald City citizen, then Lord High Underling, and finally the Tinman. He performed in the 1986 revue *Uptown…It's Hot!* and was dance captain of *Truly Blessed*, a 1990 musical tribute to Mahalia Jackson. He was a standby for *Jelly's Last Jam*, the 1992 musical based on the life of jazz musician Jelly Roll Morton. He also played the Rev in *Play On!*, a 1997 musical modernization of Shakespeare's *Twelfth Night*. In *Ragtime*, a musical based on E. L. Doctorow's novel, Hamilton played the lead role of Coalhouse Walker, a black man who suffers racist attacks.

In addition to performing on Broadway, he also served as a musical director for opera star Jessye Norman; was a vocal coach for pop-music group New Kids on the Block; and was a member of the Southern Ballet Theater, Brooklyn Dance Theater, Ballet Tap USA, and the Arkansas Opera Theater. He performed at the White House for Ronald Reagan and at the Vatican for Pope John Paul II.

At the Arkansas Repertory Theatre, he appeared as Whining Boy in *The Piano Lesson*, created *Souvenir* (featuring the works of Randy Goodrum), and directed the 2006 production of *Crowns*.

Hamilton died at Lenox Hill Hospital in New York City on April 3, 2014, due to complications from surgery. At the time of his death, he was on the faculty of Philander Smith College in Little Rock, Arkansas, where he had served as the cultural affairs director and as an associate professor of the humanities and director of choral activities.

✦ ✦ ✦

Deborah Mathis

(1953–)

Deborah Mathis is an acclaimed journalist and author who has been a reporter and columnist for newspapers and a television reporter and news anchor.

Deborah Myers was born in Little Rock, Ar-

kansas, on August 24, 1953. Her father, Lloyd H. Myers, was a businessman and Baptist minister, while her mother, Rachel A. Helms Myers, was an educator. She has two brothers and one sister. Myers attended Gibbs Elementary, Rightsell Elementary, and Westside Junior High. She graduated from Little Rock Central High in 1971. She got her start in journalism as the first female and the first African American to edit the *Tiger*, Central's school newspaper.

Rather than leave home to go to college, she remained in Little Rock and married Bill Mathis. They had two daughters and a son; the couple later divorced. She started as a clerk typist at the *Arkansas Democrat* newspaper in 1971 and moved on to reporting a few months later. When she was twenty years old, she was invited to audition for a job at WTTG-TV in Washington, D.C. She worked there until she moved back to Little Rock to become a reporter and morning anchor for KARK-TV, then for KATV Channel 7. She also worked for a time for the Winthrop Rockefeller Foundation.

After she had worked at Channel 7 for six years,

she resigned, and agreed to let the *Arkansas Demo-crat* publish her letter of resignation. She explained in a 2007 interview, "Paul Johnson, who wrote about television for the *Arkansas Gazette*, called me and said, 'I hear that...you turned in your resignation.' 'Yes.' 'Well, the general manager of Channel 7 tells me that you wrote one of the best resignation letters that he's ever seen. Do you mind if I publish some of it in my column?'"

Mathis began writing for the op-ed page of the *Arkansas Gazette* and soon was on staff at the newspaper. In 1991, she went to the Middle East to report on the Gulf War. She was also one of the first to report on "the newspaper war" between Little Rock's two major daily statewide publications, the *Gazette* and the *Democrat*; she was working for the *Gazette* when it closed in October 1991 to become part of the *Arkansas Democrat-Gazette*.

She became the staff opinion columnist for the *Clarion-Ledger* in Jackson, Mississippi, where she wrote three columns per week on the op-ed page. Her column was nationally syndicated by Tribune Media Services in more than eighty newspapers.

The *Clarion-Ledger*'s parent company, Gannett, wanted her to cover the Washington, D.C., beat while Bill Clinton was running for president, so she moved to Washington to become the White House correspondent for Gannett in January 1993. Still writing her syndicated column, she covered the White House news until the end of 2000.

Mathis then began a one-year fellowship at the Shorenstein Center on Media, Politics, and Public Policy at Harvard University, during which time she did a case study of the racial makeup of the media discussions of the disputed 2000 presidential election. However, she ran afoul of the Harvard administration when she personally invited long-time associate Bill Clinton to speak at a conference to discuss the results of her study.

She became a full-time consultant for the public-interest group the Advancement Project, which conducts civil-rights litigation. In that role, she traveled with a client to Africa to report on the AIDS epidemic there. She spoke in Turkey for a global business conference and then moved to Turkey for a year after her son left for college.

Mathis moved back to the Washington, D.C., area to become an instructor for a satellite graduate program of Northwestern University. She then be-

came the director of communications for the Public Justice Foundation, a public-interest law firm.

Mathis has published three books. She has said that she considers her first book, *Yet a Stranger: Why Black Americans Still Don't Feel at Home* (2002), to be a twenty-first-century follow-up to W. E. B. DuBois's 1903 classic, *The Souls of Black Folk*. She also wrote *What God Can Do: How Faith Changes Lives for the Better* (2005) and *Sole Sisters: The Joys and Pains of Single Black Women* (2005), for which she interviewed 125 black women.

◆ ◆ ◆

J. Donald Rice, Jr.
(1958–)

James Donald "Don" Rice, Jr., is founder, president, and chief executive officer of Rice Financial Products Company in New York, the only minority-owned derivatives firm in the nation.

J. Donald Rice, Jr., was born on August 22, 1958, to the Reverend James Donald Rice, Sr., and Ellen Rice. In 1962, his family moved from Kansas City, Missouri, to Hot Springs, Arkansas. His father founded and served as the pastor of Roanoke Baptist Church and was president of the Hot Springs chapter of the National Association for the Advancement of Colored People (NAACP). Ellen Rice funded and operated the first Head Start program in Hot Springs. She died when Rice was seven years old. He has an older sister, Donnellda.

After several failed efforts to enroll in Jones Elementary School, Rice and his sister eventually attended Eastside Elementary School, where they were the first African-American students to integrate that school. Rice also attended Central Junior High School for a short time. He became the first seventh-grade student elected as student-body vice president. At the age of thirteen and after a decade in Arkansas, Rice and his family moved to Oklahoma City, Oklahoma, and then eventually to Philadelphia, Pennsylvania. He graduated there from Central High School, a prestigious all-boys public school at the time.

Rice attended Kettering University in Flint, Michigan, and graduated with honors in 1981 with a bachelor's degree in industrial engineering. He worked at General Motors as an automotive manufacturing engineer for several years before receiving a full scholarship to Harvard University School of Business. Rice became interested in securities while studying finance. He graduated with a Master of Business Administration with distinction.

In 1985, Rice began working for the public finance department at Merrill Lynch. He was one of the founding members of the Municipal Derivatives Products Group, which developed large, complex bond refunding techniques to reduce the borrowing costs for state and local governments, specifically the District of Columbia. This technique was named an *Institutional Investor* Deal of the Year and became a common Wall Street practice. He spent a short time with Bankers Trust.

Rice secured his foothold in the derivatives market in 1993 when he founded Rice Financial Products Co. (RFP) in New York City. The company focused on borrowing for municipal governments. He expanded the company later that year with the formation of Rice Securities LLC, headquartered in Houston, Texas. This expansion included safe and customized debt management and investment

products and returns for municipalities. In 1998, Rice led the company's acquisition of minority-owned brokerage company Apex Securities and gained a significant share of the Southwest. The next year, RFP expanded further into the Northeast through the acquisition of Pryor, McClendon, Counts & Co. (PMC), the oldest black-owned investment bank in the country. Both Apex and PMC were combined to form a new subsidiary, Apex Pryor Securities, Inc. The company continued to expand in the twenty-first century by opening additional offices across the country, tripling the number of trading professionals employed, and hiring experienced bond bankers from firms such as Merrill Lynch, Goldman Sachs, Citigroup, and Morgan Stanley. In 2015, RFP held ten percent of municipal and state government borrowing throughout the country and was notably the largest investor for historically black colleges and universities. Today, Rice continues to underwrite bonds for municipalities and nonprofit organizations, including educational institutions. He currently serves as president and chief executive officer for RFP.

Rice has received a number of awards over the years. In 2000, RFP was named *Black Enterprise Magazine*'s Financial Company of the Year. Rice has twice been named among *Black Enterprise Magazine*'s "75 Most Powerful on Wall Street," once in 2011 and again in 2014. The National Association of Securities Professionals selected him as the 2002 Entrepreneur of the Year.

In 2004, *Fortune Magazine* featured him in "The New Black Power of Wall Street." He was also inducted into National Commission for Cooperative Education for 2009. He was appointed by New York Governor David Paterson to serve on the board of the directors of the New York State Thruway Authority. He was confirmed in May 2010. He also serves as the chair of the Audit Committee for the New York State Canal Corporation, with his tenure ending in June 2018.

Rice has served on several boards. He served on the Board of Directors for New York City's United Neighborhood Houses, as the chair of the Finance Committee for Board of Trustees for Kettering University, and on the Governing Board for New York City's Administration for Children Services, which oversees the New York City Head Start programs.

Rice has donated to a number of organizations, nonprofits, and institutions, including the National Urban League, Summer on the Hill, and the Democratic Congressional Campaign Committee.

Rice is a licensed pilot, frequently flying small planes around the New Jersey area.

Judge Lavenski R. Smith

(1958–)

Lavenski R. Smith, the son of a black county farm agent at Hope, Arkansas, became a justice of the Arkansas Supreme Court at age forty-one and became only the second African American to serve on the U.S. Eighth Circuit Court of Appeals, the second-highest level of courts in the country. He became chief judge in 2017.

Lavenski Roy Smith was born on October 31, 1958, to Cayce B. Smith and Olee M. Smith in Hope. He began school in racially segregated schools, but the city's schools soon integrated under court orders. He graduated from Hope High School, the school from which future Arkansas Governor Mike Huckabee had graduated a few years before. Huckabee later appointed Smith to his first judicial position.

After he graduated from the University of Arkansas (U of A) at Fayetteville in 1981, he entered law school there and graduated in 1987. He went to work for Ozark Legal Services in Fayetteville as a staff attorney who specialized in consumer defense and represented juveniles as a guardian *ad litem*. In 1991, he opened a general law practice in adjacent Springdale, which was the first minority-operated law firm in the city. Three years later, he became a professor of business law at John Brown University at Siloam Springs, Arkansas. He married Trendle Joyce of Camden, Arkansas; the couple had two children.

When Lieutenant Governor Mike Huckabee became governor in 1996 after Governor Jim Guy Tucker resigned, Smith moved to Little Rock and became Huckabee's liaison with government regulatory agencies. The next year, Huckabee appointed him chairman of the Arkansas Public Service Commission, which regulates utilities, and then in 1999 to the Arkansas Supreme Court to succeed Justice David Newbern, who retired. The term ended on January 1, 2001, and he returned to the Public Service Commission as a commissioner.

Smith established a reputation as a social conservative. He was associated with the Rutherford Institute, a national nonprofit group that approached the Constitution's First Amendment protection for civil and religious liberties from a conservative point of view. Smith was the lead attorney in a lawsuit in Pulaski County Circuit Court that sought to prevent the hospital at the University of Arkansas for Medical Sciences (UAMS) from performing abortions for women who paid for them privately. The Arkansas Supreme Court ruled unanimously in 1997 (*Unborn Child Amendment Committee, et al. v. Dr. Harry Ward, et al.*) that the hospital could perform such abortions under the Constitution and statutes.

His strong conservative religious upbringing guided his approach to legal practice and judging.

He defended that approach in a *University of Arkansas at Little Rock Law Review* article in 2009 called "Honest to God," which cited biblical references to support the notion that Christian doctrine and constitutional interpretation were not antithetical.

On May 22, 2001, President George W. Bush nominated Smith for the U.S. Eighth Circuit Court of Appeals to the seat left empty by the death of Judge Richard S. Arnold. His nomination was somewhat controversial owing to his strong opposition to abortion. Abortion rights groups opposed him. His nomination was first returned to the president, who renominated him. The American Bar Association rated him as qualified. Four senators tried to block his confirmation vote, but the U.S. Senate confirmed him easily by a voice vote in July 2002. He became only the second African American on the court, following Theodore McMillian of St. Louis, Missouri.

Unlike McMillian, Smith did not take an expansionist view of the federal Voting Rights Act. In a 2009 case which arose from racial turmoil in the schools of Farmington, Missouri, he wrote a unanimous opinion by an Eighth Circuit panel holding that the school district did not violate the free-speech rights of students who insisted on wearing Confederate symbols to school after the district banned the symbols to curtail turmoil (*B.W.A. v. Farmington R-7 School District*). The tiny minority of African Americans were bullied at the school until a few withdrew. Judge Smith said students who had been suspended during the incident were not suspended merely for the content of their speech but for the threat of violence and disruption that their actions caused. "This can hardly be considered an environment conducive to educational excellence," he wrote.

It was not surprising that when the controversial issue of same-sex marriage came before the Court of Appeals, starting in 2005, Judge Smith ruled against allowing the unions. In 2005, he sat on the appellate panel that overturned a lower-court ruling that Nebraska's ban on same-sex marriages was unconstitutional. He was on another panel that blocked implementation of a ruling favoring same-sex marriages in Nebraska as the last same-sex marriage case went to the U.S. Supreme Court.

However, Smith was not so doctrinaire that he refused to follow the Supreme Court's landmark ruling on such marriages after it came down in 2015. Seven weeks after the Supreme Court ruled that state bans against such marriages violated the equal-protection, due-process, and interstate-commerce clauses of the Constitution (*Obergefell v. Hodges*), Smith's three-judge panel took up appeals of federal district court decisions in Arkansas, South Dakota, and Nebraska that permitted same-sex nuptials and delivered instructions to each state that marriage equality was indeed the law in those states.

In March 2017, Smith became the first African-American chief judge of the U.S. Eighth Circuit Court of Appeals.

2004

W. Harold Flowers

Hazel Shanks Hynson

Patricia Washington McGraw, PhD

Fatima Robinson

Pharoah Sanders

John Stroger, Jr.

W. Harold Flowers
(1911–1990)

Throughout the 1940s, Flowers was the leading advocate for civil rights in Arkansas. He set up the Committee on Negro Organizations (CNO) in Stamps on March 10, 1940, to coordinate voter registration campaigns in the state. As a result of his efforts, the number of eligible black voters in Arkansas rose from 1.5 percent in 1940 to 17.3 percent by 1947. When the NAACP set up an Arkansas State Conference of Branches in 1945, Flowers was appointed as its chief recruitment officer. He also served as president of the NAACP branch in Pine Bluff.

In a 1947 case, Flowers won a landmark victory in the courts by winning death sentence commutations for two brothers accused of killing two white men. The victory was partly due to the fact that he demanded and was granted the appointment of black jurors, who served for the first time in the county since Reconstruction.

In February 1948, Flowers was instrumental in desegregating the University of Arkansas (U of A) Law School in Fayetteville when he served as chief counsel to Silas H. Hunt, the first successful black applicant. Later that year, Flowers was elected as president of the NAACP State Conference of Branches. In 1949, Flowers sued to equalize school facilities for black and white children in DeWitt, Arkansas, thereby paving the way for school desegregation cases in the state after the U.S. Supreme Court decision in *Brown v. Board of Education of Topeka, Kansas* in 1954.

In the 1950s, Flowers's civil rights leadership was eclipsed by friends and protégés, such as Daisy Bates and Wiley A. Branton. Nevertheless, he remained an important and influential figure in Arkansas. In 1953, he served as president of the African-American National Bar Association. He was ordained as a United Methodist minister in 1971 and remained active in the church until his death. In 1977, Flowers became the first black special circuit judge in Jefferson County. In 1980, Governor Bill Clinton appointed him as an associate justice on the state court of appeals. A year later, the Arkansas Black Lawyers' Association was renamed the W. Harold Flowers Law Society in his honor.

Flowers died on April 7, 1990, in Pine Bluff and is buried in Forest Lawn Memorial Gardens there.

William Harold Flowers was a lawyer, minister, social and political activist, and one of the leading figures in the civil rights movement in Arkansas in the 1940s. He was the first African-American special circuit judge in Jefferson County and a president of the African-American National Bar Association. He was also active in the National Association for the Advancement of Colored People (NAACP) in the state and the NAACP State Conference of Branches.

Born on October 16, 1911, in Stamps, Arkansas, W. Harold Flowers was the eldest of the three sons of Alonza (often spelled Alonzo) Williams Flowers, Jr., a businessman, and Beulah Lee Sampson, a schoolteacher.

In 1927 on a trip to Little Rock to visit his father, Flowers witnessed the lynching of John Carter; he resolved then to fight for civil rights. He enrolled in the Robert H. Terrell Law School in Washington, D.C., and later passed the Arkansas Bar examination in 1935. He set up a law practice in Pine Bluff, Arkansas, in 1938. He married Margaret J. O. Brown, and the couple had nine children.

Hazel Shanks Hynson

(1903–2005)

Hazel Shanks Hynson was a classically trained pianist who served as the choir director at Arkansas Baptist College in Little Rock, Arkansas, and in her studio taught many students who went on to become well-known musicians.

Hazel Shanks was born on August 8, 1903, in Atlanta, Georgia, to Christopher Columbus Shanks, who worked as an insurance auditor, and Luna Craig Shanks; she had one younger brother. She attended private schools and studied music. Shanks received a Bachelor of Arts degree in music with a major in piano from Atlanta University. She later traveled to England to pursue further musical studies at the University of London and back in the United States at Oberlin College in Ohio. She also studied at the renowned Juilliard School in New York.

In 1940, Shanks married William Edward Hynson, and the couple moved to Little Rock. They had no children, and he died in 1968.

After moving to Little Rock, Hynson joined Mount Zion Baptist Church and served as pianist there for more than a quarter century. She also founded the Hazel Shanks Hynson Music Studio and trained many accomplished musicians, includ-

ing jazz and classical musician Art Porter, Sr., of Little Rock. She served as pianist for the Arkansas State Baptist Convention for twenty-six years, as pianist for the National Baptist Convention for twenty-seven years, and as director of the Arkansas Baptist College Choir. The college later named its multipurpose center in her honor.

In 1990 in recognition of her service, Hynson received an honorary doctorate degree from Arkansas Baptist College. When she was inducted into the Arkansas Black Hall of Fame, the program described Hynson as "a grand lady of grace and elegance, a superb teacher and pianist, arranger, composer, and musician's musician." She was a charter member in 1956 of the Little Rock Chapter of The Links, Incorporated, an international volunteer group. She was also a charter member of the Little Rock Alumnae Chapter of the Delta Sigma Theta Sorority, Inc.

Hynson remained active into her later years, maintaining a driver's license until 1999. In the spring of 2005, she broke her hip for the second time in four years and never recovered. She died on May 22, 2005, and is buried at Miller Cemetery in Pine Bluff, Arkansas.

Patricia McGraw, PhD

(1935–)

Patricia Washington McGraw, a scholar, professor, and author, has made a significant impact throughout the country and the world as an educator and African-American cultural preservationist.

Patricia Washington was born in Little Rock, Arkansas, to William and Ruth Washington on May 6, 1935. She grew up during the period of school segregation and Jim Crow laws, so her parents instilled in her the value of education and the importance of embracing her African-American heritage. In 1953, she graduated from all-black Dunbar High School in Little Rock.

McGraw graduated from San Francisco State College in California in 1957 and earned a master's degree in American literature from the college in 1967. She was the first African-American member

of the Phi Beta Kappa Honors Society there. She taught at Philander Smith College in Little Rock in the late 1960s and was the first African-American faculty member at the University of Arkansas Little Rock.

She married Tyrone Power McGraw (1943–2015), who was a professor and coach at Philander Smith College; together, they reared three children.

In 1982, she received a PhD in sociolinguistics and black studies from Washington University in St. Louis, Missouri. In 1987, McGraw joined the faculty of the University of Central Arkansas (UCA) in Conway, where she served as a professor of English and African/African American Studies.

From 1983 to 1994, she owned and operated the McGraw Learning Institute: Abilities Unlimited in Little Rock. The private school, which was state certified to teach through sixth grade, emphasized the importance of African and African-American history.

McGraw has traveled throughout Africa numerous times performing humanitarian work and educational training. In 1999, on Lake Kivu, between the East African countries of Rwanda and the Democratic Republic of the Congo, members of the Rwandese Parliament presented an island to her due to her ongoing humanitarian work in the country; she was also granted the name mPata (meaning "one of noble birth"). She serves as Queen Mother of Imani Temple, her spiritual affiliation.

McGraw retired from UCA in 2000, but she remains active in her community and abroad. She has published several books, including the novel *Hush! Hush! Somebody's Calling My Name* (2000), and more than 500 articles and poems.

She has also received more than 300 teaching excellence and community service awards on the local, state, and national levels. She is a longtime member of National Association of Black Storytellers, a founding member of the Afro-American Genealogical and Historical Society in Arkansas, and a member of the Rufus K. Young Christian Church. She has co-hosted television shows and is the creator of a one-woman show, *A Profile of Four Black Women: Look Upon Them and Be Renewed*, which has been performed more than 400 times in Africa, the West Indies, and Canada. She continues to pass on the legacy of cultural pride and academic excellence at the Washington Heritage House, the former residence of her parents, located across the street from the historic Central High School in Little Rock.

Fatima Robinson

(1971–)

Fatima Robinson was described in the *New York Times* as "one of the most sought-after hip-hop and popular music choreographers in the world" and was once named by *Entertainment Weekly* as one of the 100 most creative people in the world of entertainment. Her dance choreography has been featured in numerous music videos, movies, and television shows.

Fatima Robinson was born on August 29, 1971, in Little Rock, Arkansas. At age four, she, along with her mother, Kadijah Furqan, and two younger sisters, moved to Los Angeles, California. She graduated from high school at age sixteen and started to work in her mother's hair salon after becoming a certified cosmetologist. However, she dreamed of a life in professional dance, having taught herself various moves by watching *Flashdance* and other movies. Robinson soon won a competition to be a dancer in a music video and followed this up with other contest wins and performances.

She quickly made the transition to choreography and became widely known for her ability to blend modern hip-hop styles with more classical dance moves. In 1992, director John Singleton, who had just released the hit movie *Boyz N the Hood* the previous year, recruited Robinson to do the choreography for a Michael Jackson music video he was filming, "Remember the Time." The video, which is nine minutes long, featured not only Jackson but also actor Eddie Murphy, model Iman, and basketball legend Magic Johnson, among other noteworthy personalities.

Working on such a high-level project launched Robinson into the upper echelons of choreography, and she began to land music and television work. She worked with renowned director Michael Mann on three of his movies: *Ali* (2001), *Collateral* (2004), and *Miami Vice* (2006); on the 2005 television movie *Their Eyes Were Watching God*, produced by Oprah Winfrey; television specials such as the *NAACP Image Awards* and the *VH1 Hip-Hop Honors*; and the Oscar-nominated 2006 movie *Dreamgirls*. She has also continued to choreograph music videos, being nominated several times for the MTV Video Music Award for Best Choreography in a Music Video and winning in 2004 for the Black Eyed Peas video "Hey Mama."

Robinson has also choreographed network television commercials for Pepsi, Gap, and Verizon. As

of 2016, she was one of only two women of color to have choreographed the Academy Awards. She also choreographed *The Wiz Live!*, which aired on NBC on December 3, 2015. This was a live television presentation of *The Wiz*, a modern reinterpretation of *The Wizard of Oz* (and featured Arkansan Ne-Yo as the Tin Man). Critical reception was immensely positive, and the production was nominated for several awards.

Robinson lives in Beverly Hills, California. She has one son, Xuly.

Pharoah Sanders

(1940–)

Pharoah Sanders is a noted jazz saxophonist who is recognized as a pioneer of the "free jazz" movement. Collaborations with artists such as Sun Ra and John Coltrane remain his most noted work, but his solo efforts stretch over five decades from 1964 to the present.

An only child, Pharoah Sanders was born Ferrell Sanders on October 13, 1940, in Little Rock, Arkansas. His mother worked as a cook in a school cafeteria, and his father worked for the City of Little Rock. Sanders began his musical career accompanying church hymns on his clarinet. His initial artistic accomplishments were in art, and it was not until he was at Scipio Jones High School in North Little Rock that Sanders discovered the tenor saxophone. The band director, Jimmy Cannon, was also a saxophone player and introduced Sanders to jazz. When Cannon left Scipio Jones High School, Sanders—still a student—took over as the band director until a permanent director could be found.

During the late 1950s, Sanders sneaked into African-American clubs in downtown Little Rock to play with acts that were passing through. At the time, Little Rock was part of the touring route through Memphis, Tennessee, and Hot Springs, Arkansas, for rhythm and blues (R&B) and jazz musicians, including Junior Parker. Sanders found himself limited by both the state's segregation and the R&B and jazz standards that dominated the Little Rock music scene.

After finishing high school in 1959, Sanders

moved to Oakland, California, and lived with relatives. He briefly attended Oakland Junior College and studied art and music. Once outside the Jim Crow South, Sanders could play in both black and white clubs. His Arkansas connection stuck with him in the Bay Area with the nickname of "Little Rock." It was during this time that he met and befriended John Coltrane.

Sanders transplanted himself again in 1961, this time to New York City. He often found himself financially destitute and on more than one occasion had to sell his saxophone. A year after moving to New York, Sanders joined Sun Ra's Arkestra and received another nickname, "Pharoah," which proved to have more staying power than the name "Little Rock."

Sanders formed his first band in 1963 while still collaborating and making appearances on records with Don Cherry and Sun Ra. Beginning in 1964, Sanders and Coltrane began to work together on a regular basis. Critics have often claimed that Sanders pushed Coltrane into a more radical and experimental direction, but it is a claim that Sanders denies. Sanders continued to play with Coltrane and his "free" group until Coltrane's death in 1967.

The same year that Sanders began playing with Coltrane, Sanders's first album, *Pharoah's First*, was released on the Calibre label. Along with other experimental musicians, Sanders began to restructure and re-conceptualize the boundaries of jazz compositions. This movement was called "free jazz" and

earned both acclaim and ridicule from critics. In 1966, Sanders released the first of a string of albums with Impulse! Records. Among these was his most critically acclaimed, *Karma* (1969), containing his most recognized recording, "The Creator Has a Master Plan."

Sanders left Impulse! in 1973 and redirected his compositions back to earlier jazz conventions. He continued to explore the music of different cultures and refine his compositions. However, he found himself floating from label to label. He found a permanent home with a small label called Theresa in 1987, which was sold to Evidence in 1991. Frustration with record labels continued to plague Sanders for most of the 1990s. Also during this time, he went to Africa for a cultural exchange program for the U.S. State Department.

Sanders's major-label debut would finally come in 1995 when Verve Records released *Message from Home*, followed by *Save Our Children* (1998). Again, Sanders's disgust with the recording business prompted him to leave that label, as well. In 2000, Sanders released *Spirits* and, in 2003, a live album titled *The Creator Has a Master Plan*.

Sanders lives in the Bay Area. He continues to compose music, including ballets, and he tours in Europe and the United States. In October 2015, he was named one of the recipients of a 2016 Jazz Masters Award from the National Endowment for the Arts.

John Stroger, Jr.

(1926–2008)

John Herman Stroger, Jr., was an Arkansas native who became a powerful figure in Illinois government and politics, especially in Chicago. He became the first African-American president of the Cook County Board of Commissioners.

John H. Stroger, Jr., was born on May 19, 1926, in Helena, Arkansas, to Ella Stroger and John H. Stroger, Sr. He attended the local all-black elementary school, as well as Eliza Miller High School, from which he graduated in 1949. He attended the Catholic and historically black Xavier University in New Orleans, Louisiana, and received a Bach-

elor of Science degree in business administration in 1953.

After graduation, Stroger briefly taught school, coached, and worked with the National Association for the Advancement of Colored People (NAACP). However, his mother urged him to move to Chicago, Illinois, in the latter part of 1953. He soon became involved in the city's South Side Democratic Party and became acquainted with important black political figures such as William Dawson, Ralph Metcalfe, and Harold Washington. In 1954, Stroger was appointed as an assistant auditor with the Chicago Municipal Court. From 1955 until 1961, he served as the personnel director of the Cook County Jail. He then became an aide to the financial director of the State of Illinois.

Stroger received a Juris Doctorate degree in 1965 from DePaul University.

He became an ally of Mayor Richard Daley early in his career and was elected a ward committeeman in 1968. In 1970, he was elected to the Cook County Board of Commissioners and began a thirty-five-year tenure on the powerful body. He

was first elected board president in 1994 and was re-elected in 1998 and 2002. He won the Democratic primary for the same position in 2006 before a stroke forced him to withdraw. His son Todd, selected to replace him on the ticket, won the election in November. Stroger served as chairman of every major committee over the years, including finance, health, building, and zoning.

His efforts over his long career involved many areas. He sponsored legislation aimed at supporting woman- and minority-owned businesses, and he was a co-sponsor of the Cook County ordinances relating to human rights and ethics, as well as a weapons ban. He appointed a commission on women's issues and created a court for juvenile drug offenders.

Yet nothing was more important to Stroger than the issue of healthcare, and he was an unrelenting advocate of greater access to quality healthcare for all. (Stroger's brother had died after he was turned away from a segregated hospital in the South.) His efforts are memorialized in the hospital that bears his name: John H. Stroger, Jr., Hospital of Cook County. His efforts on the Cook County Board also included achieving a balanced budget and opening a new AIDS treatment facility. He served on the Chicago Metropolitan Healthcare Council, as well as on the board of the South Shore Hospital.

Stroger served as president of the National Association of Counties and was appointed by President Bill Clinton to serve on the Advisory Committee on Intergovernmental Relations.

He battled a number of health problems during his life, including diabetes and prostate cancer. He underwent a quadruple bypass in 2001. Shortly after his sudden and major stroke in March 2006, he resigned as president of the Board of Commissioners. He did not appear in public again.

Stroger had a daughter and two sons with his wife, Yonnie. He died on January 18, 2008, and he is buried in Saint Mary Catholic Cemetery in Evergreen Park, Illinois.

2005

Fran Bennett

Lou Brock

Martha Dixon

David Evans

Sybil Jordan Hampton, PhD

Louis Jordan

Fran Bennett

(1937–)

Fran Bennett is an actress who has worked in theater, television, and films. She has appeared on stage across the nation and in Europe, and she has played roles on television from the 1960s onward in such hit shows as *Guiding Light*, *Star Trek: The Next Generation*, and *Scandal*.

Fran Bennett was born on August 14, 1937, in Malvern, Arkansas. She earned Bachelor of Science and Master of Arts degrees from the University of Wisconsin at Madison and went on to earn credit toward a PhD there before leaving the program. She studied voice under Kristin Linklater, a Scottish actress who relocated to the United States in 1963 to work at the Guthrie Theater in Minneapolis, Minnesota; Bennett was in Linklater's first voice teacher training program and later became the voice and movement director for the Guthrie Theater, a position she held for twelve years while also acting for the company. Under the sponsorship of the Rockefeller and Ford foundations, she studied movement with Litz Pisk, who was the head

of movement at the Central School of Speech and Drama in London, England, at that time.

Bennett made her first appearance in television with the long-running soap opera *Guiding Light* in 1965–1966, playing the role of Mrs. Matson. However, her television career did not really take off until the late 1970s, starting with appearances in *Diff'rent Strokes* and *Roots: The Next Generations*. In the 1980s, she played small roles in such shows as *Lou Grant* (two episodes), *General Hospital* (three episodes), *Dallas*, *Trapper John, M.D.*, *Benson*, *Cagney and Lacey*, *Knots Landing* (three episodes), *L. A. Law* (two episodes), and *The Bold and the Beautiful* (thirteen episodes). In 1991, she played Fleet Admiral Shanthi in the *Star Trek: The Next Generation* episode "Redemption II." (Her later appearance as a Vulcan midwife in the 2009 *Star Trek* reboot was cut from the theatrical release but restored in the DVD special edition.) Also during the 1980s, she had prominent roles in *Quantum Leap*; *In the Heat of the Night*; *Murder, She Wrote*; and *Crisis Center*.

Bennett has also had a modest presence on the big screen with such films as *New Nightmare* (1994), *Foxfire* (1996), and *8MM* (1999), as well as several lesser-known movies. The twenty-first century has seen her act in several well-known television series, including *The Book of Daniel* (eight episodes), *Boston Legal*, *ER*, *Community*, and *Scandal*.

She perhaps remains best known for her work in theater. She was the head of acting and the director of performance at the CalArts School of Theater from 1996 to 2003, and, for the school's professional arm, the Center for New Theater, she played the title role in *King Lear* at its 2002 premiere in Los Angeles, California, and at the 2003 Frictions Festival in France. In 2006, Bennett starred in Euripides's *Hippolytus* for the inauguration of the Greek-style theater at the Getty Villa in Los Angeles. In addition, she is a member of the Antaeus Theatre Company and the Los Angeles Women's Shakespeare Company.

Bennett also has a long history of serving as an educator. While studying in London, she taught at the London Academy of Dramatic Art. She has served as a master voice teacher with Shakespeare and Company in Lenox, Massachusetts, and led voice workshops at various universities throughout the United States, including Fisk University and Carnegie Mellon University.

Bennett has been the recipient of many honors, including an NAACP Theatre Award, the first AEA/AFTRA/SAG Diversity Award, and Watts Village Theater Company's 2008 "Blazing the Trail" Award. August 7, 2005, was named Fran Bennett Day in her hometown of Malvern.

Lou Brock

(1939–)

Lou Brock, a member of the Arkansas Sports Hall of Fame and the National Baseball Hall of Fame, used the stolen base technique as an important offensive weapon to effect a major change in the way baseball was played. He retired as Major League Baseball's all-time stolen bases leader, a record that stood until 1991.

Louis Clark "Lou" Brock was born on June 18, 1939, in El Dorado, Arkansas. He was the seventh of nine children born to Paralee Brock, who worked as a domestic and a field laborer. When Brock was two years old, his father, Maud, left the family, which forced Paralee and her children to move to nearby Collinston, Louisiana, where Brock grew up in the poverty and segregation of the Deep South.

Upon his graduation from high school in 1957, Brock received an academic scholarship to Southern University in Baton Rouge, Louisiana. Because of poor grades his first semester, he lost the scholarship, but he was able to replace it with an athletic scholarship after he impressed Southern's baseball coach in a tryout. He struggled on the field his freshman year, hitting .140 and striking out so often that he said, "I kept the air around home plate cool." In his sophomore year, he broke out with a .545 average and was invited to play in the 1959 Pan-American games in Chicago, Illinois. The next year, he returned to Chicago to try out for the White Sox and the Cubs; both clubs made offers, and he chose the Cubs.

Before he embarked on his professional career in late 1960, Brock married Katie Hay; they had two children together. He began play with St. Cloud in the Northern League but did not have to spend much time in the minors: by 1962, he was a starting outfielder for the Cubs. Brock was considered to be a promising power hitter, and he became the second player to hit a home run to dead center at New York's Polo Grounds. His Cubs career would prove to be a disappointment, however, in that he hit .263 and .258 his first two seasons and was a poor fielder. He was fast but stole only forty bases combined over the two seasons. During the 1964 season, he was traded to the St. Louis Cardinals.

The trade was widely considered a steal for the Cubs. They received a pitcher, Ernie Broglio, who had won eighteen games the previous year. Cardinals first baseman Bill White later said, "If anybody tells you they approved of that trade, they're lying." Brock's play in St. Louis quickly changed minds. In Chicago, Brock had been allowed to steal only occasionally, but in St. Louis his manager simply told him, "Go when it seems right to go." Brock stole thirty-three bases over the rest of the 1964 season while also hitting .348 in the more relaxed atmosphere. The Cardinals advanced to the World Series, where Brock hit .300 and helped the Cardinals beat the Yankees in seven games.

At a time when baseball teams largely focused

on hitting for power and were hesitant to attempt steals, Brock demonstrated the threat posed by a dangerous base stealer. In 1966, he stole seventy-four bases to lead the National League in steals and began a streak where he would lead the league in steals in eight of nine years. He helped St. Louis win the World Series in 1967 by setting a series record with seven stolen bases while batting .414. The Cardinals returned to the World Series in 1968, and Brock hit .464 while stealing seven bases again, though the team lost in seven games. St. Louis struggled in the following years, and the team became more dependent on Brock's ability to score runs, encouraging him to steal more often. In 1974, Brock stole 118 bases, setting a major league single-season record.

On August 29, 1977, Brock got his 893rd career stolen base, breaking Ty Cobb's longstanding record. He played two more seasons, finishing with 938 career stolen bases. Before retiring he achieved another milestone when he became only the fourteenth player to reach 3,000 career hits. Brock was elected to the National Baseball Hall of Fame in 1985, the fifteenth player to be elected in his first year of eligibility. He was listed as number fifty-eight in *The Sporting News*'s list of the 100 greatest players. After retiring, he worked briefly as a baseball analyst on television for ABC and the Chicago White Sox.

Brock and his third wife, Jacqueline, live in the St. Louis, Missouri, area. They both became ordained ministers in the Abundant Life Fellowship Church. Brock also works with the company he founded, Brockworld Products, a marketing and promotional firm, and he serves as a spring-training instructor with the Cardinals.

Brock established the Endowment Scholarship Fund at Southern University to provide scholarships for low-income students. In 2002, he received the Horatio Alger Association of Distinguished Americans Award. In November 2015, he had his left leg amputated below the knee due to a diabetes-related infection.

Martha Dixon
(1946–)

Martha Smith Dixon is an internationally recognized clothing designer and entrepreneur, whose couture gowns worn by First Lady Hillary Clinton helped to launch her career in fashion design and sales.

Martha Smith was born in Clark County, Arkansas, on February 2, 1946, the seventeenth of twenty children of James G. Smith and Beatrice Cook Smith, impoverished cotton pickers and sharecroppers in the South Central community of the county. She attended public school in Gurdon, Arkansas, when work allowed and graduated from Peake High School in Arkadelphia in 1965. The first in her family to attend college, Smith spent two years at Henderson State University before dropping out to work at Levi Strauss and Co. In 1967, she married Huie Dixon; the couple adopted a son, Chris, in 1973, and she became a stay-at-home mother. After her son reached middle school, Dixon returned to her early passion of clothes-making and completed a college correspondence program in fashion offered by the Commercial Technical Institute in Little Falls, New Jersey.

She started her first business, Martha's Designs, to cater to a diverse clientele. She walked door-to-door to boutiques in the Heights neighborhood in Little Rock before she received her first break when the Casey's Cachet boutique placed an order for twelve silk dresses. Within two weeks, one of Dixon's dresses had been selected for Hillary Rodham Clinton, then Arkansas's First Lady, to wear for the Governor's Inaugural Ball in 1987 following the re-election of her husband, Bill Clinton, as governor of Arkansas. The jade-green jersey gown was later put on display at the Old State House Museum in Little Rock.

The dress couture business picked up after the high-profile order, which allowed Dixon to place her designs in boutiques in surrounding states. In a local show of support, Arkadelphia business leaders helped pay for the initial material costs for a gown designed to adorn Hillary Clinton for special events during President Bill Clinton's 1993 inauguration. The red gown made of silk, satin, and lace is now on exhibit at the Harry S. Truman Library & Museum in Independence, Missouri.

With a $50,000 loan from the Arkansas Industry Development Council, Dixon created her second business, Dixon Manufacturing, in 1989. A children's clothing line called Dixon Kids was created in 1997 to supply school uniforms. Dixon's commercial clients have included Tyson Foods, CARTI, and Walmart. After a devastating fire in 2006 at the Dixon Manufacturing Clinton Street facility in Arkadelphia, Dixon sold the school uniform part of the company, gave the hospital uniform portion to an employee, and retained the food-services uniform portion to run from home.

Dixon became involved in the Democratic Party in Arkansas, serving in leadership roles at the county and state level, including as Arkansas Democratic National Committeewoman for Arkansas in 2000 and co-chair of the 2008 presidential campaign for Hillary Clinton in Arkansas.

Dixon was recognized as one of the "Top 100 Women of Arkansas" by *Arkansas Business* magazine. She used her influence as a prominent business owner to gain representation for African Americans in the Arkadelphia and Clark County community. In 2011, Dixon published her autobiography, *Triumph Beyond Measure*.

Over the years, she has served on numerous boards and committees, including the board of the Winthrop Rockefeller Foundation. She is a member of the Arkadelphia Rotary Club. Her accomplishments are prominently featured in a community mural in downtown Arkadelphia, and she has been featured in *Southern Living* and *Emerge* magazines.

Dixon resides in Clark County with her husband on land that Dixon's family first worked as sharecroppers.

◆ ◆ ◆

David Evans
(1939–)

David Evans worked as an engineer on significant aerospace projects but became best known later for his recruitment efforts on behalf of Harvard University, where his work led to a much greater diversity of the student body.

David L. Evans was born in 1939 in Wabash,

Arkansas, near Helena to sharecropper parents; he was the fourth of seven children. His father died when he was ten years old. Family members encouraged his mother, pregnant with her seventh child, to move to Chicago, Illinois, or Cleveland, Ohio. Instead, his mother left tenant farming and became a maid. When Evans was sixteen, his mother died in her employer's kitchen from a cerebral hemorrhage. His second-oldest sister, Maxine, left college two months before her graduation and returned home to work as a substitute teacher to care for Evans and his siblings. Evans worked part-time jobs to help generate family income, including picking cotton, chopping weeds, and working in local shops in downtown Helena. Support and love were common themes among his family and community, which he credits with helping his mother keep everyone focused.

Despite only having a combined education of six years between them, Evans's parents valued religion and education. Their belief in the importance of education impacted their seven children, all seven of whom attended college. His sister Maxine eventually received her degree from LeMoyne–Owen College in Memphis, Tennessee, and became an elementary school teacher. A younger sister, Darnetta Clinkscale, became the head of the medical department of Barnes Jewish Hospital in St. Louis, Missouri. Two other siblings completed post-graduate degrees from Northwestern University and the University of California, Los Angeles.

Evans was devoted to the written word and originally wanted to pursue creative writing in college but realized quickly that he needed to do something that would contribute to supporting his family. His talents in math and science led him to enroll at Tennessee State University, a historically black institution, and he received an electrical engineering degree. After graduation he worked for Boeing and Lockheed. In 1964, Evans then enrolled at Princeton University and pursued a PhD. He ended his study early and instead earned a master's degree in electrical engineering in 1966.

Evans headed back to the South to assist his family and gained employment with the National Aeronautics and Space Administration (NASA) in Huntsville, Alabama. He worked as an aerospace scientist in quality control for IBM's Federal Systems Division for the Saturn rockets and Apollo moon landing missions. Evans was present during Huntsville's integration and sought to address the high drop-out rate of black students. He located a local program and began an unpaid, one-man recruitment and tutoring service for black students seeking higher education. He reached out to roughly 100 colleges around the country, which all responded. However, Chase Peterson, Dean of Admissions at Harvard University, replied with a three-page letter hoping to work with Evans to diversify Harvard's student body. During his first year of recruitment, Evans successfully recruited five students to Princeton University, Brandeis University, Smith College, and Washington State University.

With local media attention, Evans received job offers from Harvard, the College Entrance Examination Board, and Massachusetts Institute of Technology (MIT). He also caught the attention of the local Ku Klux Klan and was placed under surveillance. In 1969, Evans accepted a two-year leave of absence in engineering to join the faculty and staff in the Harvard Admissions Office. Weeks after his arrival, Evans met Mercedes Sherrod; they married and had two children. During the turmoil of the late 1960s and early 1970s, Evans came to consider his recruitment work more influential on society and left engineering for education permanently.

During his time at Harvard, Evans has served as a proctor and advisor for first-year students in Harvard Yard and as assistant dean of freshman. He then became the senior admissions officer at Harvard. He has been a member of the advisory committee to the Harvard Foundation on Race Relations since 1981. He has also served as a trustee of St. George's School in Newport, Rhode Island; on the board of trustees of Roxbury Latin School; on the community advisory board of WGBH in Boston, Massachusetts; on the board of directors of Harvard Student Agencies; and as a tutor in the Charles Street African Methodist Episcopal Church after-school program.

For Helena's 150th anniversary, Evans was honored as one of six prominent citizens and the only black honoree. He received the C. Clyde Ferguson Award in 1986 and the Harvard Administrative/ Professional Prize in 2002. In October 2003, the David L. Evans Scholarship Fund was established, and it has raised over $1,000,000. In 2004, artist Stephen Coit painted his portrait, which now hangs in Harvard's Lamont Library. Evans has been featured in *Newsweek* and on *Good Morning America*; he is also a published author.

Evans has worked with his friend and colleague Henry Louis Gates, Jr., in exploring his genealogy, eventually discovering that his maternal grandmother was born a slave in Tallahatchie County, Mississippi, in 1861. He and his family established a scholarship at LeMoyne–Owen College in honor of his sister Maxine, who died in Los Angeles, California, in 2009.

Sybil Jordan Hampton, PhD

(1944–)

Sybil Jordan Hampton has served as a higher education administrator, leader in philanthropy, and political advisor during her career.

Sybil Jordan was born on September 1, 1944, in Springfield, Missouri, to Leslie W. Jordan and Lorraine H. Jordan. Her mother was a longtime educator, and her father was a World War II veteran who worked for the U.S. Postal Service. Jordan grew up in Little Rock, Arkansas, under the Jim Crow system of racial segregation, having to drink from "colored" water fountains and attend segregated schools. After the 1954 *Brown v. Board of Education of Topeka, Kansas* decision ruling that racial segregation in public education was unconstitutional, Little Rock schools began the process of desegregation. In 1959, she was recruited to be a member of the second group of pioneering black students to integrate Central High School, following the Little Rock Nine's entrance into the school in 1957. Her brother, Leslie Jordan, Jr., followed her in the school's integration.

While growing up in Little Rock, she attended Bethel African Methodist Episcopal (A.M.E.) Church and observed her parents' civil rights activism as members of the National Association for the Advancement of Colored People (NAACP). She credits her church for providing a nurturing environment and social infrastructure that produced strong citizens dedicated to making life better for people of color in the community and throughout the world.

Upon her graduation from Central High School in 1962 as the first African American who attended the school from tenth through twelfth grades, she received the National Service Scholarship, a Fund for Negro Students Supplemental Scholarship, and the Freedmen's Scholarship.

Jordan earned a bachelor's degree from Earlham College in Indiana, a master's degree in elementary education at the University of Chicago, and master's and doctorate degrees from the Teachers College, Columbia University in New York City. She married educator Alfred Hampton.

Throughout her career, Sybil Hampton served in leadership roles at Southwestern University in Georgetown, Texas; the University of Wisconsin–Madison; and the School of Arts and Science at Iona College in New Rochelle, New York. In 1996, she returned to Little Rock to serve as president of the Winthrop Rockefeller Foundation (WRF), which focuses on racial and social justice. During her ten-year tenure as president of the foundation, she helped to fund a variety of educational and cultural programs throughout the state. Hampton used her position and influence in philanthropy to provide opportunities to those disenfranchised based on race and economics. She retired from WRF as president emeritus in 2006.

Hampton has received numerous awards and honors. She was named to *Arkansas Business*'s Top 100 Women in Arkansas several times, was honored with the Earlham College Outstanding Alumni Award in 1998, was named a Woman of Achievement by Iona College in 1986, and was the 2002 recipient of the National Conference for Community and Justice Humanitarian Award.

Hampton works as a consultant, and she and her husband serve as volunteers at their church. She serves on the boards of numerous organizations, including the Arkansas Blue Cross Blue Shield Foundation and the Japanese American National Museum. Attorney General Dustin McDaniel appointed her to a four-year term on the Arkansas Ethics Commission in January 2014. Hampton began writing a memoir titled *Guest in a Strange House* with the goal of inspiring young people.

Louis Jordan

(1908–1975)

Louis Jordan—vocalist, bandleader, and saxophonist—ruled the charts, stage, screen, and airwaves of the 1940s and profoundly influenced the creators of rhythm and blues (R&B), rock 'n' roll, and post–World War II blues.

Louis Thomas Jordan was born on July 8, 1908, in Brinkley, Arkansas. His father, James Aaron Jordan—who was a Dardanelle, Arkansas, native—led the Brinkley Brass Band; his mother, Mississippi native Adell, died when Louis was young. Jordan studied music under his father and showed promise in horn playing, especially clarinet and saxophone. Due to World War I vacancies, young Jordan joined his father's band himself. Soon, he was good enough to join his father in a professional traveling show—touring Arkansas, Tennessee, and Missouri

by train instead of doing farm work when school closed. Show settings included churches, lodges, parades, picnics, and weddings; bands had to be ready to handle Charlestons, ballads, and any requests.

Jordan briefly attended Arkansas Baptist College in Little Rock in the late 1920s—he was later a benefactor to the school—and performed with Jimmy Pryor's Imperial Serenaders in Little Rock. He played saxophone and clarinet with the Serenaders and with Bob Alexander's Harmony Kings in El Dorado and Smackover during their boom lumber and oil eras, getting twice the going five-dollars-per-gig rate in Little Rock. The Harmony Kings then took a job at Wilson's Tell-'Em-'Bout-Me Cafe in Hot Springs; Jordan also performed at the Eastman Hotel and Woodmen of the Union Hall and with the band of Ruby "Junie Bug" Williams at the Green Gables Club on the Malvern Highway near town, as well as at the Club Belve-

dere on the Little Rock Highway. He rented a room at Pleasant and Garden streets in Hot Springs.

The lengths and legitimacy of his marriages are in some dispute. He first married Arkadelphia native Julia/Julie (surname unknown). He met Texas native singer and dancer Ida Fields at a Hot Springs cakewalk and married her in 1932, though he may have still been married to his first wife. He and Fields divorced in the early 1940s when he resumed dating his childhood sweetheart Fleecie Moore of Brasfield, about a dozen miles from Brinkley. They married in 1942. Moore is listed as co-composer on many hit Jordan songs, such as "Buzz Me," "Caldonia Boogie," and "Let the Good Times Roll." Jordan used her name to enable him to work with an additional music publisher; he had cause to regret it later, however, after she stabbed him during an argument, and though they reconciled for a time, he ended up divorcing her. Jordan married dancer Vicky Hayes in 1951 (and separated from her in 1960) and married singer and dancer Martha Weaver in 1966.

In the 1930s, in Philadelphia, Pennsylvania, Jordan found work in the Charlie Gaines band—playing clarinet, and soprano and alto sax, in addition to doing vocals—and he recorded and toured with Louis Armstrong. The two Louises would later play duets when Jordan became a solo star. In the meantime, he learned to play the baritone sax. In 1936, he joined nationally popular drummer Chick Webb's Savoy Ballroom Band, featuring the legendary singer Ella Fitzgerald. Jordan played sax and got the occasional vocal, such as "Rusty Hinge," recorded in March 1937. In 1938, he was fired by Webb for trying to convince Fitzgerald and others to join his new band.

Jordan's band, which changed American popular music, was always called the Tympany Five, regardless of the number of pieces. The small size of Jordan's Tympany Five made it innovative structurally and musically in the Big Band era. Among the first to join electric guitar and bass with horns, Jordan set the framework for decades of future R&B and rock combos. Endless rehearsals, matching suits, dance moves, and routines built around songs made the band, but Jordan's singular brand of sophisticated yet down-home jump blues and vocals made it a success. His humorous, over-the-beat monologues and depictions of black life are a prototype of rap;

his crossover appeal to whites calcified his popularity. Jordan charted dozens of hits from the early 1940s to the early 1950s—up-tempo songs like "Choo Choo Ch'Boogie" (number one for eighteen weeks) and "Ain't Nobody Here But Us Chickens" (number one for seventeen weeks), and ballads like "Is You Is Or Is You Ain't (My Baby)."

Jordan's musical talent was often overshadowed by his humorous stage antics set to rouse the crowds. He could play a solo and delve into a rapid-fire vocal or routine without missing a beat. He demanded no less from his groups, among the most polished of their peers. Although his songs could depict drunken, raucous scenes—like "Saturday Night Fish Fry" (number one for twelve weeks) and "What's the Use of Gettin' Sober?"—he did not drink or smoke and could be quiet and aloof, in contrast to the jiving hipster he portrayed. Jordan was also a fine ballad singer, as heard in songs such as "Don't Let the Sun Catch You Crying" and "I'll Never Be Free," sung with Ella Fitzgerald. He helped introduce calypso music to America, and, still clowning around on stage, Jordan toured the Caribbean in the early 1950s fooling natives with his faux West Indian singing accent.

Jordan said he chose to play "for the people"—no be-bop or self-indulgent solos, just Jordan's unique, fun urban blues. He also starred in early examples of music video—"Soundies," introduced in 1940—and longer films based around his songs, such as *Beware!* (1946), *Reet, Petite, and Gone* (1947), and *Look Out Sister* (1948). He cameoed in movies like *Follow the Boys* (1944) and *Swing Parade of 1946* (1946). Loved by World War II GIs, and selected to record wartime "V-discs," he remains known overseas today.

The sounds Jordan pioneered conspired to slow his record sales as R&B and rock 'n' roll emerged. His more than fifteen years on Decca—not counting his time there with Webb—ended in 1954; he sold millions of records for the company and performed duets with Armstrong, Bing Crosby, and Fitzgerald. During the late 1950s and early 1960s, Jordan released consistently engaging material, but he played for a variety of labels (Aladdin, Black Lion, RCA's X, Vik, and Ray Charles's Tangerine) and to decreasing results. Jordan continued to tour, including in Europe and Asia in the late 1960s. He returned to Brinkley in 1957 for Louis Jordan Day.

He spent much of the late 1960s and early 1970s without a recording contract. In 1973, Jordan issued a final LP, *I Believe in Music*, on the Black & Blue label.

On February 4, 1975, he died in Los Angeles, California. Jordan is buried in St. Louis, Missouri, hometown of his widow, Martha.

A host of prominent musicians claim his influence, including Ray Charles, James Brown, Bo Diddley, and Chuck Berry. His songs have appeared in commercials, on television, and in movies, and have been recorded by dozens of popular artists. Tribute albums include Clarence "Gatemouth" Brown's *Sings Louis Jordan* (1973), Joe Jackson's *Jumpin' Jive* (1981), and B. B. King's *Let the Good Times Roll* (1999).

Jordan was named an American Music Master by the Hall in 1999. A musical revue of Jordan's songs, *Five Guys Named Moe*, played on London's West End and Broadway in the 1990s. A nine-CD Decca retrospective was released by Germany's Bear Family in 1992. In Little Rock, the first Louis Jordan Tribute concert was held in 1997, with proceeds benefiting a Jordan bust in Brinkley by artist John Deering. Jordan was inducted posthumously into the Rock and Roll Hall of Fame in 1987 and the Arkansas Entertainers Hall of Fame in 1998. In 2008, the U.S. Postal Service released a stamp featuring Jordan as he appeared in the 1945 short film *Caldonia*.

2006

Oliver Baker, PhD

Charles Bussey, Jr.

Judge Glenn T. Johnson

Emma Rhodes, EdD

Henry Shead

Lencola Sullivan

Oliver Baker, PhD

(1959–)

Oliver Keith Baker is a Yale University physicist who has conducted groundbreaking research in particle physics and is a nationally known educator for his work on integrating technology into the classroom.

Oliver Baker was born on July 18, 1959, in McGehee, Arkansas, to Oliver Walter Baker and Yvonne Brigham Baker of Tillar, Arkansas; he has ten siblings. His parents were both college educated, having met at what is now the University of Arkansas at Pine Bluff (UAPB). He discovered a talent for science and mathematics while in junior high. His family moved to Memphis, Tennessee, when he was in middle school.

After he graduated from high school, Baker went on to study physics at the Massachusetts Institute of Technology, earning his Bachelor of Science degree in 1981. He went on to earn Master of Science degrees in physics and mathematics from Stanford University in 1984, followed by earning his PhD in physics there in 1987. His dissertation expounded upon the nuclear resonance effect on atomic electron capture by protons. He pursued a

post-doctoral fellowship at the Los Alamos National Laboratory after graduation before taking a position as instructor at North Carolina State University in 1988.

In 1989, Baker was appointed staff scientist at the Thomas Jefferson National Accelerator Facility (commonly called the Jefferson Lab) in Virginia and as an associate professor at Hampton University. He has also served as a visiting professor at Wayne State University (1993) and an adjunct professor of physics at Columbia University (2000–2001), in addition to serving as a consultant for the Los Alamos National Laboratory, on the Nuclear Science Division Review Committee at the Lawrence Berkeley National Laboratory, and on the Committee of Visitors for the Department of Physics at Harvard University. In 2000, Baker was named the Endowed University Professor of Physics at Hampton University. The following year, he was named dean of the School of Science. In 2002, he became the founding director for the Center for the Study of the Origin and Structure of Matter (CSOM), a National Science Foundation Physics Frontier Center that is a partnership between Hampton University, Norfolk State University, and North Carolina A&T State University. Since 2006, Baker has served as professor of physics at Yale University.

In 2010, he was appointed director of the Yale Wright Laboratory, which houses the world's most powerful tandem Van de Graaff particle accelerator. Baker was also a researcher on the ATLAS experimental team at the European Organization for Nuclear Research (CERN) in Geneva, Switzerland, playing a role in the discovery of the elusive Higgs boson particle. Baker conducted the first measurement of the muon sticking probability in muon catalyzed fusion, as well as the first accurate measurement of the elementary amplitudes in kaon electroproduction. With various co-authors, Baker has published in such journals as *Physical Review C*, *Nuclear Instruments and Methods in Physics Research Section A*, and *Physical Review Letters*.

For his contributions to nuclear and particle physics, Baker received the Edward Bouchet Award from the American Physical Society and the Elmer Imes Award from the National Conference of Black Physics Students and the National Society of Black Physicists. He has also received commendations for his teaching abilities, including the E. L. Hamm Sr. Distinguished Teaching Award and the National Award for Teaching Learning and Technology.

Charles Bussey, Jr.

(1918–1996)

Charles Bussey, Jr., was the first African American elected to serve on the Little Rock City Board of Directors since Reconstruction, the first African-American deputy sheriff of Pulaski County, and the first African-American mayor of Little Rock. Charles Bussey Avenue in Little Rock was named for him in 2005.

Charles E. Bussey—often called Charlie—was born in Stamps, Arkansas, on December 18, 1918, the eldest child of Annie Bussey and Charles Bussey, Sr. Acclaimed author Maya Angelou, who also grew up in Stamps, recalled that her uncle gave Bussey a job in his store and taught him his multiplication tables and a love of learning. Many years later, Angelou met Bussey, who told her, "I am the man I am today because of your Uncle Willie."

Bussey graduated from Stamps public schools and attended Bishop College in Marshall, Texas, a historically black college. He served in the U.S. Army as a private during World War II. After the war, he settled in Little Rock and organized and led the Veterans' Good Government Association to encourage other black World War II veterans to actively participate in government. In 1947, he was elected as Little Rock's "bronze mayor," an unofficial office designed to give the black community a feeling of participation in local government.

Bussey married Maggie B. Clark on October 6, 1945; they had two sons.

Long active in central Arkansas politics, especially in Little Rock, Bussey was a pioneering black leader in many areas of local and regional public and community service. He was a Mason and an active Shriner, who obtained the Thirty-third Degree. Professionally, he worked as a court investigator. In 1968, he was the first African American elected to serve on the Little Rock City Board of Directors since Reconstruction, where he served from 1969 to 1976 and then again from 1979 to 1990. He became the first black deputy sheriff of Pulaski County and served from 1950 to 1969, and then he became the first black mayor of Little Rock and served from November 1981 through December 1982. He also served eight and a half years as vice mayor, longer than anyone else in that position in history. His local focus during these years was involvement of youth and disadvantaged young people in civic and community activities, concentrating on leadership and active citizenship. His national focus was on presenting Arkansas—and especially Little Rock—in a positive light, reflecting the community healing that was required following the desegregation of Little Rock Central High School.

Bussey was elected to the board of directors of the Arkansas Municipal League and of the U.S. League of Cities. He was close to most members of the Arkansas congressional delegation, especially Congressman Wilbur D. Mills, and was active in all of Mills's campaigns, including the "Draft Mills for President" initiative in 1971–1972. He was also close to the Kennedy family, especially Senator Ted Kennedy of Massachusetts.

He organized and produced a television show,

Center Stage, and was influential in negotiating the formation of the Black Access Channel 14 in Little Rock.

Bussey also served as president of the Arkansas Lung Association, West Little Rock Rotary Club, Arkansas Livestock Association, Shriners, and Elks. He organized the Junior Deputy Sheriffs, where he managed baseball teams and other activities to keep young people off the streets, and served on the board of directors at St. Vincent Infirmary Medical Center.

Bussey died on June 15, 1996. In addition to the city street in Little Rock, the Charles Bussey Child Development Center in Little Rock also bears his name.

Judge Glenn T. Johnson

(1917–2010)

Glenn T. Johnson was a trailblazing judge in the latter half of the twentieth century. He spent most of his professional life in Illinois, where he served in a number of positions dedicated to a career in public service.

Glenn T. Johnson was born in Washington, Arkansas, on July 19, 1917, to Floyd Johnson and Reola Thompson Johnson. As the family moved around the state, he received his early education in Washington, then in Hope, and finally in Hot Springs, where he graduated from Langston High School. He graduated in 1941 with a Bachelor of Science degree from Wilberforce University in Ohio. After college, he served in the army, and after he was released from active duty, he continued to serve as a member of the U.S. Army Reserves. He later served in the Illinois National Guard.

Following his military discharge, Johnson moved to Chicago, Illinois. There, he enrolled in the John Marshall Law School. He earned both an undergraduate law degree in 1949 and a master's in law in 1950. Johnson also received additional professional training and graduated from the National College of State Trial Judges, while also completing the New York University Law School's Appellate Court Judge Seminar.

Johnson served as an assistant attorney general for the State of Illinois from 1957 to 1963. This was followed by three years as the senior attorney for the Metropolitan Sanitary District of Greater Chicago. In 1966, he was elected associate judge of the Circuit Court of Cook County and, two years later, he was elected a full circuit judge, a post he held until 1973. On April 2, 1973, Johnson became the second African American to serve on the Appellate Court for Illinois for the First Division, a seat he held until his retirement in December 1994. One of his better-known cases involved a jury award to a man who was left a quadriplegic after plummeting over a forty-two-inch guard rail and falling twenty feet onto a crowded concourse at Chicago's Soldier Field. Johnson upheld the $6.6 million jury verdict, affirming the decision that the conditions were unduly dangerous.

Johnson served as president of the Cook County Bar Association and was active in both the Illinois and National Bar Associations. He was chairman of the Judicial Council of the National Bar Association, as well as chairman of the Bench and Bar Section of the Illinois Bar Association. In addition, Johnson was a member of the World Judges Association. He was a loyal alumnus of John Marshall

Law School, serving on the school's board of trustees for twenty-five years.

Over the course of his career, Johnson earned a reputation as a particularly effective mentor to younger attorneys, with many of his clerks going on to judgeships and significant professional achievement. His alma mater named the law school's chapter of the Black Law Students Association in Johnson's honor. Among his many honors, Johnson was awarded the prestigious Heman Sweatt Award by the National Bar Association in 2008.

In 1948, Johnson married Evelyn F. Johnson, whom he had met in law school. Evelyn Johnson would also go on to be a judge, and the couple had two children. Two years after Evelyn's death in 1991, he married Elaine Bailey. Retired and living in Chicago, Johnson died at home on November 30, 2010.

Emma Rhodes, EdD

(1937–)

Emma Kelly Rhodes is a prominent educator and social activist who has established a series of nonprofit education centers across Arkansas. Using her own life as an example, she worked to increase access to education, especially for those who have dropped out of high school. Rhodes has sought to give these people the education and training necessary to allow them to recast their lives.

Emma Kelly was born on May 9, 1937. She grew up in a family of fourteen, was a tenth-grade dropout at age fifteen, became a mother at sixteen, and was a widow at twenty-nine. Despite all this, she reared and educated seven children, each of whom earned at least a degree from a technical college, with a number going on to earn four-year degrees. She obtained her own GED at the age of twenty-nine.

Kelly started taking classes at Capital City Business College, and that training helped her obtain a secretarial position at Philander Smith College in Little Rock. She worked during the day and attended classes at night, and she earned her Bachelor of Arts degree in 1972. She then studied vocational counseling at the University of Houston before returning to Arkansas to earn a master's degree in education from the University of Central Arkansas (UCA) in Conway. She went on to earn an EdS degree from the University of Arkansas (U of A) at Fayetteville, and she followed that with a doctorate in education from the U of A in 1987. She also earned a post-doctoral degree in adult education from the University of Arkansas at Little Rock.

In 1972, she went to work for the Arkansas Department of Education as a business education teacher, while she endeavored at night to further her own education. Eventually, Kelly met and married Clyde E. Rhodes, Jr. She would ultimately become the statewide coordinator of adult education before she retired in 1998 to allocate her time to provide training and opportunities for others who had seen their educational pursuits interrupted by life and choices, and she established a nonprofit organization to facilitate that effort: the Emma Kelly Rhodes Education Center (EREC), which opened in 2001. It later expanded to include the Dr. Emma Kelly Rhodes Education and Multi-Purpose Center for Adult Education, as well as the E. K. Rhodes Activity Center, all located in Little Rock. In 2009, she founded the House of Vision; its purpose is to provide jobs, skills, and entrepreneurial training for felons and others whose prison records have made their efforts to return to mainstream society particularly difficult.

The Rhodes Center and its affiliate operations offer courses in basic education and ADE/GED preparation, as well as technical training that prepares students to become certified nurse assistants and home health aides. The center also offers training in vocational areas such as heating and air conditioning/refrigeration, as well as painting and dry-wall work. Rhodes has developed partnerships to help provide these technical skills. The center is licensed and approved by the Arkansas State Board of Private Career Education, which also helped develop the program's curriculum and certified the instructors. In addition, EREC worked with the Little Rock School District to offer free classes to prepare students for the Arkansas High School Diploma/GED test. Having one time been a volunteer probation officer, Rhodes is particularly attuned to providing opportunities for those with minor criminal records.

Rhodes has received numerous accolades and honors, including being recognized by the *Arkansas Times* as an Arkansas Hero, as well as being named one of the "Top 100 Women in Arkansas" by *Arkansas Business*. Rhodes has also been featured in the nationally distributed *Parade* magazine.

She and her husband reside in Little Rock.

◆ ◆ ◆

Henry Shead

(1941–2012)

Henry Wallace Shead, Sr., who was also known as Henry Shed, was a pianist, vocalist, composer, recording artist, actor, choral director, and teacher. He grew up playing and singing in his father's church, and by the time he had finished college, he had developed the singing and piano-playing styles for which he became famous.

Henry Wallace Shead was born in Fordyce, Arkansas, on March 31, 1941, the third of five children born to the Reverend Henry Arthur Shead and Willie Labehel Reed Shead. He was reared in Little Rock and was introduced to the piano at the age of six by his mother. He later continued his lessons with a private teacher. Shead played in the Colored Methodist Episcopal Church (renamed Christian Methodist Episcopal Church—C.M.E.—in 1954) where his father was pastor, and he later had his own small jazz combo, which played at school dances and in small clubs. Shead and his combo were the star attraction of a local television program called *Center Stage*, which was patterned after *American Bandstand* but with all live music.

When Shead graduated from high school, he was awarded a choral scholarship to Arkansas Agricultural, Mechanical, and Normal (AM&N) College (now the University of Arkansas at Pine Bluff—UAPB), where he majored in music. During this period, he kept his combo going. After college, he became the choral director and music teacher at Southeast High School in Pine Bluff. Soon, he left teaching to devote all his time to performing. He played in Little Rock clubs such as the Drummers Club, the Top of the Rock, and the Diplomat. He refused to conform to the Jim Crow laws at the

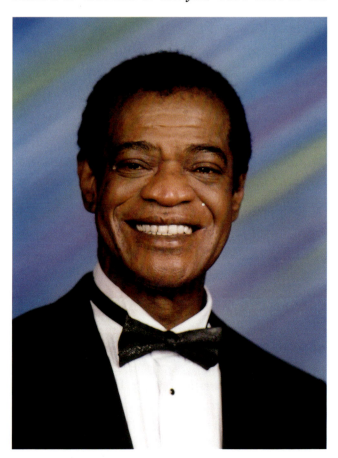

white clubs in which he played, thus helping to integrate them.

Shead married his college sweetheart, Edna Jeanette Mazique, on January 23, 1964. They had four children: Henry Jr., Todd, Lori, and Rohn.

Shead served as the music director and performed on Vic Ames's talk show in Little Rock. A favorite of Governor Winthrop Rockefeller, he accompanied Rockefeller to benefits and parties, performing at the National Urban League with President Lyndon Johnson in attendance, as well as at the United Service Organizations (USO) 1969 Woman of the Year event honoring Pearl Bailey. While performing at a governors' conference in Palm Springs, California, he was heard by fellow Arkansan Alvin Bennett of Liberty Records, who asked Shead to record for him. Shead moved to Los Angeles, California, in 1971. Later, Bennett took Shead with him when he formed a new company, Cream Records.

Shead made his acting debut within his first six months in Los Angeles when he performed in the stage play *The Time of Your Life*, for which he also arranged and composed the incidental music. Written by William Saroyan, the play starred Henry Fonda, Jane Alexander, Richard Dreyfuss, and Gloria Grahame, and it toured Washington, D.C.; Chicago, Illinois; and Los Angeles. After the play ended, Shead continued playing piano and singing at Los Angeles clubs such as Nicky Blair's, Stefanino's, the Hungry Tiger, and Derrick's Supper Club. After seeing Shead perform, Sammy Davis, Jr., requested that he appear on the bill with him in Toledo, Ohio, and in Little Rock.

In 1973, Shead acted in and composed the theme song for an ABC television movie. He also wrote the score for the educational television movie *Somewhere* (1972), and he sang the theme song "Groove Into It" for the movie *Pussycat, Pussycat, I Love You* (1970), a sequel to *What's New Pussycat* (1965). He also appeared on the national television show *Soul*; played after-theater parties given for the Carpenters, Henry Mancini, Sergio Mendes, and Barbra Streisand; and appeared on *The Tonight Show with Johnny Carson*, *The Dinah Shore Show*, and *The Jerry Lewis Telethon*. While in Los Angeles, Shead was a co-writer with Johnny Bristol, a longtime staff writer for Motown and a popular recording artist with Columbia Records. He also was

a studio pianist on the 1974 album *The Heart of a Woman* by Johnny Mathis.

In 1974, he began performing at many Las Vegas hotels and casinos, including the Aladdin (where he enjoyed the longest consecutive run of any entertainer). His band was also the house band for the weekly television program *The Frank Rosenthal Show* and won the "Lounge Act of the Year" award in 1977. He sang in the 1997 movie *Vegas Vacation*, for which he wrote the song "Rusty's Rave."

Shead played at the fiftieth anniversary of the desegregation of Central High School in Little Rock in 2007. There, Ernest Green, one of the Little Rock Nine, recalled how Shead had encouraged him to attend Central High: "Without Henry's continued support throughout the year, I am not sure I could have endured the arduous journey."

Henry Shead died on October 5, 2012, and is buried at the Forest Lawn Cemetery in Los Angeles.

Lencola Sullivan

(1957–)

Lencola Sullivan of Morrilton, Arkansas, broke many color barriers in Arkansas and became a nationally known public figure. She won four scholarship pageants from 1977 to 1980 and was the first African American to win those pageants. She was Miss Morrilton in 1977, Miss University of Central Arkansas in 1978, Miss White River in 1979, and Miss Arkansas in 1980. In September 1980, Sullivan competed in the Miss America Pageant and won the preliminary swimsuit competition. Overall, she was the fourth runner-up in the national pageant, the highest placement achieved by an African-American contestant up to that time.

Lencola Orean Sullivan was born on October 29, 1957, to Richard and Macie Sullivan of Morrilton. She was the oldest of five children. Her father was employed by Missouri Pacific Railroad, and her mother was a school teacher. Sullivan graduated from Morrilton High School in 1975 and received a Bachelor of Science in theatre arts and

speech with an emphasis in broadcasting in 1980 from the University of Central Arkansas (UCA) in Conway. While at UCA, Sullivan was a member of Alpha Epsilon Rho Broadcasting Society and *The Echo* newspaper staff, as well as a co-anchor and reporter at KUCA-FM radio. After she graduated from UCA, Sullivan pledged Delta Sigma Theta sorority, an organization predominately made up of college-educated black women.

Sullivan won the Miss Arkansas Pageant the third time she entered. According to the *Arkansas Gazette*, "She wowed the audience and judges, singing W. C. Handy's 'St. Louis Blues,' and became the first contestant in the history of the pageant to win both the H. S. (Boots) Coleman Talent Award and the Miss Arkansas title."

Prior to winning the Miss Arkansas Pageant, Sullivan was employed by NBC affiliate KARK Channel 4 in Little Rock and was an assistant to news producer Deborah Mathis. While at Channel 4, Sullivan traveled to Hollywood, California, and took part in a pilot show for television produced by Dick Clark Productions, titled *All Kinds of Stuff*. The pilot was not put into production.

In recognition of being named Miss Arkansas, Sullivan received an Arkansas Senate citation, an Arkansas House of Representatives citation, and an Arkansas Certificate of Merit from then-Governor Bill Clinton. Though she graduated from UCA, Sullivan was made an honorary member of the University of Arkansas at Pine Bluff Alumni Association, Inc., and given a life membership certificate. She was also made an honorary citizen of Tulsa, Oklahoma, and was selected as an Outstanding Young Woman of America. Sullivan was named in Personalities of the South in 1980, Directory of Distinguished Americans in 1981, and Community Leaders of America in 1982.

In 1981, Sullivan was named the *Arkansas Democrat*'s Woman of the Year for 1980. When told of her award, she elaborated on why she entered the Miss Arkansas Pageant the third time: "The main reason I fought so hard to win the third time was that I thought that I could do something positive for the state." On the subject of race, Sullivan stated, "I'm representing Arkansas first of all, but I think that my experience has encouraged more black women to enter pageants."

Winning the Miss Arkansas Pageant opened many doors for Sullivan, but it was her considerable talent in public speaking and singing that brought her to the attention of leaders of the entertainment industry and corporate world. For example, Sullivan's close friend Stevie Wonder sang at her father's funeral in Morrilton in 1989.

In 2002, Sullivan married Roel P. Verseveldt of The Hague in the Netherlands. She and her husband are involved in international business activities. Sullivan has served as a board member of the New York National Speakers Association and was a founding member of the Toastmasters Chapter in The Hague. She has spoken internationally on empowering women, diversity, inclusion, multiculturalism, corporate social responsibility, and leadership skills. She is a frequent lecturer at Hanze University of Applied Sciences in Groningen, Netherlands.

Sullivan had studied piano for seven years and voice and organ for one year. As a vocalist, she performed with the Lionel Hampton Orchestra, with Stevie Wonder, with Kool and the Gang, and at both of President Bill Clinton's inaugural balls, in 1993 and 1997. She has also performed throughout the Netherlands, on Dutch National Television, and at Jazz Club 606 in London. Sullivan has also appeared on several television soap operas, in industrial films, and in many television commercials.

She resides with her husband in The Hague and has two step-daughters.

2007

Milton P. Crenchaw

Judge L. Clifford Davis

Willie Davis

Little Rock Nine

John Stubblefield

Sheryl Underwood

Milton P. Crenchaw

(1919–2015)

Milton Pitts Crenchaw, of the original Tuskegee Airmen, was one of the first African Americans in the country and the first from Arkansas to be trained by the federal government as a civilian licensed pilot. He trained hundreds of cadet pilots while at Alabama's Tuskegee Institute in the 1940s and was the catalyst in starting the first successful flight program at Philander Smith College in Little Rock, Arkansas, which operated from 1947 to 1953. His combined service record extends for over forty years of federal service from 1941 to 1983 with the U.S. Army (in the Army Air Corps) and eventually the U.S. Air Force.

Milton Crenchaw was born on January 13, 1919, in Little Rock, Arkansas, to the Reverend Joseph C. Crenchaw, a local civil rights leader with the local National Association for the Advancement of Colored People (NAACP) and a professional tailor, and his wife, Ethel Pitts Crenchaw, who was a door-to-door beautician. He had three siblings. Crenchaw graduated from Dunbar High School in 1937 and attended Dunbar Junior College while completing the teaching certificate in auto mechan-ics. He pursued a bachelor's degree in mechanical engineering at the Tuskegee Institute in 1939 but did not complete his degree after becoming a pilot there. In 1939, Crenchaw was the first Arkansan to arrive at Moton Airbase in Tuskegee, Alabama.

After Pearl Harbor was bombed on December 7, 1941, his focus shifted from living the life of a normal college student to flying in the Civilian Pilot Training Program (CPTP), sponsored by the Army Air Corps, and becoming a flight instructor. This was possible due to the landmark government decision of December 1940 regarding the training and inclusion of black pilots in the army. This idea was first initiated by President Franklin Delano Roosevelt and then revisited by the Department of War in response to the shortage of personnel in the aviation, pilot, and engineering sectors of government. Crenchaw received partial training and physical examinations at Maxwell Air Force Base in Montgomery, Alabama, before returning to Tuskegee for another phase of primary instruction and advance courses in aviation piloting. He graduated with his civilian pilot license and then commercial pilot certificate on August 11, 1941. Crenchaw became a primary civilian flight instructor and eventually one of the two original supervising squadron commanders under Chief Pilot Charles A. Anderson. He and Charles Foxx were the first instructors for the first group of student pilot trainees between 1941 and 1946.

Crenchaw married Ruby Hockenhull in Tuskegee on December 22, 1942; they had four children.

Early in his career, Crenchaw worked as a civilian pilot training officer contracted by the military. He instructed scores of pilots and cadets, including Judge Robert Decatur, Charles Flowers, Lieutenant Colonel Charles "Chuck" Dryden, Earl V. Stallcups, and fellow Arkansan Woodrow Crockett. After the end of his tenure at Tuskegee, he served as a flight instructor at several airbases, including Fort Sill in Oklahoma (1953–1954), Camp Rucker (now Fort Rucker) in Alabama (1954–1966), and Fort Stewart in Georgia (1966–1972). While at Camp Rucker, Crenchaw became the first black flight instructor, and he trained other instructors. Others under him at Tuskegee followed; Sherman T. Rose and James E. "Muscles" Wright were both employed with Crenchaw in Alabama's predominately white airbase, Camp Rucker.

In 1947, Crenchaw returned to Little Rock, where he presented an idea to then-president of Philander Smith College, Dr. M. L. Harris, regarding the implementation of aviation/piloting courses. Harris agreed, and Philander Smith held those classes at Little Rock's Adams Field (now the Bill and Hillary Clinton National Airport) in the building of the Central Flying Service. Crenchaw taught aviation at Philander Smith from 1947 to 1953. He was also employed by the Central Flying Service and worked as a crop-duster in the central Arkansas and Delta regions.

In 1972 with over 10,000 hours on record logged in the air, Crenchaw was signed on as an equal employment opportunity officer with the Department of Defense and as a race relations officer at Fort Stewart in Georgia until 1983. He had also been involved with U.S. Senator Mark Pryor and U.S. Congressman Vic Snyder regarding educational programs and veterans' benefits; he actively pushed for veteran status for individuals who were involved in various service capacities at Tuskegee, including cooks, groundskeepers, medical assistants, support personnel, and flight instructors.

Crenchaw was inducted into the Arkansas Aviation Hall of Fame in 1998. On March 27, 2007, he was honored by Governor Mike Beebe for his historic efforts as a Tuskegee flight instructor and his service to his country. On March 29, 2007, Crenchaw, along with the other members of the Tuskegee Airmen, was awarded the Congressional Gold Medal by President George W. Bush in Washington, D.C. The Tuskegee Airmen are the largest group to ever receive this medal. Crenchaw died on November 17, 2015, in Stockbridge, Georgia. He was buried with full military honors at Arkansas State Veterans Cemetery in North Little Rock.

Judge L. Clifford Davis

(1924–)

Attorney L. Clifford Davis, whose active participation in the legal challenges of the civil rights movement began when he first sought admission to the all-white University of Arkansas School of Law in Fayetteville, went on to

a distinguished career in the legal profession, one that included two decades of service as a judge in the Texas court system.

L. Clifford Davis was born on October 12, 1924, in Wilton, Arkansas. The youngest of seven children of Augustus Davis and Dora Duckett Davis, he was reared on the family farm and received his early education in the Wilton schools. The town's educational offerings ended at eighth grade, so Davis moved to Little Rock to live with older siblings and attend Dunbar High School. He then went to Philander Smith College. He graduated in 1945 with a Bachelor of Arts degree in business administration.

He was admitted to the historically black Howard University School of Law in Washington, D.C., and attended for one year. Due to the high cost of Howard compared with state schools, as well as a desire to return home, he applied in 1946 for admission to the historically all-white law school at the University of Arkansas (U of A) at Fayetteville. While the university's policies on race were clear, the Supreme Court had recently opened up the formerly segregated graduate school at the University of Missouri to African Americans; with suits seeking similar change under review in Oklahoma and Texas, administrators at U of A looked for ways to address the increasingly volatile situation.

Hearing nothing from the university and with another school year getting under way, Davis spent the 1946–47 school year doing graduate work in economics at Atlanta University.

His application to the U of A was denied, but he was determined to apply again. Meanwhile, Robert Leflar, dean of the law school, recognized the legal inevitability that the Supreme Court's Missouri ruling represented and urged the governor and the school's board to make the necessary changes. Consequently, in the fall of 1947, Davis was offered admission—under highly regulated circumstances, ones that included instruction in a separate classroom, a separate study room, and no direct access to the library or restrooms used by the other white students. It was, as one historian put it, an invitation designed to maintain "internal segregation," and it was an invitation that L. Clifford Davis declined.

Between the realities of what life would be like under those conditions and the fact that he was about to embark on his third and final year at Howard, Davis decided to remain in Washington and graduate there. However, it soon became obvious that Davis's application for admission to the University of Arkansas School of Law, as well as the admittedly restrictive offer of admission that he received, represented a first and a very powerful step in an effort that would, the next year, see a black student enter the law school—though under the same restrictions as those accompanying the offer to Davis.

Davis graduated from Howard in 1949 and returned to Arkansas, where he passed the bar exam and was admitted to practice on July 4, 1949. For a few years, he had a private practice in Pine Bluff. In 1952, he moved to Waco, Texas, and took a job teaching at Paul Quinn College. After being admitted to the bar in Texas in 1953, he settled in Fort Worth and opened one of the first African-American-run law offices in the state. He soon organized the Fort Worth Black Bar Association, while he also assisted attorney Thurgood Marshall of the National Association for the Advancement of Colored People (NAACP) on the case that would ultimately be *Brown v. Board of Education of Topeka, Kansas* (1954). In the aftermath of *Brown*, Davis zealously and successfully pursued the issue of desegregation back in Texas. He filed suits aimed at desegregating schools in both the Mansfield and Fort Worth districts, an accomplishment later recognized when a local elementary school was named in his honor. Davis also sought to use the law to end discrimination in housing and employment.

After over three decades as a practicing attorney, Davis ascended to the bench in 1983 after Governor Mark White appointed him as a criminal district court judge. He won re-election and held the post until 1988, when he moved to the district court. There, he served in various capacities, including senior district judge in Tarrant County until 2004.

Davis remains of counsel for the Fort Worth firm of Johnson, Vaughn and Heiskell, where he does primarily pro bono work, continuing the tradition he had established during his many years of volunteering with both Legal Aid of North Texas and the NAACP Justice Project.

Davis has earned numerous awards and recognitions, including the NAACP's William Robert Ming Award and the Blackstone Award, the highest honor bestowed by the Tarrant County Bar Association. Davis has also been inducted into the National Bar Association's Hall of Fame, and he was the 2015 recipient of a Lifetime Achievement Award from *Texas Lawyer*. He received an honorary Doctor of Law degree from the U of A in 2017.

Davis lives with his wife, Ethel. They have two daughters.

Willie Davis

(1934–)

Willie Davis is a business executive, civic leader, and former football standout who grew up in Texarkana, Arkansas. Davis achieved athletic success in football at the high school, college, and professional levels. After he retired from a National Football League (NFL) career of twelve seasons (1958–1969), he moved into the business world, where he attained equal success.

William Delford "Willie" Davis was born on July 24, 1934, in Lisbon, Louisiana, to David and Nodie Davis. After his parents separated when he

could not decide if he were best suited for offense or defense) before he was traded to the Green Bay Packers, then considered to be the Siberia of pro sports. In fact, that trade briefly made him consider quitting the game. However, legendary Packer coach Vince Lombardi had different plans. He recognized immediately that Davis's catlike speed and agility would be best utilized as a defensive lineman. Thus began one of the greatest careers ever at that position. In his pro career, he played in 162 consecutive games—138 of which were during his ten years with the Packers. As a Packer, the 6'3", 245-pound defensive lineman played on six championship teams including Super Bowl I in 1967 and Super Bowl II in 1968. He set the Packer record of twenty-one career fumbles recovered and was named to the All-Pro team five times, in 1962 and in 1964 through 1967. Lombardi once said that Davis could "handle a tackle and fight off a block as well as anyone in the game."

When Davis retired from football in 1969, the Packers honored him with Willie Davis Day. In 1975, he was inducted into the Packers Hall of Fame, and in 1981 he was inducted into the National Football Hall of Fame, the first Grambling alumnus to be inducted. In 1999, *The Sporting News* listed him as sixty-ninth on its list of the 100 greatest professional football players.

During his last years as a player, Davis attended the University of Chicago and earned a master's degree in business administration in 1968. In 1969, he purchased the West Coast Beverage Company and served as the company president for the next eighteen years. At about this time, he served as a color commentator for NFL broadcasts for the National Broadcasting Company (NBC). In 1976, he became president and CEO of All Pro Broadcasting, Inc., a Los Angeles, California, company that owned several radio stations in southern California and the Midwest. He eventually bought or started several radio stations himself. In 1984, he served as the director of the Olympic Committee in Los Angeles; that same year, President Ronald Reagan appointed him to the President's Commission on the Executive Exchange.

Davis has served on numerous company boards, including those of the National Association of Broadcasters, Metro-Goldwyn-Mayer, Schlitz Brewing Company, and the Kauffman Foundation.

was eight, his mother moved the family to Texarkana. She supported the family by working as a cook at the Texarkana Country Club. Willie Davis worked two jobs while attending high school, including working in the locker room at the country club shining shoes and picking up towels.

He loved football and excelled on the defensive line at Texarkana's segregated high school, Booker T. Washington High School. Davis had not even told his mother he was on the team until the end of the third week when he came home late from a game. After his senior season for the Washington Lions, he was recruited by the legendary college coach Eddie Robinson at Louisiana's Grambling College (now Grambling State University—GSU). Davis served as the defensive team captain for two years and was twice named to the All America team for black colleges. He also excelled in the classroom and made the dean's list for two years. He graduated from GSU in 1956 with a Bachelor of Science degree in math and industrial arts.

In 1956, Davis was drafted in the fifteenth round by the NFL's Cleveland Browns. Just two weeks into his NFL career, he was drafted into the U.S. Army. In 1958, after approximately two years in the military, he began his professional football career.

Davis played two seasons for the Browns (which

He has also been an emeritus trustee for both the University of Chicago and Marquette University. In 2001, he founded and served as co-chairman of the Vince Lombardi Titletown Legends, a charitable organization. He was named the Walter Camp Man of the Year by the NFL and received the Career Achievement Award from the NFL Alumni. He has also served as independent director of Fidelity National Financial, Inc.

Davis had a son and daughter with his first wife, Ann, whom he married in the 1960s. His son, Duane Davis, is an actor with several television and movie credits. After his divorce from Ann, he married Andrea Erickson in the mid-1990s. Davis lives with his wife, Carol Davis, and remains active in his many business and charitable endeavors.

Little Rock Nine

1957

The Little Rock Nine, as they came to be known, were the nine African-American students involved in the desegregation of Little Rock Central High School. Their entrance into the school in 1957 sparked a nationwide crisis when Arkansas's governor Orval Faubus, in defiance of a federal court order, called out the Arkansas National Guard to prevent the Nine from entering. President Dwight D. Eisenhower responded by federalizing the National Guard and sending in units of the U.S. Army's 101st Airborne Division to escort the Nine into the school on September 25, 1957. The military presence remained for the duration of the school year.

Before transferring to Central, the Nine attended segregated schools for black students in Little Rock, Arkansas. Carlotta Walls, Jefferson Thomas, and Gloria Ray attended Paul Laurence Dunbar Junior High School, while Ernest Green, Elizabeth Eckford, Thelma Mothershed, Terrence Roberts, Minnijean Brown, and Melba Pattillo attended Horace Mann High School.

On May 24, 1955, the Little Rock School Board adopted a plan for gradual integration, known as the Blossom Plan (also known as the Little Rock Phase Program). The plan called for desegregation to be-gin in the fall of 1957 at Central and filter down to the lower grades over the next six years. Under the plan, students would be permitted to transfer from any school where their race was in the minority, thus ensuring that the black schools would remain racially segregated, because many people believed that few, if any, white students would opt to attend predominantly black schools. Federal courts upheld the Blossom Plan in response to a lawsuit by the National Association for the Advancement of Colored People (NAACP).

On September 4, 1957, the Nine attempted to enter Central but were turned away by Arkansas National Guard troops called out by the governor. When Elizabeth Eckford arrived at the campus at the intersection of 14th and Park streets, she was confronted by an angry mob of segregationist protestors. She attempted to enter at the front of the school but was directed back out to the street by the guardsmen. Walking alone and surrounded by the crowd, she eventually reached the south end of Park Street and sat down on a bench to wait for a city bus to take her to her mother's workplace. Of her experience, Eckford later said, "I tried to see a friendly face somewhere in the mob—someone who maybe would help. I looked into the face of an old woman and it seemed a kind face, but when I looked at her again, she spat on me." Others of the Nine arrived the same day and gathered at the south, or 16th Street, corner where they and an integrated group of local ministers who were there to support them were also turned away by guardsmen.

The Nine remained at home for more than two weeks, trying to keep up with their schoolwork as best they could. When the federal court ordered Gov. Faubus to stop interfering with the court's order, Faubus removed the guardsmen from in front of the school. On September 23, the Nine entered the school for the first time. The crowd outside chanted, "Two, four, six, eight…We ain't gonna integrate!" and chased and beat black reporters who were covering the events. The Little Rock police, fearful that they could not control the increasingly unruly mob in front of the school, removed the Nine later that morning. They once again returned home and waited for further information on when they would be able to attend school.

Calling the mob's actions "disgraceful," Eisenhower called out 1,200 members of the U.S. Army's 101st Airborne Division—the "Screaming Eagles" of Fort Campbell, Kentucky—and placed the Arkansas National Guard under federal orders. On September 25, 1957, under federal troop escort, the Nine were escorted back into Central for their first full day of classes. Melba Pattillo later wrote, "After three full days inside Central, I know that integration is a much bigger word than I thought."

After the Nine suffered repeated harassment—such as kicking, shoving, and name calling—the military assigned guards to escort them to classes. The guards, however, could not go everywhere with the students, and harassment continued in places such as the restrooms and locker rooms. After the 101st Airborne soldiers returned to Ft. Campbell in November, leaving the National Guard troops in charge, segregationist students intensified their efforts to compel the Nine to leave Central. The Little Rock Nine did not have any classes together. They were not allowed to participate in extracurricular activities at Central. Nevertheless, they returned to school every day to persist in obtaining an equal education.

Although all of the Nine endured verbal and physical harassment during their year at Central, Minnijean Brown was the only one to respond;

she was first suspended and then expelled for retaliating against the daily torment by dropping her lunch tray with a bowl of chili on two white boys and, later, by referring to a white girl who hit her as "white trash." Of her experience, she later said, "I just can't take everything they throw at me without fighting back." Brown moved to New York City and graduated from New Lincoln High School in 1959.

The other eight students remained at Central until the end of the school year. On May 27, 1958, Ernest Green became Central's first black graduate. Dr. Martin Luther King, Jr., attended his graduation ceremony. Green later told reporters, "It's been an interesting year. I've had a course in human relations first hand." The next year, the other eight, like all high school students across the district, were forced to attend other schools or take correspondence classes when voters opted to close all four of Little Rock's high schools to prevent further desegregation efforts.

The Little Rock Nine and their mentor Daisy Bates were awarded the prestigious Spingarn Medal by the NAACP in 1958. In 1999, President Bill Clinton presented the nation's highest civilian award, the Congressional Gold Medal, to the members of the Little Rock Nine: Melba Pattillo Beals, Elizabeth Eckford, Ernest Green, Gloria Ray Karlmark, Carlotta Walls LaNier, Terrence Roberts, Jefferson Thomas, Minnijean Brown Trickey, and Thelma Mothershed Wair.

◆ ◆ ◆

John Stubblefield

(1945–2005)

John Stubblefield was one of the most highly respected jazz saxophonists of his generation. He played with legendary musicians across the jazz spectrum and left a legacy of quality studio work over more than three decades as a bandleader, studio musician, and go-to saxophonist for live performances and tours.

John Stubblefield was born on February 4, 1945, in Little Rock, Arkansas, one of two children of John and Mabel Stubblefield. His father served in the U.S. Navy during World War II but was injured

ation for the Advancement of Creative Musicians (AACM). A year later, he played on Joseph Jarman's album *As If It Were the Seasons*. Stubblefield studied with AACM co-founder Muhal Richard Abrams and the accomplished be-bop and hard bop saxophonist George Coleman, Jr. While in Chicago, Stubblefield taught music in public schools and at the AACM School of Music. He also continued his academic music training at Vandercook College in Chicago and at the University of Indiana in Bloomington.

In 1971, Stubblefield moved to New York City, where he continued his work in the modern and avant-garde jazz scenes. He began to play with Charles Mingus soon after arriving in the city. However, after a major disagreement between the two men, Mingus used his influence to make it difficult for Stubblefield to find work for a time. Over the next decade, Stubblefield played alongside such jazz giants as Miles Davis, Gil Evans, and fellow AACM alumnus Lester Bowie on international tours and at major festivals including the Montreux Jazz Festival. He recorded at New York's Town Hall with another former member of AACM, free jazz innovator Anthony Braxton. He also played with legendary Latin jazz performer and band leader Tito Puente, as well as Kenny Baron, McCoy Tyner, Freddie Hubbard, and the World Saxophone Quartet.

Stubblefield's first album as a band leader was *Prelude*, recorded in 1976. Before joining the Mingus Big Band, Stubblefield went on to record several other albums as a band leader, including *Midnight over Memphis* (1979), *Midnight Sun* (1980), *Confessin'* (1985), *Bushman Song* (1986), *Countin' on the Blues* (1987), *Sophisticatedfunk* (1990), and *Morning Song* (1995). He also taught music and participated as an instructor in the Jazzmobile program, a pioneering jazz education organization established in New York City in 1964. He was inducted into the Arkansas Jazz Hall of Fame in 1998.

Stubblefield was described by fellow musicians to be a "preacher" as a soloist because of his deeply emotional style. Although his main instrument was tenor saxophone, he was also a respected soprano saxophonist. He was sought after by traditional jazz, avant-garde, and big band groups.

Stubblefield was instrumental in preserving the legacy of renowned bassist and composer Charles

and discharged; back in Little Rock, he worked as a laborer, machinist, and painter while passing his love of music along to his son.

Stubblefield began studying piano after he became interested in music while attending church with his mother. She later discouraged his transition to saxophone and involvement with jazz, rhythm and blues (R&B), and other forms of what she called devil's music. His first professional work came playing at clubs in the predominately black Ninth Street area in Little Rock, often sitting in with blues, R&B, and jazz musicians when they passed through town. Stubblefield's first recording credit came at age seventeen with the R&B group York Wilburn & the Thrillers. Next, he spent a year on the road with soul singer Solomon Burke before he enrolled at Arkansas Agricultural, Mechanical, and Normal (AM&N) College (now the University of Arkansas at Pine Bluff—UAPB) to study music. While at AM&N, he led a jazz combo and established his pattern of playing with many musicians in a variety of styles from gospel to modern jazz. He received his Bachelor of Science degree in music in 1967.

Stubblefield relocated to Chicago, Illinois, and joined the avant-garde jazz collective the Associ-

Mingus, despite their professional differences earlier in his career. After Mingus's death, his widow, Sue Mingus, founded a big band in Mingus's honor. Stubblefield led the Mingus Big Band for over thirteen years and was one of the only members who had actually played with Mingus. He proved to be a dedicated band leader and steward of the Mingus legacy, once leaving his hospital bed toward the end of his life to conduct the band from his wheelchair to record three of his arrangements for the album *I Am Three* in October 2004.

Stubblefield died of prostate cancer on July 4, 2005. President Bill Clinton was among the many friends, fellow musicians, and fans who visited him in the hospital in his final days. His memorial service at St. Peter's Church at 54th Street and Lexington in New York City was attended by scores of musicians and included three hours of musical tributes. Stubblefield was survived by his wife, Katherine Gogel of Massachusetts, and his son, John Stubblefield V.

Sheryl Underwood

(1963–)

Comedian and actress Sheryl Underwood has gained national recognition in comedy, television, politics, and philanthropy.

Sheryl P. Underwood was born in Little Rock, Arkansas, at St. Vincent Infirmary on October 28, 1963, to Cleo Underwood and Joyce Evelyn Underwood. She and her twin sister were premature and placed in an incubator shortly after birth. Her twin died soon afterward. Underwood revealed in 2011 that she carries her twin's birth certificate with her and considers her twin to be her guardian angel. Underwood has two other siblings: her brother Michael and her older sister Frankie. Frankie, who has developmental delays, requires around-the-clock care, which was provided for years by Underwood and her brother. As an adult, Underwood stated that she pays for her sister's care. Underwood experienced domestic violence between her parents and spoke about it during her first episode as a member of *The Talk*, a CBS talk show. Eventually, Underwood moved to Atwater, California, and graduated from high school there.

She holds an Associate of Arts degree in liberal arts from Fresno City College, a Bachelor of Arts degree in liberal arts from the University of Illinois at Chicago, a master's degree in media management and mass communication from Governors State University, and an Attorney Assistant Certificate from the University of California, Los Angeles (UCLA). She also served in the Air Force Reserves.

Little is known about Underwood's personal or family life. She revealed that she was raped between her college graduation and her military service. She married her husband, Michael, after dating four years. Underwood stated that Michael suffered from clinical depression and died from suicide in 1990 after three years of marriage.

Underwood began her comedy career as the first female finalist in the 1989 Miller Light Comedy Search. She starred in minor roles in *I Got the Hook-Up* and *Beauty Shop* and had guest spots in numerous television programs, including *Def Comedy Jam*, *Holla*, *The Young and the Restless*, *The Bold and the Beautiful*, *Fox News' Fox and Friends*, and *The View*. Underwood joined the CBS morning show *The Talk* in 2011. Underwood hosted and contributed to several nationally syndicated radio programs such as *The Tom Joyner Morning Show*, *The Steve Harvey Morning Show*, *Sheryl Underwood and Company*, and Jamie Foxx's *The Foxxhole*.

Underwood owns and operates Pack Rat Productions, Inc., and Pack Rat Foundation for Education (PRFFE), and she is currently raising money for students pursuing higher education at the 105 historically black colleges and universities. She founded the African American Female Comedian Association and is a member of both the National Association for the Advancement of Colored People (NAACP) and the National Council of Negro Women. She has been featured in *Ebony*, *Essence*, *People*, and other media outlets. She won an Emmy for *The Talk*. Underwood considers herself to be "a sexually progressive, God-fearing, black Republican," although she campaigned for Democrat Barack Obama's 2012 re-election and Democrat Hillary Clinton's 2016 presidential run.

Underwood is a Diamond Life Member of Zeta Phi Beta Sorority, Inc. She first joined the Zeta Tau Zeta Chapter, became a member of the Alpha Psi Zeta Chapter in Los Angeles, and helped charter the Omicron Rho Zeta Chapter in Inglewood, California, in 1993. Underwood served in several elected roles in the sorority, including as the twenty-third international president (Grand Basileus). Under her guidance, the sorority focused on organizations like the March of Dimes, the American Diabetes Association, and the American Cancer Society.

Underwood also initiated support for survivors of the 2010 Haitian earthquakes and the 2011 tornadoes across the United States. Under her leadership, a health center opened in 2011 for an all-girls' high school in Ghana, providing health services to more than 2,000 students. Underwood participated in USO tours to Kuwait and Afghanistan, and addressed service members at the Academy of Country Music's All-Star Salute to the Troops in 2014.

2008

Torii Hunter

Rose Marie McCoy

Joseph Daniel McQuany

Michelle Revere

A. D. Washington

Sterling B. Williams, MD

Torii Hunter
(1975–)

Torii Hunter was considered one of major league baseball's biggest stars during his career. An elite center fielder, he won nine consecutive Gold Glove awards, was a five-time All-Star selection, and won two Silver Slugger awards as the best offensive player at his position. He also recorded the most home runs by an Arkansan in major league history (353). In 2,372 games, Hunter hit safely 2,452 times—890 for extra bases—for a lifetime batting average of .277. He stole 195 bases, drove in 1,391 runs, and committed only fifty-two errors in center field (and later right field). He played for the Anaheim Angels and the Detroit Tigers but ended his professional career on October 26, 2015, with the Minnesota Twins.

Torii Hunter was born on July 18, 1975, in Pine Bluff, Arkansas, to Shirley Hunter (an elementary school teacher) and Theotis Hunter (an electrician). He had four brothers and a sister. He excelled at any sport, and in fact would later call football his first love and the position of quarterback the best

expression of his talent. However, at age thirteen, he flew to New Mexico to play in a Little League tournament. After he hit a walk-off home run (one that ends the game), he was interviewed by reporters. From then on, he considered baseball the more sophisticated, preferable route to the kind of professional athletic life he had in mind for himself.

Hunter was the Minnesota Twins' first pick in the 1993 draft, but it was not until 1997 that he actually made an appearance in a big-league game (as a pinch-runner). It was 1999 before he entered the game as a starter. He was perhaps the best hitter in the Twins' 2002 run to the American League Championship Series, when he led the team in home runs, runs batted in (RBIs), and slugging percentage. He finished third in hits.

Though he would continue a streak of Gold Glove–winning campaigns in center field through 2009 (he won his first in 2001), his hitting dropped off slightly in 2003 and 2004, and a broken ankle placed him on the disabled list for much of 2005. His numbers peaked again when he hit a career-high thirty-one home runs in 2006 and 107 RBIs in 2007. Perhaps on the strength of this stretch of hitting—helped no doubt by his stellar fielding—he was offered a five-year, almost $90 million contract with the Anaheim Angels.

In some ways Hunter underwhelmed the California fans, and indeed his home run production dipped (he never again hit more than twenty-five home runs in a season after 2007), but in 2012, he had a career-high season for batting average and on-base percentage. Except for an injury in 2009, he played in at least 140 games each of the five seasons he played in Anaheim.

After the 2012 season, the Angels failed to extend his contract, and the Detroit Tigers offered Hunter a two-year, $26 million contract as a right fielder. With career highs in at-bats (606) and hits (184) while striking out only 113 times, Hunter finished the 2013 season with a .304 batting average, and the Tigers reached the American League Championship Series.

Hunter's production in 2014 tailed off a bit—with fifty-seven fewer at-bats, he posted a .286 batting average (with the same home runs, seventeen, as the year before)—and in the fall the team did not compete for his contract. He was picked up by the Minnesota Twins for about $10.5 million. In

2015, though he stepped to the plate 521 times, hit twenty-two home runs, and collected eighty-one RBIs, he hit just .240, his lowest career batting average over a full season. He announced his retirement in late October 2015.

Hunter is the philanthropist behind the Torii Hunter Project (in partnership with the nonprofit Heart of a Champion). He is also active in his church, New Life Community Church, in Frisco, Texas.

Hunter's relationship with his hometown of Pine Bluff is ambivalent. He has said the smell that most immediately triggers nostalgia for him is that of a paper mill, which "remind[s] me why I left that area of Pine Bluff." He has also made a significant contribution to the baseball field and complex that now bears his name on the campus of the University of Arkansas at Pine Bluff (UAPB). Hunter has said that in retirement he would like to transition into the business of sports and/or sports analysis.

Hunter and his wife, Katrina, have a son; he has three other sons.

Rose Marie McCoy

(1922–2015)

Rose Marie Hinton McCoy emerged onto the white, male-dominated music scene in the early 1950s to become a highly sought-after songwriter whose career lasted over six decades. More than 360 artists have recorded her tunes, including Nat King Cole, Elvis Presley, and Sarah Vaughan.

Marie Hinton was born in Oneida, Arkansas, on April 19, 1922, to Levi Hinton and Celetia Brazil Hinton. She and her older brother and sister attended the area's two-room elementary school, went to church regularly, and worked on the forty-acre farm their parents rented. Though Oneida was located in the Mississippi Delta (often referred to as the birthplace of the blues) and except for the occasional singing of a field hand, the blues was not heard in that small town. Many considered it to be "the devil's music."

It was eighteen miles away in Helena that Marie became acquainted with the blues, where she often

stood outside a club called The Hole in the Wall to hear top bluesmen perform. Her grandparents lived in Helena, Arkansas, and she was sent there to attend Eliza Miller High School, the area high school for black students. Marie sang in shows and saw top black jazz bands perform, which left her dreaming of becoming a professional singer.

At age eighteen, she legally added Rose to her name. In 1942, Rose Marie Hinton moved to New York and began singing in small clubs in Harlem. On a trip back to Arkansas in 1943, she married former sweetheart James McCoy, who was in the U.S. Army and was about to be sent to Germany; they had no children. While he was away, she began traveling the so-called Chitlin' Circuit (a group of performing venues located mostly in the South). She opened for such top performers as Pigmeat Markham and Moms Mabley.

McCoy had started writing songs when she was a child. The first of her songs to appear on a record was "After All," recorded in 1946 by a group called the Dixie-aires. The royalties for writing were so small, she decided to concentrate on her singing career.

In 1952 ten years after moving to New York, she recorded two of her songs for Wheeler Records, a new company formed to capitalize on the growing popularity of black music. As soon as her record was released, music publishers began seeking her out not as a singer as she had hoped but as a songwriter. One of the first songs she was asked to write reached No. 3 on *Billboard*'s Rhythm & Blues chart in 1953. "Gabbin' Blues" gave the singer Big Maybelle her first hit record and McCoy the first of her seven BMI Awards. That same year, Big Maybelle scored another top-ten hit with McCoy's "Way Back Home."

At first, McCoy worked on her own and wrote both words and music. Then, in 1953, she teamed up with her first writing partner, Charles Singleton. From 1954 to 1956, they wrote seven top-ten hits: "Well All Right" (Big Joe Turner, 1954), "Mambo Baby" (Ruth Brown, 1954), "Hurts Me to My Heart" (Faye Adams, 1954), "Pitter Patter" (Nappy Brown, 1955), "If I May" (Nat King Cole, 1955), "Don't Take It So Hard" (Earl King, 1955), and "Letter from My Darling" (Little Willie John, 1956). Their song "Trying to Get to You" (1957) was included on Elvis Presley's first album (1956), and though it did not become a top-ten single, it has been part of many of Presley's albums and live performances. The song has since been recorded by more than thirty other artists.

Some of her other songwriting partnerships created hits for Nappy Brown ("Don't Be Angry," 1955), Elvis Presley ("I Beg of You," 1957), Ike and Tina Turner ("It's Gonna Work Out Fine," 1961), Maxine Brown ("We'll Cry Together," 1961), and Jerry Butler ("Got to See if I Can't Get Mommy to Come Back Home," 1970). McCoy also produced many recordings, which include the five songs she wrote for Sarah Vaughan's 1974 album *Send in the Clowns*. She also wrote jingles for artists such as Aretha Franklin and Ray Charles and formed her own publishing firm.

Though having her songs recorded by major artists was getting more and more difficult, McCoy kept promoting her tunes from her office in Manhattan's iconic Brill Building and later from her home in Teaneck, New Jersey. Her last songs were written with Billy Joe Conor and appear on his 2013 self-titled country album.

Rose Marie McCoy died of pneumonia on January 20, 2015, in Carle Foundation Hospital in Urbana, Illinois.

Joseph Daniel McQuany
(1928–2007)

Joseph McQuany was the founder of Serenity House in Little Rock, Arkansas, as well as the Kelly Foundation, Inc.—organizations both dedicated to helping people work through drug and alcohol addiction. He was also the author of books on recovery. His work has been influential in local, state, national, and international communities relating to the problems of addiction.

Joseph Daniel McQuany was born on November 16, 1928, to Kelly McQuany and Ada Beaty McQuany in Louisville, Kentucky. He had a brother and a sister. He eventually moved to Little Rock, where he made the decision to become sober after suffering from alcoholism. At the time, African Americans suffering from alcoholism were admitted as mental patients to the Arkansas State Hospital because programs for addiction treatment were segregated. After leaving the Arkansas State Hospital and despite resistance from some white members of the group, he started attending local Alcoholics Anonymous (AA) meetings and became the first black person to go through the program in Arkansas.

The Twelve-Step program and AA's Big Book became an integral part of McQuany's life. He soon began organizing other AA groups locally, eventually starting his own program. In 1972 using a $330 grant, he founded an offshoot of AA called Serenity House. It was originally based in a house on Broadway Avenue; as the program grew, Serenity House moved several times before settling on Roosevelt Road at a site that is now called Serenity Park. He also began to develop the Recovery Dynamics Model, which constitutes a method by which treatment counselors break down the Twelve-Step program of AA into discrete group counseling sessions. McQuany copyrighted the Recovery Dynamics Model in 1977 and incorporated the nonprofit Kelly Foundation the following year in order to assist other treatment facilities in the implementation of this treatment model. Numerous treatment centers across the nation and world now use his model, with some of them even borrowing the "Serenity" name from McQuany's original center.

McQuany toured the nation and spoke to hundreds of thousands of people on AA and Recovery Dynamics. Additionally, he wrote the books *The Steps We Took* (1990) and *Carry This Message* (2002). On March 10, 2005, ground was broken at Serenity Park for a treatment center for women, which the area had been lacking since the last one closed in the 1980s.

McQuany died on October 25, 2007, in Little Rock. He was survived by his wife of forty-eight years, Loubelle, and his two children. He is buried at Haven of Rest Cemetery.

Michelle Revere

(1960–)

Michelle Revere is a fashion and home designer who has embraced the finest European and American designs.

Michelle Revere was born in Little Rock, Arkansas, on August 30, 1960, one of two daughters of Preston Revere and Futhie Mae Holmes Revere, a licensed cosmetologist. Her father was a master brick mason from Louisiana. When he moved to the Little Rock area, he noticed that there was a lack of skilled artisans in the area but a good supply of young men who desired to learn a skill. He set out to make a difference and became the director of a government training program, Outreach Training Program, and trained electricians, brick ma-

sons, plumbers, carpenters, and the like. Education was important to the Reveres, and they stressed that with their daughters. They family is Catholic, and Revere graduated from Mount Saint Mary Academy in Little Rock. She earned a Bachelor of Arts degree in political science at the University of Arkansas at Fayetteville (U of A). One day she was spotted studying on a bench and was talked into modeling for a fashion show at the Springdale Country Club. That spurred an interest for her in the fashion and textile industry. After she graduated from the U of A, Revere took a job at the Arkansas State Capitol but also pursued her newfound interest in fashion by taking a second job at Something Special, a clothing outlet located in the Pulaski Heights neighborhood of Little Rock.

This soon became a full-time job when Revere became chief purchaser for the store. She later worked as a buyer for B.P.'s Place and Barbara Jean, Ltd., both local high-end fashion boutiques. While working at Barbara Jean, she met Hillary Rodham Clinton, whose husband, Governor Bill Clinton, was then campaigning for the presidency of the United States. Revere was contacted by Hillary to select her clothing and to create the design of the First Lady's 1993 inaugural ball gown. The hand-beaded gown was the result of Revere's vision, which she had sketched on a napkin and commissioned then slightly known designer Sarah Phillips to design. That gown now resides in the Smithsonian National Museum of American History. Afterward, Revere was commissioned by the first lady to join her in Washington, D.C., to continue as Hillary Clinton's personal wardrobe and design consultant. She later became a buyer for Nordstrom.

In 1999 upon completion of her time in the nation's capital, Revere continued in fashion and moved to London, England, where she served as design consultant and vice president of sales for British designer Tomasz Starzewski for the next three years. Her time in Europe contributed to her love for home textiles, antique porcelain, and furniture.

In 2003, after returning to the United States without her beloved French Poodle "Co Chanel," Revere launched the "Cokie Home Collection" of decorative porcelain accessories for humans and canines. She also began making beds for canines and donating the money to rescue shelters because "Cokie" had been a rescue dog.

Numerous requests to continue in the fashion industry led Revere in 2006 to launch the Christopher Whyte Collection, named for her nephew. The new collection embraced her love for designing with fur. She has created a collection of luxury fur accessories which includes hand bags, scarves, shawls, and capes, as well as a line of luxury fur home-throws and home accessories. Her designs have been represented in fine specialty stores in Japan and across North America, as well as having gained popularity with celebrities including Patti LaBelle, Lynn Whitfield, Vivica Fox, Paris Hilton, and Oprah Winfrey.

Revere is still going strong in the fashion and textiles industry and resides in the New York City metropolitan area. She maintains Arkansas ties through her sister, Phyllis White; her nephew; and her great-niece.

A. D. Washington
(1942–)

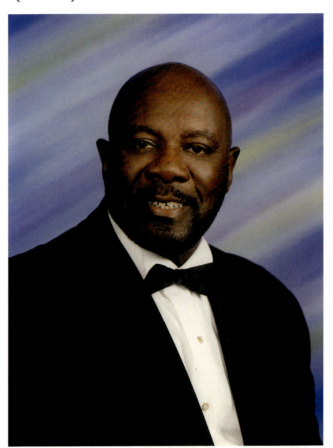

A. D. Washington has worked as a promoter for Capitol Records, Warner Bros., and MCA Records, with artists such as Patti LaBelle, Bobby Brown, and Gladys Knight.

A. D. Washington was born in Little Rock, Arkansas. He grew up in nearby Scott. After he graduated from high school, he attended the University of Arkansas at Pine Bluff (UAPB). He began his music industry career in 1973 as a regional promotion representative at Stax Records in Memphis, Tennessee, where he worked under legendary promotion pioneer Dave Clark (who himself had been hired by native Arkansan Al Bell). In 1979, he was hired by MCA Records to handle Southwest regional promotion.

The October 6, 1990, issue of *Cash Box*, the trade magazine of MCA Records, described Washington, then the senior vice president of promotion and marketing for the label's black music division, as "probably one of the best black promotional people that we have in this business." One of his most noteworthy achievements was perhaps with the R&B/soul quartet Shai, whose single "If I Ever Fall in Love" was released in October 1992 and quickly sold more than two million copies and hit the number-two spot on the Billboard Hot 100, beaten only by Whitney Houston's "I Will Always Love You." Washington was featured on the cover of the June 18, 1993, issue of *Gavin* alongside other executives such as Quincy Jones.

Washington departed MCA in 1996 as the label revamped its black music staff. Later that year, he was named the senior vice president of marketing and promotion for black music at Warner Bros. In 1999, he was named the vice president of R&B field promotion at Capitol Records.

Throughout his career, Washington has emphasized the importance of a personal connection to the artists he promoted. In the January 29, 1994, issue of *Billboard*, he said, "You always want to allow an artist to grow, and each project should allow them to show their creative talent." In addition to his work, he has also served on the board of the Living Legends Foundation, which was founded in the early 1990s to provide assistance to those who have served the music industry. Washington currently lives in Little Rock.

Sterling B. Williams, MD

(1941–2013)

Dr. Sterling B. Williams was a groundbreaking leader in the field of obstetrics and gynecology (OB-GYN) who served in several important roles in national organizations dedicated to medicine and medical education. In addition, he was a gifted vocalist who performed with numerous choral groups.

Sterling Williams was born in Little Rock, Arkansas, on April 3, 1941. He grew up in Little Rock and graduated from Horace Mann High School. He earned a Bachelor of Science degree in zoology from the University of Illinois at Urbana-Champaign, followed by a Master of Science degree in physiology from Northern Illinois University in 1966 and an MD from what is now the University of Arkansas for Medical Sciences (UAMS) in

1973. He also completed work toward his PhD in physiology but was not awarded the degree before leaving for his residency; he was eventually awarded that degree from UAMS in 2012, along with the Dean's Distinguished Alumni Award.

Williams served his OB-GYN residency at the University of Kansas (KU) Medical Center. After he completed his residency in 1976, he served in various faculty positions at KU, including as chairman of the Department of Obstetrics & Gynecology at the KU Medical Center, and became a professor at Columbia University. From 1987 to 1997, he was the residency program director at the Harlem Hospital Center in New York City. From 1997 to 2001, he was the Kermit E. Krantz Professor and chair of the department of obstetrics and gynecology at the KU. In 2001, he accepted the position of vice president of education at the American College of Obstetricians and Gynecologists (ACOG), based in Washington, D.C., where he also directed the Council on Resident Education in Obstetrics and Gynecology (CREOG).

Williams was a dedicated volunteer for the Accreditation Council for Continuing Medical Education (ACCME), and he served on the ACCME board of directors from 2006 to 2010. He served as chairman and vice chairman of the Finance Committee. He also served as a member of the Executive Committee; Compensation Committee; Nominating, Elections, and Awards Committee; the Workgroup on Cost Reduction; and the Monitoring Task Force. Williams also served on the ACCME Accreditation Review Committee from 2002 to 2005 and was elected to the board of the Council of Medical Specialty Societies (CMSS). When this nine-member board discussed placing more CEOs of specialty organizations on the board, he asserted that while it was important to have CEOs engaged, it was counterproductive to have only CEOs. Thus, he led a movement to increase but limit the number of CEOs on the board to five. Williams was also well respected for his leadership in and dedication to the National Medical Association (NMA), which represents African-American physicians and patients. Williams also published extensively in the field of medical education throughout his life, including co-authoring an article for the *Journal of Graduate Medical Education* that was published the year of his death.

Outside the medical field, Williams was a noted choral performer who sang numerous times with the Washington Chorus at the Kennedy Center in Washington, D.C., and at Carnegie Hall in New York City. He also sang with the Mormon Tabernacle Choir, the Kansas City Philharmonic, and the Kansas City Civic Chorus. An alumnus of the New York Choral Society, he was invited to join the chorus to sing with legendary folk music group Peter, Paul and Mary in one of its later concerts at Carnegie Hall.

After a brief illness, he died on May 19, 2013. He was survived by his wife, Joice, and three children, Sterling, Spencer, and Angela.

2009

Bishop Charles E. Blake, Sr.

Erma Glasco Davis, PhD

Delores Handy-Brown

James E. K. Hildreth, MD

Pastor W. R. "Smokie" Norful

Samuel W. Williams, PhD

Bishop Charles E. Blake, Sr.
(1940–)

Charles Edward Blake, Sr., is the presiding bishop of the Church of God in Christ (COGIC). He is also pastor of West Angeles Church of God in Christ (COGIC), which has a membership of more than 24,000. In addition, Blake founded Save Africa's Children, which provides orphan care programs across the continent of Africa.

Charles E. Blake was born on August 5, 1940, in North Little Rock, Arkansas, the son of Junious Augustus Blake and Lula Champion Blake. His father, a native of Camden, Arkansas, pastored various churches throughout Arkansas before moving to California. Charles Blake was ordained as a minister himself in 1962. He received his Bachelor of Arts degree from California Western University (now Alliant International University), following that with a Master of Divinity degree from Inter-

national Theological Center in 1965. He received his Doctorate of Divinity degree from the California Graduate School of Theology in 1982. He is married to Mae Lawrence Blake, and the couple has three children.

In 1969, Blake was appointed as pastor of West Angeles Church of God in Christ, which then had about fifty members, and under his leadership, the church grew by leaps and bounds, becoming one of the fastest-growing COGIC congregations in the world and the largest African-American church in the western United States, as well as a significant economic force in the community. In 1982, *Ebony* magazine recognized Blake as one of the greatest preachers in the United States and has frequently labeled him as one of the nation's most influential African Americans.

In 1985, Blake was named the Jurisdictional Prelate of the First Ecclesiastical Jurisdiction of Southern California, which oversees more than 250 churches. He served in this role until 2009. In 1988, he was named to the General Board of the Church of God in Christ. After serving as the First Assistant Presiding Bishop of COGIC, Blake became Presiding Bishop following the March 20, 2007, death of Gilbert E. Patterson. Later that year, he was elected to complete Patterson's term in office; in November 2008, he was elected to his first full four-year term. He has since been re-elected in 2012 and 2016.

Bishop Blake has served on the boards of Charles H. Mason Theological Seminary, International Theological Seminary, Oral Roberts University, and International Charismatic Bible Ministries, as well as being on the advisory committee of the Pentecostal World Conference and the leadership council of the Pentecostal/Charismatic Churches of North America. He founded the Los Angeles Ecumenical Congress and, in 2009, was appointed to the Inaugural Advisory Council of the Office of Faith-based and Neighborhood Partnerships by President Barack Obama.

Blake has received numerous awards, including the Salvation Army's William Booth Award, the Greenlining Institute's Big Heart Award, and the Los Angeles Urban League's Whitney M. Young Award. In 2003, Blake was awarded the Harvard Foundation Humanitarian Medal for his work with Save Africa's Children. The Los Angeles County

Board of Supervisors designated February 5, 2004, as "Bishop Charles E. Blake Day." Blake has also received honorary doctorates from several institutions, including Biola University and Oral Roberts University.

Erma Glasco Davis, PhD

(1928–)

Erma Glasco Davis is a historian, civic leader, and educator. She is best known for preserving and communicating the legacy of her alma mater, Paul Laurence Dunbar High School and Junior College (the building is in use in the twenty-first century as Dunbar Magnet Middle School), and highlighting the impact this historically black institution has had in Arkansas.

Erma Lee Glasco was born on December 31, 1928, in Eagle Township of Pulaski County, near Keo, Arkansas, to Anderson Glasco and Rodelia Glasco. Her father was a stone and masonry contractor, a deacon at Mount Zion Baptist Church,

a member of the Arkansas Minority Contractors Association, and a former board member of the Little Rock YMCA. Her mother was head baker at the bakery shop at Central High School (then known as Little Rock High School) in Little Rock during World War II. After the desegregation of Central, which led to the closing of Little Rock public schools for the 1958–59 school year, Rodelia Glasco earned her high school diploma and then a Bachelor of Science degree and a Master of Education degree in curriculum instruction from the University of Wisconsin at Madison; she eventually became a faculty member at Arkansas Baptist College in Little Rock.

The family moved to the South End neighborhood of Little Rock, where Erma Glasco and her brother Otis attended primary school. The South End is roughly outlined by Roosevelt Road to the north, Interstate 30 to the east, Fourche Creek to the south, and Woodrow Street to the west.

Erma Glasco graduated from Dunbar High School in May 1945. She received a Bachelor of Science degree from Arkansas Agricultural, Mechanical, and Normal (AM&N) College (now the University of Arkansas at Pine Bluff—UAPB) in 1949. That same year, she married Jim Davis; they had one daughter, Marilynn.

After the Central High School desegregation crisis of 1957–59, Erma Davis relocated with her husband and child to Detroit, Michigan. She enrolled in Wayne State University, from which she earned a Master of Secondary Science Education. She later received a doctorate in educational administration and supervision from the University of Michigan.

Davis's career flourished in Detroit. She was a teacher, counselor, and administrator who served on numerous boards and civic organizations. She was awarded the Spirit of Detroit Award in 1987, the city's highest community service award. She returned to Arkansas, however, in 1990 because of her desire to share the legacy of Dunbar High School, which, according to author Sharon G. Pierson, "was considered among the best black high schools during the era of segregation for its academic excellence in college preparatory and liberal arts curriculum."

During her time as president of the National Dunbar Alumni Association (now the National

Dunbar Horace Mann Alumni Association) from 1993 to 1999, Davis was the co-chairman of the Dunbar History Project (1994–1998) with fellow alumna Barbara Long Hill (deceased). This project produced the National Dunbar Historical Collections for the University of Arkansas at Little Rock, and the collection is housed at the Arkansas Studies Institute. The project also produced the traveling exhibit "Paul Laurence Dunbar High School: The Finest High School for Negro Boys and Girls, Dunbar High School in Little Rock, Arkansas, 1929–1955." This exhibit was unveiled in 1996 at Arkansas Territorial Restoration (now Historic Arkansas Museum); the Dunbar exhibit has traveled all around the state. It has since found a permanent home at the Mosaic Templars Cultural Center in Little Rock. In 2003, Davis co-wrote *Paul Laurence Dunbar High School of Little Rock, Arkansas: "Take from Our Lips a Song, Dunbar to Thee"* with fellow alumna Faustine C. Jones-Wilson.

Davis was appointed to the state Review Committee for Historic Preservation in 2005 by Governor Mike Huckabee. She was reappointed in 2007 by Governor Mike Beebe.

Delores Handy-Brown

(1947–)

Delores Handy-Brown has made a name for herself as an award-winning African-American journalist, reporter, and news anchor. In over four decades, She has won four Emmy awards for her television work in Washington, D.C., and Boston, Massachusetts.

Delores Handy was born in Little Rock, Arkansas, on April 7, 1947, to the Reverend George G. Handy, Sr., and Myrtle Handy. She is the oldest of fourteen children—nine girls and five boys. George Handy, Sr., pastored a Baptist church in North Little Rock.

Handy attended Horace Mann High School. Her interests included flag football and track and field. She graduated in 1965 and began college in the fall at Little Rock University, now the University of Arkansas at Little Rock. She graduated in 1969. After graduation she worked for KAAY-AM

1090 in Little Rock under the pseudonym Mary Donald. Handy's interest in athletics in school carried over to her career. She was an Arkansas Travelers baseball fan and attended games often. She learned how to keep game records and spent time being mentored by *Arkansas Gazette* sports editor Orville Henry, *Gazette* sportswriter Jim Bailey, and local broadcaster Jim Elder.

Handy also worked in media markets in Memphis, Tennessee; Los Angeles, California; and Washington, D.C. In 1976, she joined WJLA-TV in Washington as a co-anchor with David Schoumacher. Then, in January 1978, Handy was abruptly fired from the station, and her contract was not renewed. Her termination became a social and political issue between the District of Columbia City Council and WJLA-TV news director Sam Zelman. Amid allegations that Handy and Schoumacher frequently quarreled, additional concerns included on-air time, billing, story assignments, and salaries. Handy, twenty-nine at the time, was likely making significantly less than Schoumacher's $150,000 annual salary. Her termination came at a time when council members were fighting for passage of the Equal Rights Amendment and an increase in employment-based affirmative action, while the station was involved in a corporate ownership transfer. Hundreds of phone calls and letters were sent to city council members and the station. The story was picked up later in the year by *Ebony* magazine after Handy had been hired by an independent news outlet in the city. Simone Booker, *Ebony's* Washington bureau chief, urged the city's majority-black population to control the media and wield the power of reporting by turning their television dials to Handy's new station.

Handy moved to Boston in 1982 to work at WQTV Channel 7. She also worked as a producer, anchor, and host for WGBH 2 and WHDH 68. Boston University purchased WGBH in 1993 and changed the call letters to WABU. On February 14, 1994, Handy became one of two principal anchors on the station's *Newsbreak 68*, a two-minute news update airing at the top of the hour five days a week between noon and 11:00 p.m. In recent years, Handy has served as an anchor for CNN's *Headline News*. She also anchored for the Christian Science Church's televised Monitor Channel, which closed in 1992. She most recently worked as an anchor and journalist for WBUR, National Public Radio in Boston, and for Boston University's World of Ideas. Programming includes university faculty, staff, and community discussion of academic issues, current and relevant topics, events, and national and international politics.

The Washington Press Club named her Journalist of the Year in 1977. After twenty-five years of service, she was inducted into the Southeast Chapter's Silver Circle of the National Academy of Television, Arts, and Sciences. The Museum of African-American History in Massachusetts honored her as one of 350 people who embody the spirit of black presence. She also won the New York International Film Festival's Award for Documentaries. She has served on the board of directors for Project Step.

Handy is married to Larry Brown, a retired Boston police officer. They have a son and daughter and live in the Boston area. Handy is a cousin to the Reverend Doctor Jesse Brown and a descendant of blues music pioneer W. C. Handy.

James E. K. Hildreth, MD
(1956–)

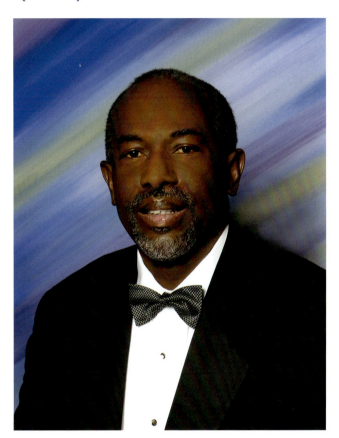

James E. K. Hildreth, a leading HIV/AIDS researcher, is dean of the University of California–Davis College of Biological Sciences. Previously, he was employed by Meharry Medical College in Nashville, Tennessee, where he was director for the Center for AIDS Health Disparities Research; program director of the Research Centers in Minority Institutions; director of the Meharry Center for Translational Research; associate director at the Vanderbilt-Meharry Center for AIDS Research; and professor of internal medicine, microbiology, and immunology. At the Center for AIDS Health Disparities Research, he worked on a cream that kills the human immunodeficiency virus (HIV).

James Earl Hildreth was born in Camden, Arkansas, on December 27, 1956, to Lucy and R. J. Hildreth. He is the youngest of seven children. In 1968, his father died of renal cancer. Around this time, Hildreth began to think about becoming a physician. He read books about medical schools and doctors and discovered that a high percentage of students from Harvard University were accepted into medical school. From then on, he worked hard in school with the goal of being accepted into Harvard.

After he earned high scores on both the ACT and SAT college admissions exams, Hildreth applied to many colleges, including Harvard. He graduated from Camden High School as the valedictorian of his class and went on to Harvard. To help pay for college, Hildreth worked as a carpenter. He also applied for the Rhodes scholarship at the end of October 1978 and became one of thirty-two American Rhodes scholars and the first African-American Arkansan to achieve that honor.

In 1979, Hildreth graduated magna cum laude from Harvard with a degree in chemistry. He then went to Oxford University in England as a Rhodes scholar. A year later, he married Phyllis King. He had to get permission from the Rhodes Trust because he was not allowed to marry as a Rhodes scholar. To honor his wife, he added King to his name. They have two children.

Hildreth lived in England for three years; in 1982, he earned his doctorate in immunology. He then returned to the United States to attend Johns Hopkins University School of Medicine in Baltimore, Maryland, where he earned a medical degree in 1987. He taught at Johns Hopkins and was an associate dean until 2005, when he left for Meharry Medical College in Nashville. He became dean of the University of California–Davis College of Biological Sciences on August 1, 2011.

Dr. Hildreth's research focuses on HIV and AIDS. HIV is a virus that attacks the cells of the immune system and leads to AIDS, or acquired immune deficiency syndrome. About fifty percent of the people infected with HIV in the United States live in the South, which is defined as a region consisting of sixteen states and the District of Columbia. African Americans make up less than fourteen percent of the population of the United States but make up forty-five percent of new HIV infections in the country. Hildreth and his researchers are studying drugs to help prevent the spread of HIV. He was given a grant from the federal Centers for Disease Control and Prevention (CDC) to partner with black churches in thirteen states in order to educate people about HIV.

In 1986, Hildreth began research on an HIV-killing cream with an objective to help developing countries lower their HIV infection rates. He traveled to Zambia in 2006 to test his product, and he later traveled to South Africa with the same goal in mind.

Hildreth has also written and co-written many publications and has received many awards and honors.

◆ ◆ ◆

Pastor W. R. "Smokie" Norful
(1975–)

Smokie Norful—a popular pastor in Chicago, Illinois, and a Grammy Award–winning gospel singer—spent most of his developing years in Pine Bluff, Arkansas. He is also one of the most commercially successful gospel recording artists to have emerged from Arkansas.

Born Willie Ray Norful, Jr., in Little Rock on October 31, 1975, to the Reverend W. R. Norful and Teresa Norful, he is the oldest of three boys. Like so many other African-American gospel singers, he found church to be a nurturing environment where his musical skills could be honed. At a 2012 taping of the Trinity Broadcast Network's flagship program, *Praise the Lord*, Norful joked before a studio audience about growing up as a "P. K." (preacher's kid) and expressed gratitude for his minister father and no-nonsense mother. Norful remarked, "Most of the family sermons came from the other end of her belt."

Having spent his earliest years in Muskogee and Tulsa, Oklahoma, Norful relocated with his family to Pine Bluff, where he attended junior high and high school. He earned a Bachelor of Arts degree in history at the University of Arkansas at Pine Bluff (UAPB). Then to prepare for his ministerial career, Norful attended Trinity International Seminary in Deerfield, Illinois, and Garrett-Evangelical Theological Seminary in Evanston, Illinois. He earned a Master of Divinity degree. Thereafter, he taught history for several years at the schools of his youth, Jack Robey Junior High School and Pine Bluff High School. He later returned to Illinois to begin a position at Evanston Township High School.

During his time in Arkansas, Norful served as the educational director for the Pine Bluff Housing Authority's after-school program, historian for the National Park Service, and congressional aide for the Fourth Congressional District. In Pine Bluff, Norful was also ordained a church elder and became a licensed minister in 1997. He served as the minister of music, youth pastor, and associate pastor under his father at Pine Bluff's St. John African Methodist Episcopal (A.M.E.) Church. He was heavily involved in the ministry by the time he launched his music career.

Norful's debut album, *I Need You Now* (2002), received gold certification from the Recording Industry Association of America (RIAA). The title track, enhanced by Norful's mastery of the piano, became the song for which he is perhaps best known. Another gold record, *Nothing without You* (2004), garnered the Grammy Award for Contemporary Soul Gospel Album of the Year. Other albums have included: *Life Changing* (2006); *Smokie Norful Live* (2009), which features Tony Award winner Heather Headley on "Jesus Is Love"; *How I Got Over: Songs That Carried Us* (2011), a project on which Norful returned to his traditional gospel roots by recording with the Twelfth District A.M.E. Mass Choir and gospel veterans Melvin

Williams, Myron Butler, and Sheri Jones-Moffett, as well as his greatest musical influence, Vanessa Bell Armstrong; and *Once in a Lifetime* (2012), an album that includes his popular compositions "No One Else," "Justified," and "God Is Able." Norful won his second Grammy in 2015 for "No Greater Love" in the Best Gospel Performance/Song category. Norful has also won multiple Dove Awards from the Gospel Music Association, as well as several Stellar Awards. He has been nominated for an NAACP Image Award, a Soul Train Award, and two BET awards for gospel music.

Norful resides in the Chicago area, where he ministers at Victory Cathedral Worship Center, the church he founded in Bolingbrook, Illinois, and its satellite location on Chicago's South Side. He also serves on the Board of Regents for Trinity International University. With his wife, Carla, Norful has two sons and an adopted daughter. The couple are entrepreneurs, with business interests in real estate, entertainment, and publishing.

Samuel W. Williams, PhD
(1912–1970)

Samuel W. Williams was an African-American Baptist minister, college professor, and civil rights activist who had a major impact on race relations in the city of Atlanta, Georgia, from the mid-to-late 1950s until his sudden death in October 1970.

Samuel Woodrow Williams was born on February 20, 1912, in Sparkman, Arkansas, the oldest of the eight children of Arthur Williams and Annie Willie Butler Williams. As a child, he enjoyed hunting, fishing, and playing baseball and basketball. Nothing, however, gave him as much pleasure as reading. Over his lifetime, he amassed a collection of more than 1,000 volumes. Lessons about racism came early for Williams. Before he reached the age of ten, he was refused service in a Sparkman drugstore for not calling a white sales clerk "sir." In his teens, his letter to a white peer regarding the community's segregated youth groups meeting to discuss important racial issues resulted in a threatened lynching.

In 1932–33, Williams attended the historically black Philander Smith College in Little Rock and subsequently transferred to Morehouse College in Atlanta, where he earned a bachelor's degree before pursuing bachelor's and master's degrees in divinity at Howard University. The Howard years (1938–1942) became important to the development of his personal philosophy concerning human liberation from oppression. In a class paper entitled, "A General Theory of the Freedom Cause of the Negro People," Williams concluded that freedom of the human species would come only when African Americans were free and that such an eventuality would require intense effort by black people themselves. He undertook doctoral studies at the University of Chicago in pursuit of a PhD. He received an honorary doctorate from Arkansas Baptist College in 1960.

Williams became a chaplain and professor at Alcorn College and Alabama A&M before joining the faculty of Morehouse College in 1946 as chairman of the Department of Philosophy and Religion. At Morehouse, Williams earned a reputation as intellectually rigorous and demanding of his students. Perhaps more importantly, he mentored students who became important leaders: Samuel DuBois Cook, who became president of Dillard University; Maynard Jackson, the first black may-

or of Atlanta; and Martin Luther King, Jr., one of the most important leaders of the twentieth century. Williams developed a close relationship with the King family, was one of two faculty members present at King's 1948 ordination, and co-taught a senior-level philosophy class with King in the fall of 1961. King also studied philosophy under Williams while he was a student at Morehouse.

In the 1950s, Williams began his association with the Atlanta branch of the National Association for the Advancement of Colored People (NAACP). He joined its executive board and later became president of the branch in 1957 when he filled the unexpired term of John Calhoun. Williams served as branch president three more terms—1959, 1960, and 1965. His leadership of the NAACP came during critical times. In 1957, he and the Reverend John Porter filed suit against the segregated Atlanta trolley system, which led to a legal victory in 1959. Williams and Porter had been inspired by the Montgomery Bus Boycott victory, one partly led by King. During Williams's leadership tenure with the NAACP, the agency filed suit against the Atlanta school board in January 1958 and forced it to begin the long and difficult process of compliance with *Brown v. Board of Education*. Although the schools were not finally desegregated until after his death, Williams provided much of the pressure that led to the final outcome.

Williams also played a key role in the Atlanta Student Movement. He was one of the adults who convinced student leaders to draft "An Appeal for Human Rights," the manifesto of the Atlanta Student Movement that was published in early March 1960 in the Atlanta newspapers and the *New York Times*. As NAACP president, Williams pledged full support for the students and often chided other adults who failed to do likewise. He was a founding member and a vice president of the Southern Christian Leadership Council (SCLC), the main organization with which King was affiliated during his activist days.

When racial progress seemed to be at a standstill in 1963, Williams helped found the Atlanta Summit Leadership Council (ASLC), aiming to pressure the school board and the rest of the city to end segregation, address poverty, and expand mass transit into the predominantly African-American west side of the city. Despite the ASLC's measured success, Williams's leadership came under serious assault in late 1967 after he advised public-housing tenants to embark on a rent strike to settle grievances with the Atlanta Housing Authority. The ASLC was forever fractured into two competing organizations, the future effectiveness of which was hampered by squabbling among leaders.

In late 1966, Mayor Ivan Allen established the Community Relations Commission (CRC) and made Williams the vice chairman. The CRC was designed to give grassroots communities a mechanism to voice their concerns to city officials at the highest level, with the CRC as an intermediary. Williams eventually became chair of the CRC and established community town hall meetings and human-relations workshops for city agency managers, as well as made recommendations to end discriminatory hiring and promotion practices at City Hall.

Williams was also a local Baptist pastor of one of the most prominent black Baptist churches in Atlanta: Friendship Baptist Church, founded in 1865. This was the institution that nurtured Morehouse College, Spelman College, and Atlanta University in their early days. In 1947, Williams became assistant pastor of Friendship, and when senior pastor Maynard Jackson, Sr., the father of Atlanta's first black mayor, died in 1954, Williams became acting pastor and then the permanent replacement. As senior pastor, Williams was the most activist-oriented pastor in Friendship's history. In a 1968 sermon to the white congregation at All Saints' Episcopal Church, he pointedly asked them: "What [is] your responsibility for justice?" Likewise, he told the Christian Council of Metropolitan Atlanta that the refusal of churches to take a stand on controversial issues was a "kind of moral pussyfooting."

Williams's high profile not only made him a greatly respected figure around Atlanta, but it also subjected him to fairly severe criticism, even from within his own community. In particular, younger men such as John Boone, Joseph Boone, and Otis Smith attacked him as a dictatorial and ineffective leader and accused him of failing to hold elections as mandated by the ASLC and of supporting an ill-advised rent strike by public housing tenants that put public housing residents at risk of eviction without giving any real solutions to their grievances. Even more serious was the charge that he had abandoned the very people he had pledged to fight for when he sided with white officials who were behind the firing of Eliza Paschall, whose contract as the director of the CRC was not renewed because she was viewed as too "pro-Black" by conservative whites on the CRC board of directors.

Williams weathered all of these storms, yet he left an often forgotten legacy of racial progress in Atlanta. The city hung his portrait in City Hall in September 1973 as a symbol of what his life had meant to the people of Atlanta.

Williams died on October 10, 1970, after a surgical procedure. He was survived by his wife, Billye, who later married baseball great Hank Aaron.

2010

Annie Abrams

ReShonda Tate Billingsley

Judge Timothy C. Evans

Brig. Gen. William J. Johnson

Shaffer Chimere "Ne-Yo" Smith

Reece "Goose" Tatum

Annie Abrams

(1931–)

Annie Abrams is a retired educator and a political, social, civic, and community activist in Little Rock, Arkansas. She led the campaigns to rename various Little Rock streets in honor of local and national trailblazers. Abrams was also instrumental in the institution of Little Rock's first Martin Luther King, Jr., Day parade.

Annie Mable McDaniel was born on September 25, 1931, in Arkadelphia, Arkansas. She is the eldest of four children born to Queen Victoria Annie Katherine Reed. McDaniel's father died when she was eighteen months old, and she was reared with the help of her grandfather James Arnold.

McDaniel attended Peake School, the segregated school in Arkadelphia, until the age of thirteen. In 1944, her mother sent her to Little Rock to pursue a better education. While in Little Rock, she lived with her cousin Louise Denton, whose husband was Herbert Denton, the principal of Stephens Elementary. McDaniel graduated from Dunbar High School in 1950 and enrolled in Dunbar Junior College, where she majored in education. After she graduated in 1952 with full licensure in education, she was offered a scholarship to

the prestigious Brandeis University in Massachusetts. Due to her financial circumstances, she was unable to attend and had to forfeit the scholarship.

McDaniel relocated to Marianna, Arkansas, to teach at the segregated three-room elementary school. She remained there until 1956, when she accepted a position with the Arkansas Teachers Association (ATA), an activist organization instituted to support equality for black teachers in Arkansas. She married Orville Abrams upon her return to Little Rock; they had four children. She later enrolled in Philander Smith College on a part-time basis and graduated in 1962 with a Bachelor of Arts degree in special education. Her husband suffered a massive stroke in 1970 and died in 2000.

Annie Abrams took an active role in community issues upon her return to Little Rock in 1956. Through her work with the ATA and in that she was a close associate of Daisy Bates, she became involved with the desegregation of Central High School. Abrams also involved herself in Democratic Party politics, at one point joining a group of Democratic women who campaigned for Republican Winthrop Rockefeller as he sought the state's governorship. She began active participation in the Young Women's Christian Association (YWCA) leadership during the 1970s. In 1978, she traveled to Geneva, Switzerland, as a YWCA delegate and represented North America at a United Nations conference as a non-governmental organization (NGO) affiliate.

The first national observance of the Martin Luther King, Jr., holiday was held on January 20, 1986, after which Abrams, with the help of other community members meeting in her living room, established what would become the annual Martin Luther King, Jr., Day parade. Abrams, along with others, also began a campaign to rename High Street in Little Rock as Dr. Martin Luther King, Jr., Drive. After years of petitioning the City of Little Rock's Board of Directors, the street was renamed and dedicated in 1992. She was also instrumental in campaigns to name streets in honor of local legends Daisy Gatson Bates and Mayor Charles Bussey.

In 2010, the Coalition of Greater Little Rock Neighborhoods, along with the New Africa Alliance and other local community organizations, submitted applications to the City of Little Rock's

Board of Directors requesting that Wright Avenue be renamed in honor of Abrams. The request caused controversy because this would replace one person's name with another, and the street would be named for someone still living. After the initial proposal was thwarted, 19th Street was suggested as an alternative. The suggestion did nothing to quell the controversy. In February 2011, at the request of Abrams, the application was withdrawn.

Abrams has been involved in many community-service organizations. She was a member of the Little Rock Central High Integration 50th Anniversary Commission, commissioner for the Fair Housing Commission, and treasurer of the Arkansas Democratic Black Caucus; she also serves as an honorary co-chairman of the state Martin Luther King, Jr., Commission.

Abrams is the recipient of numerous honors and has been recognized throughout the state for her continued community service and activism. She was awarded an honorary doctorate and the Community Service Award from her alma mater, Philander Smith College. Abrams has received the Brooks Hays Award for Civil Rights Champions and the Making of the Martin Luther King, Jr., Holiday Award by the national Martin Luther King, Jr., Commission, given by Coretta Scott King.

Abrams resides in her family home in Little Rock. She has remained active in community and political activism, and her endorsement is highly sought in local politics.

ReShonda Tate Billingsley

(1969–)

ReShonda Tate Billingsley is a journalist, public speaker, publisher, editor, ghostwriter, and producer; however, it is for her work as an award-winning national bestselling author that she is best known. Since publishing her first novel, *My Brother's Keeper* (2001), through her own publishing company before Simon & Schuster/Pocket Books began publishing it, she has authored more than forty additional novels and contributed to several anthologies. Most of her novels have been published by Simon & Schuster/Pocket Books and have spanned several genres, including nonfiction and both teen and adult fiction.

ReShonda Tate was born in Kansas City, Missouri, to Bruce Tate and Nancy Kilgore. She moved to Arkansas at a young age and was reared in her mother's hometown of Smackover, Arkansas, as well as in nearby Louann and El Dorado. She also spent time with her paternal grandparents in Norphlet. Her grandmother, Pearly Hicks, encouraged her to embrace her love for storytelling. She credits her time in the state as the foundation for her writing career and continues to visit family in Arkansas regularly.

She moved to Houston, Texas, where she graduated from Madison High School. She earned a Bachelor of Arts degree in journalism from the University of Texas at Austin. She married Arkansas native Dr. Miron Billingsley of Helena-West Helena; they had three children.

For more than twenty years, ReShonda Tate Billingsley worked in television as an anchor and reporter. In 2007, having already published several novels, she left her broadcasting job to pursue her writing full time.

She has received several awards for her faith-based and family-themed works. Three of her novels have been nominated for NAACP Image Awards for Outstanding Literature, with *Say Amen, Again* (2011) winning in 2012. Other awards and honors include Black Writers Alliance Gold Pen Award for best new author (2002), *Let the Church Say Amen* being named one of Library Journal's Best Books 2004 in Christian Fiction, National Association of Black Journalists "Spirit in the Words" award on five occasions, Texas Executive Woman on the Move (2006), *Rolling Out* magazine's Top 25 Women of Houston (2009), African American Literary Award for Best Teen Fiction for Drama Queens (2011), African American Literary Award for Best Christian Fiction for Fortune & Fame (2014) with Victoria Christopher Murray, and *Mama's Boy* being named one of Library Journal's Best Books of 2015 in African American Fiction.

In 2015, a screen adaptation of her sophomore novel, *Let the Church Say Amen*, aired on the BET network. The film was directed by actress Regina King and produced by megachurch pastor T. D. Jakes and rapper/actress Queen Latifah. The next year, adaptations of two more of her books, *The Secret She Kept* and *The Devil Is a Lie*, made on-air debuts on TV One. Billingsley acted in some of the film adaptations. BET also purchased the rights to three additional novels, *I Know I've Been Changed* (set in Arkansas) and the remainder of the Amen series: *Everybody Say Amen* and *Say Amen, Again*.

Billingsley co-founded boutique publishing company Brown Girls Books with her writing partner, bestselling author Victoria Christopher Murray. The company won Best Publisher of the Year in 2016 at the African American Literary Awards and has branded itself as a powerhouse in African-American literature. With more than forty authors on its roster, Brown Girls Books started several imprints, including Brown Girls Kids and Teens and Brown Girls Faith.

She is an active member of Alpha Kappa Alpha Sorority, Inc. (the first Greek-letter sorority established by black college women) and of Jack and Jill of America, Inc., an organization dedicated to nurturing future African-American leaders. Billingsley resides in Durham, North Carolina.

Judge Timothy C. Evans
(1943–)

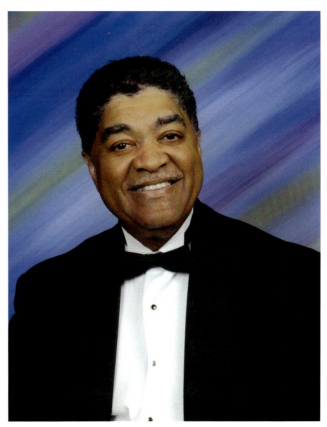

Timothy C. Evans was the first African American to be elected as chief judge of the Cook County Circuit Court of Illinois. Timothy Evans was born on June 1, 1943, in Hot Springs, Arkansas, to George Evans and Tiny Marie Evans. His father eventually became a bailiff for the Illinois State Supreme Court, a position he held for twenty-seven years. Evans has two siblings: George W. Evans and Sandra M. Johnson.

As a child in Hot Springs, Evans wanted to become a doctor. The family moved to Chicago, Illinois, shortly after Governor Orval Faubus closed Little Rock's public schools in 1958 to impede desegregation, an act which his mother saw as a threat to the education of her children. At Hirsch High School, Evans realized that racism was still prevalent in the North when he was barred from attending until he showed the administrators his birth certificate; later, he was sent home because of his mustache, which was against school policy.

When he graduated in 1961, the civil rights movement was in full force, which inspired Evans to change his career course and become an attorney. He pointed to Thurgood Marshall and leaders in the National Association for the Advancement of Colored People (NAACP) as role models. He attended the University of Illinois at Urbana-Champaign and was enrolled as a premed student, but he was advised that he could still go to law school and take those classes. He met his future wife, Thelma, an aspiring doctor, in anatomy class; they had twin daughters. He graduated with a Bachelor of Science degree in zoology and then enrolled in the John Marshall Law School in 1965. He graduated four years later.

During law school, Evans worked as a clerk in domestic relations to pay for tuition. There, he became motivated in public service. His first job was assistant corporation counsel for the City of Chicago in the Torts Division. After two years and having never lost a case, he was promoted to deputy commissioner of the Department of Investigations, a position he held for eighteen months before he became chief hearing officer of the Illinois Secretary of State's Office and made a name for himself in Chicago politics.

In 1973, after the death of Alderman Claude Holman of Chicago's Fourth Ward, a special election was held, and Evans won. He held this position until 1991. One of his primary goals was to bridge the socioeconomic gap between Oakland and the affluent Hyde Park areas of the ward. He played a role in opening several schools in the ward, as well as helped to prevent the closing of Provident Hospital of Cook County, the first black-owned hospital in the county. He served as the chairman of the budget committee and the floor leader of the city council. In 1989, an election to replace acting mayor Eugene Sawyer forced Evans to run as an independent. He received more than 428,000 votes but lost to Democratic nominee Richard M. Daley. In 1992, Evans was elected as judge of the Cook County Fifth Subcircuit. In September 2001, he was elected as chief judge by unanimous vote of the circuit judges; he is the first African American to hold the post.

As chief judge, Evans oversees approximately 400 judges over the court's ten divisions and six geographical districts. Evans has brought reforms to the court, including the creation of two court-wide divisions dedicated to domestic violence and

elder law matters; court dedication to mental health and drug treatment; and measures to support veterans. He received the William H. Rehnquist Award for Judicial Excellence from the National Center for State Courts and the Liberty Achievement Award from the American Bar Association, as well as many other prestigious awards and honors.

Brig. Gen. William J. Johnson
(1950–)

William J. Johnson became the first African-American general in the history of the Arkansas National Guard. Johnson served in the Arkansas National Guard for thirty-six years before his 2012 retirement. Brigadier General Leodis Jennings said of Johnson's 2008 promotion to deputy adjutant general that it was "significant on three levels—he is the first African American General in Arkansas, the first African American Deputy Adjutant General in Arkansas, and the highest ranking African American in the Arkansas National Guard. He routinely sets the standard of excellence." In 2013, Johnson became a member of the Arkansas National Guard Officer Candidate School (OCS) Hall of Fame.

William J. Johnson was born in Pulaski County, Arkansas, on December 11, 1950. He graduated from Scipio A. Jones High School, an African-American school in North Little Rock. He enrolled in Philander Smith College in Little Rock. He received his bachelor's degree in organizational management. (In 2001, he received a master's degree in strategic studies from the United States Army War College.)

In 1976, Johnson joined the Arkansas Army National Guard as an enlisted soldier. This was less than twenty years after the desegregation of Little Rock Central High School, of which the Arkansas National Guard was a prominent part. During the Central High School crisis in 1957, when Johnson was a child, African Americans were barred from serving in the Arkansas National Guard. When he walked into the armory to join the National Guard, Johnson sat down to fill out his paperwork with a warrant officer. In the back room, an administrative supply technician (AST) was making derogatory remarks about African Americans. Johnson knew he had to make a decision—finish filling out the forms or walk out. General Johnson recounted in 2016 that the warrant officer said, "You have a right to be in this Guard just as much as we do. Don't let that bother you. Just a minute." The warrant officer walked to the back room to talk to the AST, who then apologized. Johnson finished the forms.

As an enlisted soldier, Johnson spent his first five years in the Arkansas National Guard as part of the 212th Signal Battalion. In 1981, he was commissioned from the OCS. Before attaining the rank of brigadier general, Johnson served in several staff and command positions. These include the 212th Signal Battalion's commander; the executive officer of the First Battalion, 153rd Infantry; chief operations officer of the Marksmanship Training Unit; and chief of the Joint Staff for the Arkansas National Guard.

On January 1, 2008, General Johnson achieved the distinction of being the first African American in the Arkansas National Guard to be appointed the deputy adjutant general. Among his duties was to help lead more than 10,000 members of the Arkansas Army and Air National Guard. In addition, Johnson was in charge of the preparedness for domestic operations and homeland security in Arkansas.

He has received many awards and decorations, including the Legion of Merit Medal, Meritorious Service Medal with Three Oak Leaf Clusters, Army Achievement Medal, Army Physical Fitness Badge, Arkansas Distinguished Service Medal, and Arkansas Army National Guard General Staff Badge. General Johnson retired from the Arkansas National Guard on December 31, 2012. Of his military service, Johnson said, "Even my worst day that I had [in the Arkansas National Guard] was still a good day." During his more than three decades of service, Johnson saw the Arkansas National Guard grow into a more professional and inclusive organization. He played a significant role in this through mentoring and leadership.

Shaffer Chimere "Ne-Yo" Smith
(1982–)

Shaffer Chimere Smith, Jr., who uses Ne-Yo as his professional name, is one of the most prominent and active Arkansas-born recording artists and songwriters performing in the early twenty-first century. Initially known for songs he wrote for other artists, Ne-Yo began releasing solo rhythm and blues (R&B) albums of his own in 2006.

Shaffer Chimere Smith, Jr., was born on October 18, 1982, in Camden, Arkansas, to Lorraine and Shaffer Smith. Young Smith displayed his songwriting acumen at an early age when he wrote his first song at the age of five. After his parents separated, he relocated with his mother to Las Vegas, Nevada, where he spent the remainder of his formative years. His mother worked in a variety of jobs before becoming a bank manager, though music was a constant presence in the Smith household. While still in high school, Smith began performing with local R&B group Envy and later moved with the group to Los Angeles, California. After the group disbanded, he worked as a staff writer at a production company, which eventually led to a record deal with Columbia Records in 2000.

Smith recorded a full-length album for Columbia Records under the performing name of Shaffer,

for Best Contemporary R&B Album. His two subsequent albums, *Year of the Gentleman* (2008) and *Libra Scale* (2010), have also been top sellers, and Ne-Yo received two additional Grammy Awards in 2009 for the song "Miss Independent." His fifth studio album, *R.E.D.*, was released in 2012, and his sixth, *Non-Fiction*, was released in 2015.

While Ne-Yo's prominence as a performer grew, he continued to stay active as a songwriter. In addition to Mario's "Let Me Love You," Ne-Yo has written songs for Beyoncé ("Irreplaceable") and Rihanna ("Take a Bow") that have reached number one on the *Billboard* Hot 100 chart. He has also written songs for Chris Brown, Mary J. Blige, Whitney Houston, and Celine Dion, among others. Ne-Yo also works with young artists and producers through his production company, Compound Entertainment, which he founded in 2004. He opened his own recording studio, Carrington House, in Atlanta, Georgia, in 2007. Ne-Yo left Def Jam in 2012 to take a position as a senior vice president of artists and repertoire at Motown Records.

In addition to his career in music, Ne-Yo has acted in movies and television. He appeared in the movies *Save the Last Dance 2* (2006), *Stomp the Yard* (2007), *Battle: Los Angeles* (2011), and *Red Tails* (2012); he guest-starred on the television show *CSI*.

He had two children with his long-time girlfriend, Monyetta Shaw. On February 20, 2016, he wed Crystal Renay.

but it was never released. Soured by the experience, he focused on songwriting instead. The nickname Ne-Yo was given to him by producer Deon "Big D" Evans due to his songwriting prowess, as Big D felt that Smith saw music the same way that the character Neo saw the intricacies of the matrix in the movie *The Matrix*. Smith quickly adopted it as his stage name with a change of spelling due to copyright reasons. He garnered attention after the song "That Girl" from his Columbia Records album was re-recorded by Marques Houston in 2003. Ne-Yo's acclaim as a songwriter grew even more after he co-wrote Mario's 2004 single "Let Me Love You," which reached number one on the *Billboard* pop and R&B singles charts.

While Ne-Yo continued to focus on songwriting, during a visit to Def Jam Recordings, he was persuaded to perform for label executives. This led to a recording contract and his return as a performing artist. Ne-Yo's first released solo album, *In My Own Words*, came out in 2006 on the Def Jam label and debuted at number one on the *Billboard* albums chart. The album also featured three singles that reached the top ten on the singles chart, including "So Sick," which reached number one. His second album, *Because of You* (2007), also debuted at number one and won the 2008 Grammy Award

Reece "Goose" Tatum
(1921–1967)

Reece "Goose" Tatum excelled at two sports, baseball and basketball, but he is most famous for his basketball career with the Harlem Globetrotters. Known as "Goose" for his comic walk and for his exceptionally wide arm span, he is remembered more for his comic antics in games than for his athletic ability and accomplishments, which were considerable.

Reece Tatum was born on May 3 or 31, 1921, in Arkansas in either El Dorado or Hermitage—

fielding the throws of his teammates. Early in his career, he began enlivening the games with comic antics, including catching throws behind his back, kneeling in mock prayer before going to bat, and inviting fans (especially children) onto the field during a game. These performances caught the attention of Abe Saperstein, who had founded the Harlem Globetrotters as a touring basketball team from Chicago in 1926.

In high school, Tatum had played basketball and football, as well as baseball. His natural athletic ability and sense of comic timing made him a natural fit for the Globetrotters. He soon became the team's clown, eventually earning the nickname "Clown Prince" for his antics on the basketball court. Tatum's comedic routines on the court were usually played off his stature (he had an arm span of eighty-four inches). He often said, "My goal in life is to make people laugh," which he deftly accomplished with such antics as playing hide-and-seek with the referees or replacing the original basketball with a trick one. Tatum studied clowns in movies and circuses, always seeking new elements to add to his routines. By showcasing his antics of hiding in the audience during a game or pretending to spy on the opponents' huddle or pretending to faint until he was "revived" by the smell of his own shoes, Tatum helped to establish the Globetrotters' reputation as an act that exceeded the usual showmanship of professional basketball teams.

Tatum played with the Globetrotters for the 1941 and 1942 seasons, and then he was drafted into the U.S. Army Air Corps during World War II. He served at Lincoln Army Airfield in Nebraska, largely as an entertainer for the troops. After the war, he returned to play with the Globetrotters for another ten years. Tatum is credited with many inventive basketball moves, such as the hook shot, and he frequently scored more than fifty points in a game. At the same time, he continued his baseball career, playing in an all-star game in 1947 that drew the attention of major league scouts.

On occasion, Tatum failed to show up for scheduled games with the Globetrotters, sometimes missing as much as two weeks of work. In 1954, he left the team for good and created his own touring basketball teams, including the Harlem Road Kings, Goose Tatum's Harlem Stars, and Goose Tatum's Harlem Clowns.

sources differ on his birth date and birthplace. His father, Ben, was a part-time preacher and part-time farmer who also worked at the local sawmill, while his mother, Alice, mostly remained at home to rear their seven children, of whom Reece was the fifth. She also often worked as a domestic cook. Tatum attended Booker T. Washington High School in El Dorado but may not have graduated, since he was employed at the local sawmill and played baseball while still in his teens.

By 1937, Tatum was playing professional baseball for the Louisville Black Colonels of the Negro Leagues. He later played for the Memphis Red Sox, the Birmingham Black Barons (1941 and 1942), and the Indianapolis Clowns (1943 and 1946–1949). He reportedly played for a baseball team in Forester, Arkansas, one summer as a young man and acquired his nickname "Goose" there. Later, as part-owner of the team, he occasionally played for the Detroit Stars. Tatum played first base, where his long arms made him skilled at

Many sources report that Tatum was moody and even violent when he was not performing. He is said to have stabbed a pitcher from an opposing baseball team with a screwdriver and to have been arrested on several occasions on charges ranging from attacking a police officer to nonpayment of taxes. Tatum was married three times, but little information is available about his marriages; he was not married at the time of his death.

He died on January 18, 1967, in El Paso, Texas, of an apparent heart attack. He is buried at Fort Bliss National Cemetery in El Paso. Tatum was inducted into the Arkansas Sports Hall of Fame in 1974. His jersey (number 50) was retired on February 8, 2002, sixty years after his first season. His was the fourth number the Globetrotters had retired. On the same occasion, he was entered into the Globetrotters' "Legends" Ring at Madison Square Garden. Tatum was elected to be in the Naismith Memorial Basketball Hall of Fame in 2011.

2011

Abraham Carpenter, Sr., and Family

Leo Louis "Jocko" Carter

Derek Fisher

Kathryn Hall-Trujillo, PhD

Joseph "Joe" Jackson

Robert Williams, II, PhD

Abraham Carpenter, Sr. and Family

Abraham Carpenter, Sr., and his wife, Katie, along with their children, have long been an important symbol of African-American success in the field of agriculture, especially when many independent black farmers faced monumental difficulties in remaining solvent. They founded Carpenter's Produce, an agricultural enterprise based in Grady, Arkansas, that supplies produce for both regional farmers' markets and national grocery chains such as Walmart and Kroger.

In 1969, Katie Carpenter planted a one-acre vegetable garden and began selling her produce locally. At the time, Abraham Carpenter, then almost forty years old, was working at Seagram's Lumber Mill in nearby Pine Bluff, Arkansas. Using some of his earnings, he purchased thirty additional acres around Grady, which led to a more extensive operation that began employing other family members.

In a part of the state where monoculture crops are common (such as cotton, soybeans, and rice), the Carpenters set themselves apart by focusing on fruits and vegetables, including squash, greens, green beans, sweet potatoes, purple-hull peas, wa-

termelons, and pinkeye peas. This focus on produce allowed the Carpenter family to grow multiple rotations of crops on the same land throughout the year. Eventually, the operation grew to encompass more than 1,000 acres and became one of the largest employers in Grady, with approximately thirty-five members of the extended family working on the farm (along with forty to fifty seasonal workers during peak harvest times). All of the Carpenters' eight children remained involved in the family business in some capacity. Abraham Carpenter, Jr., became the manager when he joined the business immediately after graduating from high school.

Carpenter's Produce now includes two retail outlets in Arkansas (in Pine Bluff and Little Rock) and sells produce regularly at farmers' markets, having been a part of the Little Rock Farmers' Market since its inception in the 1970s. The Carpenter family was named a Farm Family of the Year in 1988 by the Arkansas Farm Bureau. The family was part of a nationwide lawsuit against the United States Department of Agriculture (USDA) alleging years of discrimination against black farmers as related to lending practices. The suit was settled in 1999, though the Carpenters were among those appealing on the basis of continuing practices of discrimination; the USDA negotiated an additional settlement in 2010.

Abraham Carpenter, Jr., has been an activist in agricultural spheres (notably in the field of water conservation) and has served in a number of organizations, including on the board of directors of the Delta Farmers' Cooperative and as president of the Arkansas Vegetable Growers Association. After Hurricane Katrina struck the Gulf Coast in 2005, Carpenter's Produce sent truckloads of produce to the area to feed people in need. Carpenter's Produce was also part of an initiative spearheaded locally by the Arkansas Land and Farm Development Corporation in 2005–06 to train farmers from minority groups on the USDA's "Good Agricultural Practices and Good Handling Practices" audit verification program.

Abraham Carpenter, Sr., was inducted into the Arkansas Agriculture Hall of Fame in 2011.

Leo Louis "Jocko" Carter
(1924–1989)

Leo Louis Carter, known as "Jocko" to his friends and listeners, was one of the first radio announcers for KOKY 1440 AM, the first station in Arkansas designed for the culture of the urban community, and became a local pioneer in African-American radio programming. He assisted in the establishment of the station's "True Heritage Today," which was designed to provide entertainment, public service announcements, and advertising to the African-American community, and later worked with several national music labels.

While at KOKY, he served in many capacities, including radio announcer, music director, and later program director. Carter quickly became one of the most versatile and successful personalities in Arkansas radio.

After years of success in Little Rock–area markets, Carter became sought after in the music industry's national arena. He went on to accept a position at FAME Records in Muscle Shoals, Alabama, as a national promotional director. He worked with several labels, overseeing southern R&B promotion for Mercury Records. He later joined Phonogram, which was then expanding its marketing division. He also worked with Stax Records. Carter was later hired by the world's leading recording company: Warner Bros. Records. He joined its team as the Southeast Regional Promotions Manager for Black Music.

Carter's presence at Warner Bros. served to increase the sale of records by black artists. In this position, Carter was directly responsible for obtaining airplay for black artists. With the professional backing of Carter, artists were able to amass sales in excess of 500,000 copies. Some of these artists and their albums include Ashford & Simpson's *Send It*, George Benson's *Breezin'*, and Parliament Funkadelic's *One Nation Under a Groove*.

In addition to his contribution to the careers of black artists and to Arkansas urban radio, Carter will always be remembered for his favorite catch phrase to his audience: "Don't meet me there; beat me there!"

He was survived by his wife, Lillie M. Walker Carter, and their three children.

Derek Fisher
(1974–)

Derek Fisher is one of the most successful basketball players to hail from Arkansas. After an exemplary high school and college career in Little Rock, Arkansas, he won five championships as a member of the Los Angeles Lakers in the National Basketball Association (NBA). He also set an NBA record for participation in the most playoff games at 259.

Derek Lamar Fisher was born in Little Rock on August 9, 1974, to John and Annette Fisher. He has an older brother, Duane Washington, who also played in the NBA, and a younger sister. The Fishers lived on West 22nd Street in Little Rock. Derek attended Wilson Elementary School, Henderson Junior High School, and Parkview Arts and Science Magnet High School.

Derek's father cultivated his interest in basketball from an early age and played the most formative role in his development. Fisher participated in youth basketball leagues at the Penick Boys and Girls Club, shadowed his brother at Parkview, and joined an Amateur Athletic Union (AAU) team as a ten-year-old. During his senior year at Parkview,

Fisher was the point guard for a team that won the state championship and finished with a record of 35-1. He received an honorable mention as a McDonald's High School All-American. After graduating from high school, he signed a basketball scholarship with the University of Arkansas at Little Rock.

Except for the first game of his freshman year, Fisher started every game of his four seasons. As a senior, he was the 1996 Sun Belt Conference Player of the Year. When the university constructed new athletic facilities in 2005, Fisher donated $700,000 for the construction of a practice court that was named in his honor.

The Los Angeles Lakers chose Fisher as the twenty-fourth pick of the 1996 NBA draft. He spent eighteen seasons in the NBA and won championships with the Lakers in 2000, 2001, 2002, 2009, and 2010, competing alongside future Hall of Famers Shaquille O'Neal and Kobe Bryant under the tutelage of legendary coach Phil Jackson. Fisher also played briefly for the Golden State Warriors, Utah Jazz, Oklahoma City Thunder, and Dallas Mavericks. He averaged 8.3 points and three assists in 25 minutes per game over the course of his professional career.

Fisher was a left-handed guard whose play was characterized by consistency and reliability. One of his most famous plays was during Game 5 of the 2004 Western Conference Semifinals versus the San Antonio Spurs. With the Lakers trailing by one point with only four-tenths of a second remaining, Fisher received an inbounds pass and made a shot to win the game.

In 2005, Fisher married Candace Patton. She gave birth to twins the following year, one of whom, it was soon discovered, suffered from a rare form of cancer, retinoblastoma. The couple agreed to an experimental surgery and a regimen of chemotherapy that saved their daughter's life and eyesight. The general public became aware of their daughter's ailment when Fisher was absent from the start of a playoff series as a player for the Utah Jazz. He arrived during the third quarter of Game 2 of the 2007 Western Conference Semifinals and helped the team beat the Golden State Warriors by scoring five points in overtime. This situation was recounted in an autobiography that Fisher published in 2009 with author Gary Brozek, *Character Driven: Life, Lessons, and Basketball*, in which he attributed much of his success in life to his Christian faith.

In 2006, Fisher was elected president of the NBA Players Association. In that role, he led the association through two significant controversies: the NBA owners' lockout in 2011 and the removal of Billy Hunter as the union's executive director in 2013. As a result of the latter action, Fisher was named in a lawsuit by Hunter for wrongful termination, but a judge dismissed the last of the claims against him in 2014.

Fisher retired as a player after the 2013–2014 season and was soon hired as the head coach of the NBA's New York Knicks whose president, Phil Jackson, was Fisher's former Lakers coach. The Knicks finished with a record of 17–65 in Fisher's first season, the worst record in franchise history, and he was fired during his second season when the Knicks were 23–31.

Fisher and Patton divorced in 2016. During the 2016–2017 NBA season, Fisher worked as a television analyst for Spectrum SportsNet, the television station for the Lakers, and Turner Network Television, which features NBA games with commentary by former players.

Kathryn Hall-Trujillo, PhD
(1948–)

Kathryn Hall-Trujillo is a public health expert and advocate who focuses on healthcare for African-American women. Best known for founding Birthing Project USA, "Mama Katt," as she has been affectionately called, was named a 2010 hero by the CNN television network for her work with at-risk mothers and babies.

Kathryn Hall was born on July 19, 1948, in Moscow, Arkansas, a small town near Pine Bluff. Her mother's name was Corrine, and she has said that her grandmother was her mentor. She said of her childhood, "Even though I came from a family that was poor, I came from a very good family; we loved one another and were part of a larger community."

She had a rough adolescence, however, and dropped out of high school. She found herself in an abusive marriage and sometimes lived at a bus station in Oakland, California, with her two daughters: Tamu and Kenya. She said, "But other women in the community said, 'Oh, no, we're not going to have this.' Those were the women who modeled caring for me." She eventually received a Bachelor of Arts degree in public health from the University of California, Los Angeles (UCLA) and went on to receive a master's degree in public health from UCLA in 1976.

She worked as a public health administrator for the State of California from 1976 to 1991. Her experience with underserved women and her concern about their lack of access to quality healthcare led her to establish the Center for Community Health & Well-Being, a health and social service agency. In the course of this work in public health, she realized how costly it was for the state to pay for babies' healthcare when they were born sick; at the same time, she saw how comparatively cost effective it was to provide care for pregnant women that could improve outcomes for their babies.

With this in mind, in 1988, she founded the nonprofit organization Birthing Project USA: The Underground Railroad for New Life, which has the goal of reducing infant mortality rates by pairing pregnant women (primarily black women) with "sister friends" to guide and support them during pregnancy and after the birth of their child. Between 1988 and 2010, the Birthing Project helped 12,000 babies in ninety-four community chapters in the United States, Canada, Cuba, Central America, and Africa.

In addition to her work with the Birthing Project, she is also an independent consultant for government, community, and private agencies in health administration, project development, and education. She directs a research project in Cuba that looks at the system for child and maternal health. She also works with the Cuban Medical Scholarship Program to train American students in Cuban medical schools to practice medicine in underserved parts of the United States.

Hall-Trujillo has received many honors. She was chosen as Woman of the Year by the California State Legislature, named a Hero in Healthcare by the Coalition for Excellence in Healthcare, and made Child Abuse Prevention Professional of the Year by the California Statewide Child Abuse Consortium. She is the recipient of the Essence National Community Service Award, the United States Public Health Service's Women's Health Leadership Award, and the California State Maternal and Child Health Certificate of Excellence. She was inducted as an Ashoka Fellow in 2008.

She met Arnold M. Trujillo when she first started visiting Cuba; the couple married in 2005. She said of her future, "The Birthing Project feels like my child who's growing up, and I am ready to be a grandparent. I want to live long enough to see the next generation take it over."

Joseph "Joe" Jackson

(1928–)

Joseph "Joe" Jackson is a talent manager who is best known as the father and manager of his children's careers, including the Jackson 5, Michael Jackson, and Janet Jackson.

Joseph Walter Jackson was born on July 26, 1928, in Fountain Hill, Arkansas. He is the oldest of five children of Samuel Joseph Jackson and Crystal Lee King. His father was a schoolteacher. Jackson remembers that his father was one of few

African Americans in the area to own a car. The elite status earned his father the nickname of "Professor Jackson."

Much of Jackson's childhood was spent in Arkansas. However, when his parents separated, he left Arkansas at the age of twelve for Oakland, California. At age eighteen, he moved to be closer to his mother in East Chicago, Indiana. Jackson pursued a career as a professional boxer but never achieved widespread success.

In Chicago, Jackson met Katherine Scruse. He had a short marriage to another woman that was later annulled, but he continued his relationship with Scruse. They were married on November 5, 1949, and settled in Gary, Indiana. They had ten children: Maureen Reillette (Rebbie), Sigmund Esco (Jackie), Toriano Adaryll (Tito), Jermaine La Jaune, La Toya, Marlon, Brandon (Marlon's twin, who died at birth), Michael Joseph, Steven Randall (Randy), and Janet Damita Jo. Jackson has another daughter, Joh'Vonnie, from another relationship.

While in Gary, Jackson worked as a crane operator for U.S. Steel. He began a music career in the mid-1950s with his brother Luther in a band called the Ford Falcons. However, the band never had much success, so Jackson continued working with U.S. Steel.

Jackson turned his musical attention toward his children once he recognized their talent and potential for success. In the mid-1960s, he trained his older sons (Jackie, Tito, and Jermaine) for a musical career. Tito played instruments, while Jackie and Jermaine sang. Jackson built on the brotherly musical act, adding younger brothers Marlon and Michael. Together, they formed the Jackson 5.

The Jackson 5 continued to practice under Jackson's direction and gained local attention. They began to travel and perform more, which earned them a record contract with Motown Records in 1968. With Motown Records, the Jackson 5 rose to international fame and, in 1970, became the first group whose first four singles reached number one on the *Billboard* Hot 100.

Jackson continued to manage the Jackson 5, as well as the solo careers of Michael and Jermaine. Management control waffled between Jackson and Motown Records CEO Berry Gordy, but Jackson regained control by managing his children's performances in Las Vegas, Nevada. However, his sons began leaving Jackson's management until all had withdrawn by 1983. Michael Jackson embarked on an extremely successful solo career in the 1980s and 1990s, earning him the name "The King of Pop."

Jackson managed the careers of his daughters Rebbie, La Toya, and Janet in the early 1980s. However, like his sons, his daughters also left his management. Janet Jackson's solo career flourished in the 1980s and 1990s. Joe Jackson resides in Las Vegas.

Robert Williams, II, PhD

(1930–)

Robert Williams, II, is a leading figure in American psychology known for his work in the education of African-American children and in studying the cultural biases present in standard testing measures, especially IQ tests.

Robert Lee Williams was born on February 20, 1930, in Little Rock, Arkansas. His father, Robert L. Williams, worked as a millwright and died in 1935; his mother cleaned houses. He had one sister. He graduated from Dunbar High School at age sixteen and attended Dunbar Junior College for a year before dropping out, discouraged by his low score on an IQ test. He married Ava L. Kemp in 1948. They have eight children.

After working a few different jobs, including in construction and as a carhop, Williams enrolled at Philander Smith College and graduated cum laude in 1953. From there, he went on to Wayne State University in Detroit, Michigan, where he earned a master's degree in educational psychology in 1955.

For several months, he was employed as the director of guidance at the high school in Mound Bayou, Mississippi. In 1955, he was hired by the Arkansas State Hospital as staff psychologist. Encouraged by his supervisor to pursue a doctorate, he went on to study clinical psychology at Washington University in St. Louis, Missouri. He earned his PhD in 1961. He subsequently served as the assistant chief psychologist for the Veterans Administration Hospital in St. Louis (1961–1966); director of a hospital improvement project in Spokane, Washington; and consultant for the National Institute of Mental Health in San Francisco, California, starting in 1968. Following the assassination of Dr. Martin Luther King, Jr., in April 1968, Williams helped to organize the Association of Black Psychologists, founded in San Francisco on September 2, 1968. He served as president of the association from 1969 to 1970.

Following the assassination of King, Williams experienced a growing consciousness of the black experience and his own blackness. After briefly serving as the chief of psychology at the Jefferson Barracks Veterans Hospital in St. Louis, Williams took a position with his alma mater, Washington University. From 1970 to 1992, he was professor of psychology there. He also developed the African and African-American Studies program, and served as its first director.

In a paper presented to the American Psychological Association in 1972, Williams described the results of a 100-question intelligence test he had created, the Black Intelligence Test of Cultural Homogeneity, or the BITCH-100. Questions employed a cultural context more familiar to African Americans. Consequently, white takers of the test scored lower than their black counterparts. This work has become part of a larger body of evidence showing how standardized IQ tests exhibit racial and cultural biases that result in lower scores for black students.

However, Williams's most well-known work is his study of black linguistic practices. In 1973, he coined the term "Ebonics" to encompass the vernacular English often spoken by African Americans, claiming that some of the features of so-called Black English can be traced back to various African languages. Two years later, he published the edited volume *Ebonics: The True Language of Black Folks*. His work on Ebonics remained relatively obscure in mainstream circles until 1996, when the Oakland School Board in California resolved to recognize Ebonics as a language employed by its students. This was done to access funding for bilingual education. The subsequent uproar from politicians and linguists resulted in Williams making numer-

ous appearances on national television to explain Ebonics.

In 1980, while serving as a visiting professor at the University of Texas in Austin, Williams wrote his second book, *The Collective Black Mind: Toward an Afrocentric Theory of Black Personality*, which argued for the employment of African philosophical concepts and terms for the study of African Americans, rather than those derived from a European philosophical tradition. Williams also published *Racism Learned at an Early Age through Racial Scripting* (2007) and a 2008 history of the Association of Black Psychologists, in addition to more than sixty scholarly papers.

After retirement, Williams served as a visiting professor at the University of Missouri in Columbia from 2001 to 2004 and held the position of interim director of Black Studies there from 2002 to 2003.

2012

Jerry T. Hodges, Jr.

Charles E. Phillips, Jr.

Pearlie S. Reed

Lt. Col. Yolonda R. Summons

Rosetta Tharpe

Lenny Williams

Jerry T. Hodges, Jr.

(1925–)

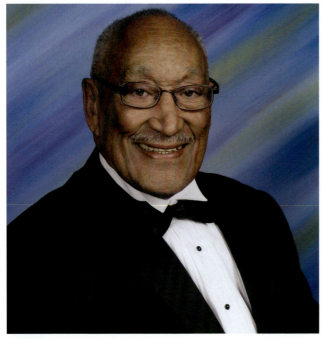

Businessman Jerry T. Hodges, Jr., who grew up in the Arkansas Delta, was one of a group of African-American men to serve as Original Tuskegee Airmen during World War II. Approximately 992 pilots advanced through the segregated Tuskegee program, with more than 450 seeing action in the war overseas. Hodges was one of the more than 500 who completed the training program but did not see action.

Jerry Hodges was born in Memphis, Tennessee, on June 29, 1925, to Jerry Hodges, Sr., and Mae Paterson Hodges. The family soon moved to Arkansas, settled in Hughes and then finally relocated to a farm in Heth. He attended the segregated Lincoln High School in Forrest City for two years. He then attended Robert R. Moton High School in Marianna, where he graduated as valedictorian in 1943.

He enrolled at Hampton Institute (now Hampton University) for three semesters. To pursue a lifelong interest in aviation, he left college and enlisted in the Army Air Corps on June 12, 1944. He was inducted into the service in the closing days of World War II at Camp Lee, Virginia, before being transferred to Kessler Field in Biloxi, Mississippi, for basic training. He was soon transferred to Tuskegee Army Air Field in Alabama, where he became one of the famous Tuskegee Airmen.

He completed his Tuskegee training on September 8, 1945, and was then transferred to Ohio's Lockbourne Air Base on July 5, 1946, where he was assigned to the 617th Bomb Squadron of the 477th Bomber Group. With the assignment coming so near the end of World War II, he never flew any combat missions.

After he was discharged in the fall of 1946, Hodges enrolled at the University of Southern California (USC) to complete his degree in business. By his junior year, he had already obtained his license as a public accountant. He graduated from USC in 1950 with a bachelor's degree in accounting and finance. He also took classes at California State University at Los Angeles and the University of California, Los Angeles (UCLA). He later received an additional degree in financial planning from the College of Financial Planning in Denver, Colorado.

After graduation, Hodges pursued a career in accounting. He became the vice president of Casualty Insurance Company, one of the first African-American-owned insurance companies in California. In about 1964, he opened his own accounting business. By 1965 he had expanded his business and was managing his own company of about ten employees.

Over the years, Hodges became a successful businessman and was involved in many civic activities. He was one of the founders of the Los Angeles Branch of the David Rockefeller Interracial Council on Business Opportunity. He also served as chairman and president of the nonprofit Tuskegee Airmen Scholarship Foundation.

Hodges is retired and lives in southern California with his wife, Lillian Reed Hodges. They have two daughters.

Charles E. Phillips, Jr.

(1959–)

Charles E. Phillips, Jr., is the CEO of Infor, a company that specializes in industry-specific software. His long career on Wall Street and in Silicon Valley includes high-level positions

in financial services corporation Morgan Stanley and computer technology corporation Oracle.

Charles Phillips was born in 1959 in Little Rock, Arkansas. His father was stationed at the nearby Little Rock Air Force Base, and the family moved frequently during his youth, including stints in Germany and Spain. Aiming to follow in his father's footsteps, Phillips enrolled in the U.S. Air Force Academy in Colorado Springs, Colorado. Although he graduated with a degree in computer science in 1981, worsening eyesight during his senior year kept him from becoming a pilot. Phillips instead enlisted in the U.S. Marine Corps, and built computer systems at Camp Lejeune in Jacksonville, North Carolina. He rose to the rank of captain and earned his MBA from Hampton University in 1986.

Phillips left the marines at the urging of his wife, Karen, whom he had married as an undergraduate; the couple had one son. The family relocated to New York, where he began working for various Wall Street companies that were struggling to make the transition to the Internet era. He also studied at New York Law School and received his Juris Doctorate in 1993. The following year, he was hired as an analyst for Morgan Stanley. He eventually became the managing director in the technology group.

In 2003, Phillips was recruited by Larry Ellison to join Oracle, which Ellison had co-founded. Within six months, Phillips was named president of the California-based firm. Under Phillips, Or-

acle undertook several major acquisitions, including BEA (for $8.5 billion) and Siebel Systems (for $5.8 billion). His business acumen led to his appointment to President Barack Obama's Economic Recovery Advisory Board, as well as to the boards of New York Law School, the American Museum of Natural History, Jazz at Lincoln Center, and Viacom. Phillips was also known for his publicly accessible toll-free telephone number, 1-800-MR-CHUCK.

In 2010, at a technology conference in Aspen, Colorado, Phillips claimed that Oracle would engage in $70 billion worth of acquisitions over the next five years. The following day, the company issued a retraction, and some of Phillips's responsibilities were given to other executives. Rumors swirled regarding his eventual removal. That fall, Phillips announced that he was leaving Oracle to join Infor.

One of the first things Phillips did as chief executive officer at Infor was to relocate the company's headquarters from Alpharetta, Georgia, to New York City. Michal Lev-Ram wrote in *Fortune* magazine in 2013 that Infor, under Phillips's leadership, was "trying to carve out a niche for itself by going after smaller companies and divisions within large corporations, unlike rivals Oracle and SAP, which focus on software that powers huge industries from retail to telecommunications." By 2016, Infor had tripled in size under the leadership of Phillips, and it had acquired seventy other companies.

Phillips and his wife have engaged in numerous philanthropic ventures, and they formed Karen and Charles Phillips Charitable Organizations (PCO) in 2010 as an umbrella for their various activities. PCO provides financial aid for single parents, students interested in engineering, and wounded veterans.

Pearlie S. Reed

(1948–2016)

Pearlie S. Reed spent more than a quarter century of his career working in agriculture, serving four major regions of the United States and initiating sweeping progressive and

anti-discrimination policies in the 1990s.

Pearlie Sylvester Reed was born in Heth, Arkansas, on June 14, 1948. He was one of eighteen children of Floyd L. Reed and Gennora Reed. Reed attended school in the nearby town of Hughes and graduated from the segregated Mildred Jackson High School. As a student at what is now the University of Arkansas at Pine Bluff (UAPB), Reed began his career in agriculture in 1968 as an intern in Walnut Ridge, Arkansas, with the Soil Conservation Service, later renamed the National Resources Conservation Services (NRCS). He graduated from UAPB in 1970 with a Bachelor of Science degree in animal husbandry. Reed later received a master's degree in public administration and finance from American University in Washington, D.C. He completed additional specialized studies from the U.S. Department of Agriculture (USDA) Graduate School and Johns Hopkins University Center for Alternative Disputes and Resolutions.

He rose through the ranks of NRCS. He served as a soil conservationist, deputy state conservationist, and state conservationist in Arkansas, Delaware, Maryland, and California, as well as in the U.S. territories of Puerto Rico and Guam. Reed then served as the associate chief of NRCS and, according to the *Congressional Record*, "spearheaded the most comprehensive reorganization of the agency in its 60-year history." He focused on Na-

tive American outreach by working directly with tribes on conservation programs and technical services. Reed assisted in the development and implementation of the Conservation Title of the 1996 Farm Bill. That same year, Reed was appointed to the USDA Civil Rights Action Team and tasked with developing recommendations to advance civil rights within the department. His team developed ninety-two recommendations, all of which were implemented by order of President Bill Clinton.

Reed operated as acting Assistant Secretary of Agriculture for the administration from 1997 to 1998. In 1998, he was promoted to chief of NRCS and remained there until he retired in 2003. In 2002, he was named regional conservationist for the western U.S. After his retirement, Reed operated a consulting firm in Marion, Arkansas. He focused on conservation, agriculture, economic development, and management.

In 2009, President Barack Obama nominated Reed to serve again as Assistant Secretary of Agriculture. U. S. senator Blanche Lincoln introduced him at his nomination testimony before the Senate Committee on Agriculture, Nutrition, and Forestry on May 7, 2009. He was sworn in on May 21, 2009. Reed retired a second time in June 2012 after an office he managed failed to follow procedures and regulations for awarding grant recipients. He returned to his firm in Marion and promised to "continue to focus on conservation and public policy issues impacting socially disadvantaged farmers and communities." Reed served as chairman for several USDA-wide initiatives during his career, including the USDA/1990 Task Force, Agricultural Air Quality Task Force, and National Food and Agricultural Council.

Reed assisted UAPB in 1991 with acquiring what became the Pearlie S. Reed-Robert L. Cole Small Farm Outreach Wetlands and Water Management Center near Lonoke and briefly served as an advisor with UAPB's School of Agriculture, Fisheries and Human Sciences during his second retirement. In 2010, he served as the keynote speaker at a National Black Farmers Association conference in Albany, Georgia. He contributed to international conservation efforts in South Africa, in Australia, and for the International Soil Conservation Organization. He supported professional development opportunities for groups such as the

National Organization of Professional Black Natural Resources Conservation Service Employees (NOPBNRCSE). The Pearlie S. Reed Excellence in Conservation Award from NOPBNRCSE is given to members who demonstrate exceptional leadership and contributions to community conservation, protection, and enhancement of natural resources. Reed received several awards and honors, including the Distinguished Presidential Rank Award for "strength, integrity, industry, and a relentless commitment to excellence in public service"; the George Washington Carver Public Service Hall of Fame Award; and the USDA Silver Plow Award in 1996 and 1998.

After Reed's first wife, Deloris W. Reed, died, he married Lesia Reed. He has two daughters, Cheryl Yvette Reed and Teresa Reed, and a stepson, Robert Charles Terrell, Jr.

Reed suffered from diabetes and heart problems during his later years. On April 8, 2016, he died shortly after being admitted to the Methodist University Hospital in Memphis, Tennessee. He is interred at Paradise Garden Cemetery in West Memphis, Arkansas.

Lt. Col. Yolonda R. Summons

(1969–)

Yolonda R. Summons has had an extensive career in the U.S. Army that includes combat service in the Middle East and leadership positions at the Pentagon and Walter Reed National Military Medical Center. She has received numerous military awards and decorations, including the Bronze Star Medal, and currently holds the rank of Lieutenant Colonel.

Yolonda Summons hails from Little Rock, Arkansas. She graduated from Little Rock McClellan High School and earned a full basketball scholarship to Ouachita Baptist University in Arkadelphia. She majored in biology and graduated with a Bachelor of Arts degree. Summons was commissioned as a U.S. Army officer in May 1992. She entered active duty in the U.S. Army in October 1993.

Summons's extensive military education encom-

passes the Combined Arms Services Staff School, the Aeromedical Evacuation Officer Course, the UH-60 (Blackhawk) Aviator Qualification Course, Initial Entry Rotary Wing (Helicopter) Course, the Army Medical Department Officer Advance Course, the Combat Casualty Course, the U.S. Airlift Planners Course, and the Army Medical Department Officer Basic Course. Her career with the U.S. Army includes multiple deployments to Iraqi and Kuwait; Brigade S1 (Director, Human Resources); Resident at the Command and General Staff College; Brigade G3 Air (Director, Aviation Operations); Battalion S1 (Director, Human Resources); Commander for a Headquarters and Headquarters' Company for a Medical Brigade; Executive and Flight Operations Officer for a Medical Air Ambulance Company; Aide-de-Camp to the Deputy Commanding General at the U.S. Army Medical Department Center and School; Executive Officer for a Medical Veterinary Detachment; and a Platoon Leader for a Mobile Army Surgical Hospital.

Summons later worked as the Army Medical Department Deputy Chief of Staff at the Pentagon in Washington, D.C. In the summer of 2013, she was made Troop Commander (Director of Hospital Operational Training and Development) for the U.S. Army Element, Walter Reed National Military Medical Center.

She received a Master of Arts degree in Organizational Leadership from Chapman University and has pursued a Doctorate of Ministry at Howard University School of Divinity.

Summons has received numerous military awards and decorations, including the Bronze Star Medal for her combat service, five Meritorious Service Medals, four Army Commendation Medals, four Army Achievement Medals, two National Defense Service Ribbons, the Armed Forces Expeditionary Medal, the Global War of Terrorism Expeditionary Medal, the Global War on Terrorism Service Medal, and the Army Service Ribbon. She proudly wears the Aviator Badge and the Expert Field Medical Badge, as well as the Order of Military Medical Merit and Order of Saint Michael's medallions.

Rosetta Tharpe

(1915–1973)

Arkansas native Rosetta Nubin Tharpe, known as Sister Rosetta Tharpe, was one of gospel music's first superstars, the first gospel performer to record for a major record label (Decca), and an early crossover from gospel to secular music. Tharpe has been cited as an influence by numerous musicians, including Bob Dylan, Little Richard, Elvis Presley, and Arkansan Johnny Cash.

She was born in Cotton Plant, Arkansas, on March 20, 1915, to Katie Bell Nubin Atkins—an evangelist, singer, and mandolin player for the Church of God in Christ (COGIC)—and Willis Atkins. She went by the first names Rosa, Rosie Etta, and Rosabell, and used both her father's last name and her mother's maiden name. She began performing at age four, playing guitar and singing "Jesus Is on the Main Line." By age six, she appeared regularly with her mother, performing a mix of gospel and secular music styles that would eventually make her famous. As a youth, she could sing and keep on pitch and hold a melody. Her vocal qualities, however, paled beside her abilities on the

guitar—she played individual tones, melodies, and riffs instead of just strumming chords. This talent was all the more remarkable because, at the time, few African-American women played guitar.

Her guitar style was influenced by her mother's mandolin playing and by pianist Arizona Dranes. She also sang the popular hymns of the day, including the compositions of bluesman turned gospel musician Thomas A. Dorsey. Indeed, elements of the blues are readily apparent in her guitar styling. Later, her music would be influenced by her work with jazz greats Lucky Millinder and Cab Calloway.

Billed as the "singing and guitar-playing miracle," she was an added attraction at her mother's church services. Both mother and daughter worked as members of an evangelistic troupe that worked throughout the South before arriving in Chicago in the late 1920s. There they became part of the growing Holiness movement, a late nineteenth-century offshoot of the Pentecostal denomination which, in the 1890s, led to the formation of COGIC and other new religious groups.

After several years of working with her mother and on the advice of several Chicago promoters, Rosetta Nubin moved to New York in the mid-

1930s. She married minister Thomas A. Thorpe in 1934. The marriage, however, was short-lived and after their divorce, Rosetta kept the last name, changing the spelling to "Tharpe" for use as her stage name. Later, in the 1940s, Tharpe married promoter Fosh Allen.

Tharpe was signed to Decca Records in 1938 and was successful immediately. Versions of Thomas A. Dorsey's "This Train" and "Hide Me in Thy Bosom," released as "Rock Me," were smash hits featuring Tharpe on guitar and Lucky Millinder's jazz orchestra as accompaniment. These releases started a trend for Tharpe, who recorded both traditional numbers for her gospel fan base and up-tempo, secular-influenced tunes for her growing white audience.

The popularity of her singles led to Tharpe's inclusion in John Hammond's black music extravaganza, "From Spirituals to Swing," held in Carnegie Hall in New York City on December 23, 1938. After this well-publicized event, Tharpe went on a concert tour throughout the northeast. She also recorded with Cab Calloway to some success but fared better with "Trouble in Mind," "Shout, Sister, Shout," and "That's All"—all recorded with Lucius "Lucky" Millinder's jazz orchestra in 1941 and 1942. Tharpe's popularity was so great that she was only one of two black gospel acts—the other was the Dixie Hummingbirds—to record "V-Discs" for U.S. troops overseas. In the late 1940s, Tharpe returned to more strictly religious songs, recording "Didn't It Rain" (1947) and "Up Above My Head" (1947) with Marie Knight. From 1944 to 1951, her main accompanist was Samuel "Sammy" Blythe Price, a boogie-woogie pianist from Texas. His trio backed her on "Strange Things Happening Every Day," a top-ten "race record."

Tharpe continued her success in the religious market. Such was Tharpe's popularity that on July 3, 1951, about 25,000 people paid to witness her marriage to Russell Morrison, her manager, in a ceremony held at Griffith Stadium in Washington, D.C. While her marriages to men were a matter of public record, it is widely accepted that Tharpe also had relationships with women.

Tharpe and Marie Knight parted ways after unsuccessfully trying to enter the blues music market. As a result of the foray into the pop music market, Tharpe's popularity waned; soon her concert dates

dropped off and she lost her recording contract with Decca. Tharpe kept working and had signed with Mercury Records by the late 1950s. She first toured Europe in 1957 and made return trips in the 1960s. She made several live recordings while overseas. Although she never realized her comeback, Tharpe continued to perform. A stroke in 1970 necessitated a leg amputation and caused speech difficulties, but it merely slowed her down. Tharpe continued to tour and perform until her death in Philadelphia, Pennsylvania, on October 9, 1973.

Tharpe's music and influence continue years after her death. Her songs have been recorded by Elvis Presley, and Johnny Cash spoke of her impact on his music. In 1998, the U.S. Postal Service issued a Rosetta Tharpe postage stamp. In 2003, the album *Shout, Sister Shout: A Tribute to Sister Rosetta Tharpe* was released, with versions of Tharpe's songs performed by female artists including Maria Muldaur, Odetta, and Marcia Ball. In 2013, the PBS series *American Masters* featured an episode on Tharpe, and she was inducted into the Arkansas Entertainers Hall of Fame.

Lenny Williams

(1945–)

Soul singer Lenny Williams is an influential rhythm and blues (R&B) artist who is best known for his time as the lead singer of funk band Tower of Power in the mid-1970s. He pursued a solo career after he left the band.

Leonard Charles "Lenny" Williams was born on February 6, 1945, in Little Rock, Arkansas; his family later moved to Oakland, California. He learned to play trumpet in elementary school. He started singing in church and considered becoming a minister before deciding to pursue a career in secular R&B.

Williams made connections with Bay Area musicians, the most notable being Sly Stone (who fronted the legendary R&B band Sly and the Family Stone) and Larry Graham, who was Sly and the Family Stone's bass player. He also knew members of Tower of Power, which was at that time a "blue-eyed soul" group called the Motowns. He signed

his first record deal with Fantasy Records and recorded two singles: "Lisa's Gone" and "Feelin' Blue" (written by John Fogerty of Credence Clearwater Revival fame). He then signed briefly with Atlantic Records.

In 1972, he put his solo career on hold and tried out to become the lead singer for funk group Tower of Power, whose front man Rick Stevens had gone to prison. The group had its heyday during the few years Williams was its lead singer, producing three hit albums: *Tower of Power* (1973), *Back to Oakland* (1974), and *Urban Renewal* (1974), with hit songs such as "So Very Hard to Go," "Don't Change Horses (In the Middle of a Stream)," "What is Hip?," and "This Time It's Real."

In 1975, Williams left the band to resume his solo career and recorded a few albums for the Motown label. He then moved to ABC Records in 1977 and recorded several albums. He garnered a number of hits, including "Shoo Doo Fu Ooh," "Choosing You," "You Got Me Running," and "Midnight Girl." *Choosing You* (1977) was his first

gold LP (selling more than 500,000 copies). In 1986, Williams sang the vocals for "Don't Make Me Wait for Love" on popular saxophone artist Kenny G's album *Duo Tones*.

Williams and his music continue to influence R&B and hip-hop artists in the twenty-first century. His 1978 hit "Cause I Love You" was sampled by Havoc of Mobb Deep for the track "Nothing Like Home," and by Kanye West for the songs "Overnight Celebrity" by the rapper Twista and "I Got a Love" by Jin. The song was also sampled in 2007 by Scarface for his single "Girl You Know." Williams's song "Half Past Love" was sampled by the Coup for their 2006 single "My Favorite Mutiny." In 2005, he won a BMI Urban Award along with Kanye West and Twista for contributing to "Overnight Celebrity." In a 2013 interview, Williams—who had three daughters in college at the time—discussed his pleasant surprise at receiving two royalty checks for $94,000 each to pay for music Kanye West/Twista had sampled; he compared it to planting a seed a long time ago and watching it grow into something substantial years later.

Williams made a number of solo albums throughout the 1980s and 1990s. In the twenty-first century, he released *It Must Be Love* (2007) and *Unfinished Business* (2009) on his own label, LenTom Entertainment, and he released *Still in the Game* in 2012. It was announced in February 2017 that he would be inducted into the Rhythm & Blues Hall of Fame in Detroit, Michigan.

Williams has been honored for his involvement in the Oakland community. On November 14, 2013, the San Leandro Unified School District and the Keep Music Rockin' Foundation unveiled the Lenny Williams Music Room at San Leandro High School, with Williams and his wife, Debbie, in attendance at the dedication. The Keep Music Rockin' Foundation Lenny Williams Golf Classic also raises funds for the foundation, which supports music in schools. Williams is also an ambassador for Lazarex Cancer Foundation.

2013

Gerald Alley

Chief Master Richard E. Anderson

Morris Hayes

Raye Jean Montague, RPE

Art Porter, Jr.

Willie Roaf

Gerald Alley
(1952–)

Gerald Byron Alley is the founder of Con-Real, LP, which is the leading African-American-owned construction and real estate firm in Texas, with other offices located in Arkansas and California.

Gerald Alley was born in Pine Bluff, Arkansas, on September 30, 1952. He was the youngest of five children of Troy Alley, a local businessman who started the Alley ESSO Service Station, and Gladys Gray Alley, an educator who had taught at Philander Smith College in Little Rock before marriage. After attending local public and private schools, and working in his father's station, Alley enrolled in the University of Arkansas (U of A) at Fayetteville at the age of sixteen. He majored in finance and graduated in 1973. He entered graduate school at Southern Methodist University (SMU) in Dallas, Texas, in 1974 and graduated the following year with an MBA degree. He carried out additional study at the Kellogg School of Management at Northwestern University in Chicago, Illinois, and was recruited by Sanger-Harris, a retail corporation based in Dallas.

In 1979, Alley founded Con-Real. In the beginning, he and an assistant, who shared a desk, made up the entire staff. His brother Troy joined him as a partner soon after the founding, and Con-Real soon grew into a major force in construction and real estate. Headquartered in Arlington, Texas, it opened offices in Dallas and Houston, as well as Little Rock and San Francisco, California. Con-Real regularly provides services to Fortune 500 companies.

Alley also founded The Alley Group (TAG), a project management services company in San Francisco, and Bravado LP, a real estate and hospitality firm based in Arlington. In addition, he co-founded the Candace Alley Family Foundation, which supports organizations providing for the needs of underprivileged students, and has served on numerous boards, including at SMU and the U of A. In 2017, Con-Real announced that it and its partners would construct the Texas Live! development in Arlington's entertainment district.

Alley and his wife, Dr. Candace P. Alley, have three children. The government leaders of Tarrant County, Texas, declared October 19, 2013, to be Gerald Byron Alley Day.

Richard E. Anderson
(1951–)

Chief Master Richard E. Anderson, an eighth-degree black belt master, became the highest-ranking African American in the American Taekwondo Association (ATA), World Traditional Taekwondo Union, and Songahm Taekwondo Federation. He has dedicated his life to helping inner-city youth and children from all walks of life, providing them with a positive path to gain self-confidence and a stable support system in their lives.

Anderson was born in Dowagiac, Michigan, the sixth of seven children born to Mary Lee Anderson. He graduated from Dowagiac High School in 1969, where he had been an All-State defensive back on the football team. After high school, he attended Southwestern Michigan College. Under the guidance of Alvin Smith, Anderson became in-

volved in martial arts.

After moving to Arkansas from Michigan in 1989, Anderson opened his Taekwondo school and became the pulse behind Anderson's Taekwondo Center Camp Positive, located in Little Rock, Arkansas. This camp is a nonprofit martial arts school, which runs a high-profile program with about 120 members. Camp Positive offers an outlet to inner-city youth and their families, which strengthens them through the moral standards of the ATA. The emphasis at Camp Positive is its motto: "Go to Church On Sunday, Practice Free On Monday."

Anderson and the instructors at Anderson's Taekwondo Center (ATC) reach out to one child, youth, or family and give those individuals life lessons. Those beneficiaries are then able to reach out to and teach others around them who are similarly situated that there is a positive alternative to the streets.

Anderson and his staff specialize in counseling at-risk youth who have discipline issues, who possess low self-esteem, and who are low achievers in school. He teaches discipline through Taekwondo, and he stresses the importance of academic achievement by encouraging good grades and a "Yes I Can" mindset. Anderson is not only concerned with inspiring youths to graduate from high school but also with helping them aspire to graduate from college and to become active contributors to society in general and to their communities in particular.

Anderson has one daughter, and she is a second-degree black belt. He has three grandsons who have achieved varying levels of mastery.

Anderson received an Arkansas Community Service Award in 1998. On November 21, 2001, Mayor Jim Dailey issued a proclamation declaring the day Chief Master Richard E. Anderson Day in Little Rock. In 2008, Governor Mike Beebe appointed him as Commissioner of the Arkansas Athletic Commission. In 2008 and 2009, he was named Arkansas Man of the Year; he is a member of the Martial Arts Hall of Fame.

Morris Hayes

(1962–)

Morris Hayes is a talented musician, producer, and band leader. As a keyboardist, Hayes has worked with superstars such as Prince, George Clinton, Elton John, Whitney Houston, and Stevie Wonder.

Morris Kevin Hayes was born on November 28, 1962, in the small town of Jefferson, Arkansas, just outside Pine Bluff. He was inspired by the religious music he heard in church as a child. He majored in art at the University of Arkansas at Pine Bluff (UAPB). When a rhythm and blues (R&B) band on campus lost its keyboard player, Hayes—who had learned to play a bit in high school—offered to fill in. Although he was still learning to play the keyboard, he played well enough to take the spot.

After graduating from college, Hayes played in churches and with various bands. He moved to Chicago, Illinois; Memphis, Tennessee; and then to Texas. He co-founded a group called the Bizness, which former Prince and the Revolution bass player Mark Brown heard. Brown asked the group to come to Minneapolis, Minnesota—which had a vibrant music scene—and record a demo. Hayes recorded the demo and then joined Brown's band, Mazarati.

When Brown's group disbanded around 1991, Hayes remained in Minneapolis. When the keyboardist for the popular group the Time quit, Hayes replaced him and toured with the group in Asia. After the tour ended, Hayes formed another group called G Sharp and the Edge. This group performed as the house band in the popular Minneapolis club Glam Slam, which was frequented by Prince (who would later purchase the club). Prince signed the group to open for him on his "Diamonds and Pearls" tour in 1992.

After the tour ended, Prince asked Hayes to join his band, the New Power Generation. Hayes played in the band for ten years. In 2003, he left for a scheduled six-week gig with funk and soul jazz saxophonist Maceo Parker. Instead, he stayed for two years before rejoining the New Power Generation as the leader of the band in 2005.

Hayes has also performed with a long list of major artists, including Sheila E., Chaka Khan, Herbie Hancock, Kanye West, Elton John, Babyface, Carlos Santana, Kenny Loggins, Lenny Kravitz, Alicia Keys, Will.i.am, Mary J. Blige, Maroon 5, Ani DiFranco, Questlove, Kool Moe Dee, Sheryl Crow, Gwen Stefani, Erykah Badu, Amy Winehouse, Bono, The Edge, and Macy Gray.

Hayes has received numerous honors for his work. He is involved in a nonprofit called No Worries Now, which helps children with terminal illnesses by organizing proms for them. The organiza-

tion also helps fund osteosarcoma research. Hayes is the owner and CEO of Ill Street, Inc., a music production company through which he has written for various films and television shows such as Flavor Flav's *Under One Roof*, Martin Lawrence's *You So Crazy*, and *Laurel Avenue* on HBO.

Raye Jean Montague, RPE

(1935–)

Raye Jean Jordan Montague was an internationally registered professional engineer (RPE) with the U.S. Navy who is credited with the first computer-generated rough draft of a U.S. naval ship. The U.S. Navy's first female program manager of ships (PMS-309), Information Systems Improvement Program, she held a civilian equivalent rank of captain.

Raye Jordan was born on January 21, 1935, in Little Rock, Arkansas, to Rayford Jordan and Flossie Graves Jordan. She attended St. Bartholomew School before moving to Merrill High School in Pine Bluff. She graduated in 1952. She attended Arkansas Agricultural, Mechanical, and Normal (AM&N) College (now the University of Arkansas at Pine Bluff—UAPB), wanting to study engineering. However, she obtained a degree in business because Arkansas colleges were not awarding engineering degrees to African-American women in the 1950s. She graduated in 1956.

She was married three times: to Weldon A. Means in 1955, to David H. Montague in 1965, and to James Parrott in 1973. After her marriage to Parrott ended, she returned to the name Montague, the same last name as her only child, David R. Montague.

In 1956, Montague began her career with the navy at the old David Taylor Model Basin (now the Naval Surface Warfare Center) in Carderock, Maryland, as a digital computer systems operator. She later advanced to the position of computer systems analyst at the Naval Ship Engineering Center and served as the program director for the Naval Sea Systems Command (NAVSEA) Integrated Design, Manufacturing, and Maintenance Program as well as the division head for the Com-

D. *Eisenhower* (CVN-69) and the navy's first landing craft helicopter-assault ship (LHA). The last project with which she was affiliated was the Seawolf-class submarine (SSN-21).

Montague retired in 1990. In 2006 after fifty years spent in the metropolitan Washington, D.C., area, she returned to Arkansas. She lives in West Little Rock, where she remains active with LifeQuest, The Links Inc., Alpha Kappa Alpha Sorority, Inc., and the American Contract Bridge League. She mentors inmates through a community re-entry program through the University of Arkansas at Little Rock as well as students at the eStem Elementary Public Charter School in Little Rock.

◆ ◆ ◆

Art Porter, Jr.

(1961–1996)

Arthur Lee (Art) Porter, Jr., was an extremely talented musician proficient on saxophone, drums, and piano. He was an energetic, engaging entertainer and a creative composer whose work ranged across jazz, rhythm and blues, funk, and ballads. The son of legendary jazz musician Art Porter, Sr., he released four albums through Polygram/Verve Records before his accidental death in 1996.

Art Porter, Jr., was born on August 3, 1961, in Little Rock, Arkansas, to Thelma Pauline Minton Porter and Arthur Porter, Sr.; he had four siblings. Porter played alto saxophone in the Benkenarteg, Inc., sound group, which was composed of the five siblings. Porter was awarded the title of most talented young jazz artist in America by the Music Educators of America at age sixteen; this honor included the chance to perform as a soloist with the U.S. Marine Band and with trumpet player Dizzy Gillespie in Dallas, Texas, at the group's annual convention in 1977. For three years consecutively, he was first-chair saxophonist in All-State Band. He also won commendations for classical solos in regional and all-state competitions before graduating from Parkview Performing Arts High School in 1979.

During Porter's youth, his playing while un-

puter-Aided Design and Computer-Aided Manufacturing (CAD/CAM) Program. On January 22, 1984, she accepted the newly created position of deputy program manager of the navy's Information Systems Improvement Program.

Montague's career spans the development of computer technologies, from the UNIVAC I, the world's first commercially available computer, down to modern computers. She successfully revised the first automated system for selecting and printing ship specifications and produced the first draft for the FFG-7 frigate (the Oliver Hazard Perry–class, or Perry-class, ship) in eighteen hours. This was the first ship designed by computer.

In 1972, Montague was awarded the U.S. Navy's Meritorious Civilian Service Award, the navy's third-highest honorary award. She was the first female professional engineer to receive the Society of Manufacturing Engineers Achievement Award (1978) and the National Computer Graphics Association Award for the Advancement of Computer Graphics (1988). She has also received a host of other honors from military branches, industry, and academia. Montague worked on the USS *Dwight*

derage in venues where liquor was sold proved controversial. Bill Clinton, then attorney general, researched and established a framework for the legislature that would allow minors to work in such venues with parental supervision. State senator Jerry Jewell and state representative Townsend authored and shepherded the "Art Porter Bill" into Arkansas law.

Porter graduated from Northeastern Illinois University in Chicago, Illinois, in 1986 with a Bachelor of Arts degree in music education and performance. While in college, he won two certificates for excellence in jazz at the Notre Dame Festival of Music in South Bend, Indiana. He later earned a few graduate hours at Roosevelt University, studying music education. He attended Virginia Commonwealth University for one semester, also studying music education and performance.

Porter married Barbi Lynn Howlett on October 15, 1988; they had two sons. They moved to Murfreesboro, Tennessee, in 1994. That same year, he performed at Carnegie Hall for the Polygram Anniversary Celebration.

Porter's first album, *Pocket City* (1992), featured "LA" and "Little People," both inspired by his son Arthur Porter, III. His second album was *Straight to the Point* (1993). In 1994, his third album, *Undercover*, was a great success, placing Porter solidly on the "wave" radio charts with R&B artists as well as "cool jazz" artists. His final album, *Lay Your Hands on Me* (1996), contained the radio favorite

"Lake Shore Drive." Many of his compositions were expressions of his spirituality, such as the song "Lay Your Hands on Me." During an inaugural prayer service for President Bill Clinton in 1993, he performed solo renditions of "Amazing Grace" and "My Tribute."

Porter died on November 23, 1996, in a boating accident in Thailand. He had just completed a performance at the Thailand International Golden Jubilee Jazz Festival commemorating the fiftieth anniversary of King Bhumibol Adulyadej's reign.

In 1998, Verve Records released the memorial album *For Art's Sake*, featuring Porter's unrecorded music, songs of tribute to him from other artists, and favorites from his previous albums. Porter received posthumous awards from the recording industry, media and production companies, and the educational community of Gary, Indiana. He was also inducted into the Arkansas Jazz Hall of Fame and the Arkansas Entertainers Hall of Fame.

Willie Roaf

(1970–)

Willie Roaf became one of the greatest football players in Arkansas sports history and one of the best offensive linemen ever in the National Football League (NFL). He was inducted into the Pro Football Hall of Fame in 2012.

William Roaf was born in Pine Bluff, Arkansas, on April 18, 1970, one of four children of dentist Clifton Roaf and attorney Andree Layton Roaf. (Andree Roaf was the first African-American female member of the Arkansas Supreme Court and the second woman ever to serve in that capacity.) Though he played football at Pine Bluff High School and graduated in 1988, he was not recruited by any major colleges. After he was told that he would need to gain more weight to be seriously considered for major college football, he briefly considered pursuing college basketball. He was finally offered a football scholarship at Louisiana Tech University in 1989.

After encouragement from coaches to further develop fundamentals and to work hard on

weights, Roaf began to transform into an able offensive player. He was named a two-time all South Independent Conference player, served as a team captain in 1992, and earned All-American honors. Roaf was part of the team that went to the Independence Bowl in 1990. He finished with an 8–3–1 record. In his senior year at Louisiana Tech, Roaf was a finalist for the Outland Trophy for the best offensive lineman in college.

In 1993, the NFL's New Orleans Saints chose Roaf as the overall eighth pick during the first round of the draft. He started all sixteen games in his first year and earned All-Rookie honors. By his second season with the Saints, he was a Pro Bowl choice. He went on with the Saints to play in seven Pro Bowls. He attained the honor of All Pro four times over his nine-year career with the team and was eventually named to the 1990s All-Decade Team and the 2000s All-Decade Team.

He joined the Kansas City Chiefs in 2002 after suffering an injury with the Saints in 2001. Over the next four years, he amassed eleven Pro Bowl selections. In 2009, Roaf took his first coaching job when he became the offensive line coordinator at Santa Monica College in California.

In 2012, Roaf was inducted into the Pro Football Hall of Fame. He has also been inducted into the New Orleans Saints Hall of Fame, the Arkansas Sports Hall of Fame, the Louisiana Sports Hall of Fame, and the College Football Hall of Fame. He is married to Angela Hernandez Roaf.

2014

Vertie Carter, PhD

Colette Honorable

Rickey Jasper

Judge Olly Neal, Jr.

Deputy U.S. Marshal Bass Reeves

Bobby Rush

Vertie Carter, PhD

(1923–)

Vertie Lee Glasgow Carter is a renowned educator whose doctorate in education paved her way into previously unattainable arenas for an African-American woman of her time in Arkansas. Over her long career in education, she influenced generations of teachers and revolutionized the way Arkansas applied employment and merit systems.

Vertie L. Glasgow was born on October 19, 1923, into the sharecropping family of Daisy James Glasgow, who was also a schoolteacher, and Thomas Glasgow in the Antioch community in Hempstead County. To buy books and pay tuition to Yerger High School in Hope, Arkansas, she raised and sold pigs. After graduating from high school in 1942, she attended Arkansas Agricultural, Mechanical, and Normal (AM&N) College in Pine Bluff—now the University of Arkansas at Pine Bluff (UAPB). She graduated in 1949, having taken time off during World War II to work at the Pine

Bluff Arsenal. Glasgow earned a Master of Science degree in education at the University of Arkansas at Fayetteville (U of A) in 1954, although she had to study with U of A professors who came to Little Rock each summer to teach graduate classes because African-American students were not allowed at that time to attend the school in Fayetteville.

By 1958, she was married to Isaiah Carter, a World War II veteran and machine operator for the Cotton Belt railroad; they had two sons: Larry D. Carter and Michael R. Carter.

Although she was courted by various colleges that offered her a significant salary, Carter decided to join the faculty of Philander Smith College in Little Rock in 1964. The school's president had told her how much the school needed someone certified in teacher education for the department to gain accreditation. She went on to receive a doctorate in education from North Texas State University (now the University of North Texas) in 1970.

Over the twenty-one years she spent at Philander Smith College, she used her own money to create a teacher education laboratory and led the school to accreditation by the North Central Association and the National Council for Accreditation of Teacher Education. She also started a similar lab at Arkansas Baptist College in Little Rock, where she was dean of instruction and an adjunct professor. She sometimes served in these roles without pay when the institutions faced financial troubles.

In 1969, Governor Winthrop Rockefeller appointed Carter to the Arkansas Merit System Council to assess equal opportunity in state employment. She was the first African American, the first educator, and the first woman appointed to the council. She served on the council for nine years, having been reappointed by Governor Dale Bumpers in 1972 and Governor David Pryor in 1975; she chaired the council for seven years. During this time, she wrote a book called *How to Get a Career Job* (1978) and held seminars to help people apply for and test for state jobs.

During her tenure on the council, she uncovered and confronted antiquated and discriminatory practices in testing, hiring, firing, promotions, and appeals. After pointing out that there were no black members of the Oral Review Board, she selected two to serve on the board—part of her effort to revolutionize the merit system. She also served as

second vice president of the International Personnel Management Association and vice president of the advisory committee on affirmative action. In 1981, she published *Arkansas Baptist College: A Historical Perspective*, 1884–1982.

Carter retired in 2001. Her husband died in 2007.

✦ ✦ ✦

Colette Honorable

(1970–)

Colette Dodson Honorable is an Arkansas lawyer and public official. A longtime member—and ultimately, chairman—of the Arkansas Public Service Commission (APSC), she was appointed to the Federal Energy Regulatory Commission (FERC) in 2014 by President Barack Obama; she began her service on January 5, 2015. Her service ended on June 30, 2017.

Colette Dodson was born in 1970 in St. Louis, Missouri, to Joyce and Harold Dodson. She and her twin sister, Coleen, have three older brothers and a half-sister. The family moved from St. Louis to California when the twins were young. After her parents divorced, Dodson moved to Little Rock, Arkansas, where she attended Forest Heights Junior High and then Central High School. An active, high-achieving student, and the president of the school's chapter of Future Business Leaders of America, Dodson originally planned to go into business. She met her future husband, Rickey Honorable, at a Future Business Leaders of America conference in high school. However, urged by family members to consider the law, she changed direction and studied criminology and criminal justice while earning her undergraduate degree from the University of Memphis. She went on to earn a law degree from the University of Arkansas (U of A) School of Law in Fayetteville.

She worked as a staff attorney for the Center for Legal Services and also served as an assistant public defender in Jefferson County, Arkansas. Having joined the Arkansas Attorney General's Office under Mark Pryor, Honorable served for five years, first as an assistant attorney general in both the Consumer and Civil Litigation departments, and then as senior assistant attorney general in Medicaid Fraud. She next served as executive director of the Arkansas Workforce Investment Board before being tapped as chief of staff for Attorney General Mike Beebe, who went on to be elected governor and, in October 2007, appointed her to the APSC. In January 2011, she was chosen as chairman of the commission.

As chairman, she oversaw an agency with jurisdiction over approximately 450 utilities whose Arkansas revenues total roughly $6 billion. Under her stewardship, the state led the South and Southeast in energy efficiency programs, consistently achieved one of the nation's lowest electricity rates, and achieved a top nationwide ranking in pipeline safety transparency. She worked to improve energy efficiency and expand access to renewable resources, while judiciously balancing energy and environmental considerations.

After completing two terms as vice president of the National Association of Regulatory Utility Commissioners (NARUC), as well as a stint as treasurer, she was elected as the group's president in November 2013. On August 28, 2014, President Obama nominated her to serve on FERC. Arkansas's two U.S. senators, Democrat Mark Pryor

2014

(who was her former boss) and Republican John Boozman, supported Honorable's nomination.

The hearings on Honorable's FERC nomination were initially delayed after her husband—banker Rickey Earl Honorable—died suddenly on September 7, 2014, less than two weeks after her nomination. However, the bipartisan support the nomination had received from the beginning allowed it to be acted upon despite the change in congressional party alignment as a result of the 2014 elections. In December 2014, she was overwhelmingly confirmed by the Senate. She officially joined the commission on January 5, 2015. She announced in April 2017 that she would not seek a second term after her term expired on June 30, 2017.

Honorable is active in the local community, volunteers at her daughter Sydney's school, and serves as president of the board of the Central High Museum, Inc. She has also served on the boards of both Arkansas Cares and Positive Atmosphere Reaches Kids. She is an active member of Alpha Kappa Alpha Sorority, Inc.

Rickey Jasper

(1963–)

Rickey Jasper is the highest-ranking African American ever to serve in the U.S. Central Intelligence Agency (CIA). He has also had a career as a minister, serving as a pastor at his church in the United States while pursuing seminary studies both at home and abroad.

Rickey Lane Jasper was born in Parkdale, Arkansas, on July 28, 1963. His mother, Louisie Mae Grayson, and her husband, Kirt Grayson, reared him and his siblings in the small town. He graduated from Hamburg High School and headed off to college. Although he had planned to join the military after graduation, the academically inclined Jasper instead decided to join his twin brother, Mickey, in college.

He ultimately earned a Bachelor of Science degree in political science with a minor in accounting from Southern Arkansas University, as well as an MBA in management from Louisiana Tech University and a Master of Science degree in account-

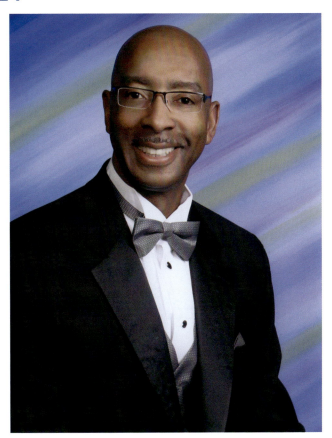

ing from Strayer University. During his tenure in Singapore, Jasper took graduate-level seminary courses at the Singapore Bible College. In the United States, he began work on a Master of Divinity degree at the John Leland Center for Theological Studies in Washington, D.C.

Jasper contemplated a career as a lawyer, but he found himself intrigued by a flyer touting the opportunities offered by the CIA. Jasper began working for the agency after graduation, beginning in Dallas, Texas, in 1987. In addition to work in the United States, Jasper's CIA assignments have taken him all over the world, with a posting in Berlin, Germany, where he served just after the Berlin Wall had fallen, as well as serving in Belize and Singapore.

Jasper became the highest-ranking African American in the history of the CIA, serving as the executive secretary to CIA Director Michael Hayden, the final director to serve under President George W. Bush. Jasper held that position at the beginning of Leon Panetta's tenure under President Barack Obama. Jasper has also served as special assistant for diversity plans and programs in the office of the director of the CIA. Much of his work, given the nature of the agency's operations and responsibilities, must go unreported.

Jasper and his wife, Sheila D. Jasper, have two sons: Rickey Lane "R. J." Jasper, II, and Desmond "Tyler" Jasper.

A licensed minister, Jasper serves as assistant pastor at First Mount Olive Baptist Church in Leesburg, Virginia. He has primary responsibility for the youth ministry, and he teaches church school and conducts workshops. He is the former pastor of the Protestant Faith Fellowship in Berlin, Germany, and First Mount Olive Baptist Church in Lincoln, Virginia.

Judge Olly Neal, Jr.
(1941–)

Olly Neal, Jr., headed up a community health clinic in Marianna, Arkansas, in the 1970s, became the first black district prosecuting attorney in Arkansas, and served as a circuit court judge and on the Arkansas Court of Appeals. He is also a civil rights activist, political agitator, and Arkansas Delta advocate.

Olly Neal, Jr., was born on July 13, 1941, on a farm eleven miles west of Marianna in the rural New Hope community to Ollie Neal and Willie Beatrice Jones Neal. Neal grew up poor in a home with no electricity. His parents impressed upon him and his twelve siblings the importance of education. Neal's father had only a second-grade education but insisted that his children complete high school, while his mother obtained her college degree in 1959, a year after Neal graduated from high school. "She would drive to school at nights through the week whether it was in Pine Bluff, Little Rock, or some extension course up at Forrest City," Neal recalled.

Neal was drafted into the U.S. Army and served two years in Vietnam, 1964–1965; he attained the rank of specialist E-5. He earned a Bachelor of Science degree in chemistry from LeMoyne-Owen College in Memphis, Tennessee, in 1974 and a Juris Doctorate from what is now the University of Arkansas at Little Rock William H. Bowen School of Law in 1979.

In 1970, Neal was asked to run the Lee County Cooperative Clinic (LCCC), a nonprofit, federally funded community health clinic based in Marianna. He served as its first chief executive officer from 1970 to 1978. In 1969, CBS *60 Minutes* correspondent Daniel Schorr had broadcast a segment titled "Don't Get Sick in America," which featured Marianna and the lack of medical care for African Americans and poor whites. LCCC was established that same year by Jan Wrede and Corrine Cass, VISTA (Volunteers in Service to America) health advocates placed in Marianna. They were joined by Dr. Dan Blumenthal, the first VISTA physician in the nation. According to author Marvin Schwartz, "Neal, more than any other figure, influenced the destiny of the clinic through his determination for its success, his articulation, and his steadfast refusal to be intimidated by any person or group that stood in his way." LCCC remains Lee County's sole healthcare facility.

During these years, Marianna and LCCC made national news. In 1971, Neal's brother Prentiss, along with Rabon Cheeks, led a boycott against white merchants in the downtown business district. Violence broke out during the boycott, and the economic damage from the boycott was estimated to be in the millions. In 1972, renowned American folk singer and activist Joan Baez held a benefit concert in Memphis, Tennessee, to raise funds for LCCC. That same year, 250 black students staged a sit-in at the local high school seeking the reinstatement of a fired black teacher and a Dr. Martin Luther King, Jr,. Day school observance.

Neal transitioned from community organizer and LCCC administrator into politics, making three unsuccessful bids for public office. In 1973, he ran for state senator against Paul Benham of Marianna. In 1982, he ran against incumbent Robert Donovan for city attorney, and in 1984 he ran for municipal judge against incumbent Dan Felton, III. Undaunted by his losses, in 1990 Neal paid part of the filing fee for a white attorney, Dan Dane, to run for prosecuting attorney for the first judicial district. Dane won and selected Neal as deputy prosecuting attorney. The next year, Dane resigned. In a news release, Dane stated that it was time for him to move on to other career opportunities. Governor Jim Guy Tucker appointed Neal to complete Dane's term, calling the appointment "historic."

In 1991, Neal became the first black district prosecuting attorney in Arkansas. He was elected circuit court judge for the First Judicial District in 1993. Governor Tucker appointed Neal to the Arkansas Court of Appeals in 1996, where he served for eleven years before retiring in 2007. This was the first time three African-American judges (Neal, Wendell Griffen, and Andree Layton Roaf) served concurrently in the Arkansas Court of Appeals.

Neal became part of a national discussion about education when National Public Radio (NPR) aired a Story Corps interview with Neal and his daughter Karama in 2009. The segment included a recollection of Neal's former English teacher and school librarian, Mildred Grady, who had confided to Neal at a high school reunion in 1972 that she had seen him steal a Frank Yerby book from the school library. Grady told Neal that she realized he stole rather than borrowed the book in order to preserve his reputation as a tough guy. After reading the book, Neal secretly returned it but was astonished to find another Yerby book in exactly the same place. Neal stole the new book. Three times that semester, Grady placed a new book there (having driven to Memphis and purchased it for him), and Neal credits Grady with fostering in him a love of reading. In 2012, *New York Times* columnist and

Pulitzer Prize winner Nicholas Kristof used their story to demonstrate the importance of good teachers and the potential they can make with "troubled, surly kids in a high-poverty environment."

Neal has two children: Karama and Nakia. In 1992, he married Karen Buchanan.

Dep. U.S. Marshal Bass Reeves
(1838–1910)

Arkansas native Bass Reeves was one of the first African-American lawmen west of the Mississippi River. As one of the most respected lawmen working in Indian Territory, he achieved legendary status for the number of criminals he captured.

Bass Reeves was born a slave in Crawford County in July 1838. His owners, the William S. Reeves family, moved to Grayson County, Texas, in 1846.

During the Civil War, Bass became a fugitive slave and found refuge in Indian Territory (modern-day Oklahoma) amongst the Creek and Seminole Indians. Reeves is believed to have served with the irregular or regular Union Indians that fought in Indian Territory during the Civil War.

After the Civil War, Reeves settled in Van Buren, Arkansas, with his wife, Jennie, and children. Oral history states that Reeves served as a scout and guide for deputy U.S. marshals going into Indian Territory on business for the Van Buren federal court. In 1875, Judge Isaac C. Parker became the federal judge for the Western District of Arkansas, which had jurisdiction over Indian Territory. This court had moved to Fort Smith. In 1875, Reeves was hired as a commissioned deputy U.S. marshal, making him one of the first black federal lawmen west of the Mississippi River.

During his law enforcement career, Reeves stood 6'2" and weighed 180 pounds. He could shoot a pistol or rifle accurately with his right or left hand; settlers said Reeves could whip any two men with his bare hands. Reeves became a legend during his lifetime for his ability to catch criminals under trying circumstances. He brought fugitives by the dozen into the Fort Smith federal jail. Reeves said the largest number of outlaws he ever caught at one time was nineteen horse thieves he captured near Fort Sill, Oklahoma. The noted female outlaw Belle Starr turned herself in at Fort Smith when she found out Reeves had the warrant for her arrest.

In 1887, Reeves was tried for murder for allegedly shooting his trail cook; but he was found innocent. In 1890, Reeves arrested the notorious Seminole outlaw Greenleaf, who had been on the run for eighteen years without capture and had murdered seven people. The same year, Reeves went after the famous Cherokee outlaw Ned Christie. Reeves and his posse burned Christie's cabin, but he eluded capture.

In 1893, Reeves was transferred to the East Texas federal court at Paris, Texas. He was stationed at Calvin in the Choctaw Nation and took his prisoners to the federal commissioner at Pauls Valley in the Chickasaw Nation. While working for the Paris court, Reeves broke up the Tom Story gang of horse thieves that operated in the Red River valley.

In 1897, Reeves was transferred to the Musk-ogee federal court in Indian Territory. His first wife died in Fort Smith in 1896. He married Winnie Sumter in 1900. In 1902, Reeves arrested his own son, Bennie, for domestic murder in Muskogee. Bennie was convicted and sent to the federal prison in Leavenworth, Kansas.

Reeves worked until Oklahoma achieved statehood in 1907, at which time he became a city policeman for Muskogee. He died of Bright's disease (a chronic kidney disease) on January 12, 1910.

On May 26, 2012, a bronze statue depicting Reeves on a horse riding west was dedicated in Fort Smith's Pendergraft Park. The statue, which was designed by sculptor Harold T. Holden and cost more than $300,000, was paid for by donations to the Bass Reeves Legacy Initiative.

◆ ◆ ◆

Bobby Rush

(1935–)

Bobby Rush is an award-winning blues artist whose music also parlays elements of southern soul, funk, and rap into a genre he calls "folkfunk." He became known as the "King of the Chitlin' Circuit," touring venues throughout the South that were popular with African-American artists.

Bobby Rush was born Emmett Ellis, Jr., on November 10, 1935, near Homer, Louisiana, to Emmett and Mattie Ellis; however, the 1940 census lists him as three years old. The son of a minister, Rush was influenced by his father's guitar and harmonica playing, and he first experimented with music by tapping on a sugar-cane syrup bucket and playing a broom-and-wire diddley bow. In 1947, his family moved to Pine Bluff, Arkansas, where his music career began. He headed a band at a local juke joint behind a sawmill. He donned a fake mustache so he would look older. It was also in Pine Bluff that he formed key associations with area blues artists such as Elmore James, "Moose" Walker, Boyd Gilmore, and others. It is unclear why he chose the stage name Bobby Rush, though perhaps he changed his name out of respect to his minister father, with whom he shared a name.

After moving to Chicago, Illinois, in the early

Since the late 1970s, Rush has made dozens of albums and has built both a national and international fan base. Interestingly, his awards and acclaim have come in his later years, as he received his first major recognition after the release of *Raw*, his twenty-second album, when he received the Soul Blues Male Artist of the Year award at the Blues Music Awards in 2007. His album *Hoochie Momma* received a Grammy nomination in the blues category in 2001. In 2006, Rush was inducted into the Blues Foundation's Blues Hall of Fame. His album *Porcupine Meat* was released in 2016.

Rush has been married twice. His first wife and three children all died from sickle-cell anemia.

Sexually suggestive, edgy, and humorous, Rush has always had a high-energy performance show that is as entertaining as his music. He touts his desire to keep these shows an integral part of his performances, especially for smaller "Chitlin' Circuit" clubs, which have limited means to attract big stars.

Rush has also become an ambassador for blues, representing the genre in cultural venues worldwide, and has also been noted as a humanitarian. In 2007, he became the first blues artist to perform in China, which earned him the title "International Dean of the Blues." He was later named Friendship Ambassador to the Great Wall of China after he performed the largest concert ever held at that site. Rush has also performed for troops in Iraq and supported projects for prisons and at-risk youth.

1950s, Rush made additional associations with legends such as Howlin' Wolf, Muddy Waters, Little Walter, Albert King, and others. By the early 1970s, he had his first *Billboard* R&B hit with the song "Chicken Heads," which reached No. 34. Rush later made his first full album, *Rush Hour*, in 1979, with another hit, "I Wanna Do the Do."

2015

Luenell Batson

Mildred Barnes Griggs, PhD

Cortez Kennedy

Bishop Donnie L. Lindsey

Eddie Reed, MD

C. Michael Tidwell

Luenell Batson

(1959–)

L uenell, who goes by only her first name professionally, is a comedian and a film and television actress known for her appearances in such movies as *Borat: Cultural Learning of America for Make Benefit Glorious Nation of Kazakhstan* (2006) and *Hotel Transylvania* (2012).

Luenell was born Luenell Batson on March 12, 1959, in Tollette, Arkansas, a historically black community. Her father was murdered while her mother was pregnant with her. As her mother already had seven other children, she was adopted by family members out of state. She became Luenell Campbell and moved to California. She attended school in the community of Castro Valley in the San Francisco Bay Area. In grade school, she became enthralled by theater and enrolled in drama classes. She continued her theatrical studies through college, studying first at Chabot Junior College (now Chabot College) and completing her bachelor's degree at California State University at Hayward (now California State University, East Bay). She began performing at the Oakland En-semble Theatre and doing stand-up comedy.

In the 1990s, Luenell began appearing on KSBT (Soul Beat) television, a black-owned public-access station, after Soul Beat owner Chuck Johnson had seen her stand-up comedy performances. She held a number of roles at Soul Beat, including video DJ and general on-air personality, as well as host of *Club 37*, a talk show with a *Tonight Show*–like format. She also picked up bit parts in television shows and movies, first appearing in *So I Married an Axe Murderer* (1993) as a public records officer (she was credited as Luenell Campbell, a name used for several of her appearances), followed by small roles in the television show *Nash Bridges* and the movie *The Rock* (1996).

In the late 1990s, Luenell faced some personal challenges. She discovered that she was pregnant; her daughter, Da'Nelle, was born in 1996. Her mother died around the same time. Luenell spent the next few years taking care of her daughter before returning to television in 2004, when she appeared on *The Tracy Morgan Show*. She also had regular small roles in *The Boondocks*, *It's Always Sunny in Philadelphia*, *Californication*, and others. However, her role in *Borat* attracted the most attention. In that movie, she played a prostitute whom Borat Sagdiyev (Sacha Baron Cohen) invites to accompany him to a private dinner club in the South. They are both thrown out of the gathering. She rejoins him at the end of the movie, and together they travel back to Borat's native Kazakhstan. The next year, Luenell appeared as herself in *Katt Williams: American Hustle* doing stand-up comedy; her stand-up has also garnered a devoted following.

Other noteworthy film appearances include *Think Like a Man* (2012) and *Taken 2* (2012). She also performed her comedy routine in *Snoop Dogg Presents: The Bad Girls of Comedy* on Showtime and continues to tour comedy venues across the country. In addition, she posed nude for the March 21, 2017, issue of *Penthouse*.

Mildred Barnes Griggs, PhD

(1942–)

Mildred Barnes Griggs is professor and dean emeritus at the University of Illinois at Urbana-Champaign. She is a native of Marianna, Arkansas. She completed her undergraduate degree at Arkansas Agricultural, Mechanical, and Normal (AM&N) College (now the University of Arkansas at Pine Bluff—UAPB) in Pine Bluff, Arkansas, in May 1963, and received her graduate degrees at the University of Illinois in 1967 and 1970.

Dr. Griggs had many varied roles at the University of Illinois that included teaching graduate and undergraduate classes; advising students; directing dissertation research and funded research projects; serving on committees at the university, state and national levels; serving in leadership capacities in professional organizations; and serving as Dean of the College of Education.

After joining the faculty of the University of Illinois in 1970, she became the first African Ameri-

can to be promoted through the academic ranks of assistant, associate, and full professor. She was also the first female dean of a college in the University of Illinois. Her peers and students frequently recognized her as an outstanding instructor and student adviser.

Griggs was named the 2006 S. A. Haley Lecturer at the 50th Annual Rural Life Conference sponsored by the School of Agriculture, Fisheries and Human Sciences at UAPB. She also spoke at the university's 1993 Homecoming Convocation. She is a life member of the UAPB/AM&N Alumni Association and was inducted into the UAPB Hall of Fame.

In addition to her academic accomplishments, she served as one of the two University of Illinois Faculty Athletics Representatives to the Big Ten and the National Collegiate Athletic Association (NCAA) for twelve years. In 2001, the University of Illinois Mothers Association named her the recipient of its prestigious Medallion of Honor Award. In 2008, the provost of the University of Illinois selected her as one of the University's outstanding alumni and hung a banner in her honor on the University of Illinois campus.

She was inducted into Delta Eta Chapter of Delta Sigma Theta Sorority at AM&N. She is currently a life member and spends considerable time on public service activities.

She retired from the University of Illinois on August 20, 2000. After retirement, she earned a Juris Doctorate degree from the College of Law at the University of Illinois and is currently licensed to practice law in the state of Illinois.

She is a consultant at the East Arkansas Enterprise Community and director of the Arkansas Delta Seeds of Change (ADSOC). ADSOC is an organization that was formed by farmers and representatives from various federal, state, and not-for-profit agencies with a grant from Heifer International to help establish a sustainable food system in the East Arkansas Delta region.

Cortez Kennedy

(1968–2017)

Arkansas native Cortez Kennedy was considered one of the best defensive tackles to have played in the National Football League (NFL). After an eleven-year career with the Seattle Seahawks, he retired in 2000. In 2012, he was inducted into the Pro Football Hall of Fame.

Cortez Kennedy was born on August 23, 1968, in Osceola, Arkansas. He spent his first eighteen years in the small Mississippi County town of Wilson, where he was raised by his mother, Ruby, and stepfather, Joe Harris. With few activities available in the rural setting, Kennedy turned to football and became a star defensive player at Rivercrest High School. His promising career nearly ended when as a sophomore he was forced to leave the team due to academic problems. Kennedy recalls his mother sending him a "wish you were here" postcard that year from the state championship game, in which he was not allowed to play. He regained his academic standing. By his senior year in 1985, he led the Rivercrest Colts to the Arkansas 3A State Championship.

Football offered great opportunities for a young man who had aspirations to follow his stepfather into the construction business or to be a state trooper. Though he was highly recruited by colleges, academics once again proved a roadblock. Instead of enrolling in a major university, he accepted a scholarship from Northwest Mississippi Community College in Senatobia. After successfully completing two years of junior college (1986–87), he transferred to the University of Miami (UM). Kennedy excelled on the field during his two years (1988–89) with the Hurricanes. During his senior year, UM won a national championship. Kennedy was named Associated Press Second Team All-America.

After completing his college eligibility (he would later return to UM and graduate), he became one of the most sought-after defensive linemen by teams of the NFL. In the first round of the 1990 draft, the Seattle Seahawks drafted Kennedy as the third overall player selected.

Kennedy's late reporting to the Seahawks training camp due to a contract dispute contributed to a rookie season in which he started in only two games. As a starter in his second season in 1991, he began the season strong, recording six quarterback sacks in the first six games. Even though a mid-season knee injury hampered his play, he made seventy-three tackles—an impressive number for an interior defensive lineman. He was selected as an alternate to his first Pro Bowl and was able to play after another player was forced to withdraw.

Kennedy received the most accolades of his career for his 1992 season. He recorded fourteen sacks. Of his total of ninety-two tackles, twenty-eight were for losses. At the conclusion of the season, he was unanimously selected as the NFL Defensive Player of the Year.

Kennedy played another eight years, all for the Seahawks. During his career, he played in 167 games, had 568 unassisted tackles, assisted in 100 more tackles, and had fifty-eight sacks, three interceptions, and one fumble recovery for a touchdown. He was selected to participate in the Pro Bowl eight times and was named All-Pro five times. Despite his outstanding play, the Seahawks fielded only two teams with winning records during his career, in 1990 and 1999.

After an eleven-year NFL career, Kennedy sat out the 2001 season. After considering leaving the

Seahawks, he announced his retirement in 2002. He soon purchased a home in Wilson and moved there. He believed that as a single father he could better rear his eight-year-old daughter, Courtney. Kennedy and his wife, Nicole, divorced in about 1996. Kennedy had received custody. He attempted to remain fairly low key in his hometown despite his celebrity, but city officials sometimes asked for his assistance in attracting businesses to the area.

After being a four-time finalist, Kennedy received a great honor in 2012 by being inducted into the Pro Football Hall of Fame. Among the honorees that year was fellow Arkansan Willie Roaf. Kennedy's many honors include induction into the Arkansas Sports Hall of Fame, the Seattle Seahawks Ring of Honor, and the University of Miami Ring of Honor; he was also a member of the 1990s NFL All Decade Team. The Seahawks also retired his jersey, number 96.

In 2012, Kennedy and his daughter moved to Orlando, Florida. He said that he wanted his daughter to be able to become her own person and escape his name. Though retired from football, Kennedy remained active in the sport. He served as an advisor for the New Orleans Saints and in 2013 was appointed a Seahawks Ambassador to work with outreach programs for the franchise.

Kennedy died on May 23, 2017.

Bishop Donnie L. Lindsey

(1924–)

Donnie L. Lindsey, longtime bishop within the Church of God in Christ (COGIC) in Arkansas and noted businessman, founded the regionally famous Lindsey's Barbecue in North Little Rock, Arkansas.

Donnie Lee Lindsey was born in Bluff City, Arkansas, on April 17, 1924, to Newton Lindsey and Anna Lindsey. His father was a sharecropper. By the 1930 census, he had one brother and four sisters. The family moved to the Maumelle, Arkansas, area when Lindsey was four years old. In an interview with the *Arkansas Democrat-Gazette*, Lindsey described himself as a rebellious youth who dropped out of school but returned at age seventeen to attend the ninth grade. In junior high school and high school, he worked at Johnson's Barbecue in Little Rock. In 1943, he began fighting in World War II. The following year, he felt himself being called to the ministry. When he returned from the war, he entered Arkansas Baptist College in Little Rock and earned a Bachelor of Arts degree in 1949. He later pursued graduate work at Fisk University in Tennessee and at what is now Tuskegee University in Alabama.

Lindsey married Irma Moore on September 1, 1946; they had three children.

In 1951, he began his first pastorate at the England Church of God in Christ in England, Arkansas. In 1959, he transferred to Revelation Church of God in Christ in Carlisle, Arkansas. In 1967, Lindsey began serving in a larger administrative capacity within COGIC, when he became the Jurisdictional Sunday School Superintendent. In 1972, he organized the Emmanuel Mission in North Little Rock, and the following year he was appointed as the first administrative assistant of the bishop of the Second Jurisdiction of Arkansas. In 1974, he was made bishop of that jurisdiction and held the office until 2009 when he retired as bishop. The next year, he was made the pastor of what later became New Calvary Temple in North Little Rock. He became senior pastor at The Worship Center COGIC (a mission of New Calvary), also in North Little Rock. During his time as bishop, he also filled in on an interim basis in other jurisdictions within the state.

Lindsey has held jobs outside the church, including serving as a teacher and as the principal of George Washington Carver School in Allport, Arkansas. However, he is perhaps best known as the proprietor of Lindsey's Barbecue in North Little Rock, which he started in 1956. The restaurant became a North Little Rock staple. In 1975, shortly after having been appointed bishop, he sold the restaurant to a nephew, Richard Lindsey (one of the North Little Rock Six). Lindsey entered the food service business again in 1989 when he opened Lindsey's Hospitality House, which was a home-cooking and barbecue restaurant that offered catering services and a banquet hall. Lindsey's son Donnie Jr. eventually took it over. In 2007, the original Lindsey's Barbecue was destroyed by fire. The business at 207 Curtis Sykes Dr. in North Little Rock became known as Lindsey's BBQ & Hospitality House.

Lindsey has also served on a number of local, regional, and state boards, including the Arkansas State Labor Board. He was the Coordinator of Citizens Participation in the Model Cities Program and on the Governor's Commission on School District Reorganization. He was the first African American to serve on the North Little Rock City Council, the North Little Rock Chamber of Commerce, and the board of directors of the North Little Rock Boys and Girls Club. He holds honorary doctorate degrees from Arkansas Baptist College and from Shorter College.

Eddie Reed, MD

(1953–2014)

Eddie Reed was a cancer researcher, medical oncologist, and leader in public policy addressing disparities in healthcare in the United States.

Eddie Reed was born on December 17, 1953, the son of Floyd and Gennora Reed, who reared a family of eighteen children on a farm near Hughes, Arkansas. Reed and his siblings received their ear-

ly education in Hughes's public schools. They each achieved a college education and had distinguished careers as lawyers, doctors, teachers, and public servants. Reed attended Philander Smith College, a historically black institution in Little Rock, Arkansas, where he achieved academic distinction. In the summer following his sophomore year, he was chosen to work in medical research at the National Cancer Institute (NCI) in Bethesda, Maryland. The laboratory chief, Bruce Chabner, recognized Reed's outstanding potential and became his mentor and lifelong friend.

At the NCI, Reed studied the metabolic disposition of allopurinol, an important medication for treating gout and complications of leukemia. His work on allopurinol during college led to his pursuit of a career in cancer drug development in the nation's foremost research institutions. After graduation from Philander Smith in 1975, he completed his medical degree from Yale Medical School in 1979 and trained in internal medicine at Stanford University Hospitals from 1979 to 1981. Dr. Reed entered the United States Public Health Service, of which the NCI is a part, as a fellow in medical oncology in 1981. He became a career officer and scientist at the NCI, where he remained for seventeen years.

At the NCI, his research focused on the new anticancer drug cisplatin and its interaction with

DNA. In the early 1970s, cisplatin became the most important new cancer drug, a key component for treating testicular cancer, lung cancer, ovarian cancer, and tumors of the head and neck. However, its toxic side effects to normal tissues were often severe and unpredictable. Reed was the first to show that inherent individual capacity to repair DNA lesions caused by cisplatin determined the degree of toxicity for both normal and human tissues. He implicated an increased capacity to repair DNA as the major factor contributing to resistance to cisplatin and its sister drug, carboplatin. DNA repair has since become a major focus for cancer drug development efforts. All the while, Reed remained a committed cancer physician and a leader nationally and internationally in the study of treatments for ovarian cancer, for which cisplatin and other platinum-based drugs remain crucial elements.

In 1995, he was promoted to chief of the Clinical Pharmacology Branch at the NCI, the first African-American scientist to hold a branch chief position at NCI. He retired from the Public Health Service after a twenty-year career in 1998 to become director of the Mary Babb Randolph Cancer Center at the University of West Virginia (1998–2003). Thereafter, he was chosen to be director of the Division of Cancer Cause and Prevention of the U.S. Center for Disease Control and Prevention in Atlanta, Georgia (2003–2008), where he led national programs to advance cancer screening and diagnosis. He left Atlanta in 2008 to become clinical director of the Mitchell Cancer Center at the University of South Alabama (2008) in Mobile and, in 2012, was chosen to become the first clinical director of the newly formed National Institute of Minority Health and Health Disparities at the National Institutes of Health (NIH) in Bethesda, Maryland, a position he held until his death in 2014.

Throughout his career, despite his growing administrative and research responsibilities, he always maintained an active laboratory and clinical agenda, with a special interest in the treatment of ovarian cancer. He was an advocate for the underserved in his various positions in West Virginia, Alabama, and nationally, and he gave his outspoken support for the advancement of minority scientists in the field of cancer research.

His scientific contributions include more than 300 scientific papers, many book chapters, and numerous lectures in the United States and abroad. He served as an advisor to the National Center for Toxicological Research in Arkansas and academic cancer centers. He was also a member of the senior advisory council of the American Association for Cancer Research. Throughout his life, he never forgot Arkansas and often reminded colleagues at the NCI, Yale, Stanford, and West Virginia of his love for the Razorbacks, the family farm, and the simpler days in Arkansas.

Reed's remarkable life came to a sudden close when he developed cancer at the age of sixty, an ironic ending to a unique career. He died on May 28, 2014, and is buried at Paradise Gardens Cemetery in Edmonson, Arkansas. His career was recognized during a celebration of his life at the American Association for Cancer Research in 2015. In his honor, colleagues and friends established the Dr. Eddie Reed Exchange Fellowship at the Massachusetts General Hospital Cancer Center (MGHCC). This fellowship supports training in cancer control and treatment at the MGHCC for cancer professionals from Sub-Saharan Africa.

Dr. Reed was survived by his wife and research collaborator, Meenakshi Reed. His only son, Edward Reed, died at the age of twenty-three in an automobile accident.

C. Michael Tidwell
(1951–)

C. Michael Tidwell was the principal dancer for Ballet Arkansas for ten years and has performed across the world. He has also served as an educator in Little Rock, Arkansas, and is the founder of the Tidwell Project, Inc., a nonprofit organization that employs dance as a means of exploring creative expression and healthy life choices among children.

Tidwell received his early education in the Little Rock public schools. He attended the University of Arkansas at Little Rock, where his dance instructor, Dot Callanen, encouraged him to pursue dance as a career.

Tidwell studied with many renowned dancers,

including Manolo Agullo of Ballet Russe de Monte Carlo; Lorraine Cranford, the founding director of Ballet Arkansas; Maureen Migden of the Royal Ballet Academy; Peter Fairweather of the Royal Ballet; Luigi at the Luigi Dance Centre in New York; Gus Giordano of Chicago, Illinois; and Alvin Ailey of New York.

Tidwell was a principal dancer for Ballet Arkansas for a decade. He also toured Asia with the Buddy Simpson Dancers and was a recipient of the Arkansas choreographers fellowship sponsored by the National Endowment for the Arts and the Arkansas Arts Council.

As a teacher, Tidwell became aware of the fact that many in the wider community had little engagement with the performing arts due to lack of exposure and economic disadvantages. In response, he established the Tidwell Project in 1990. The Tidwell Project's mission statement reads, in part, "Using dance as a portal of entry, youth are exposed to various forms of expression and given the opportunity to engage in healthy choices and behavior." He also founded the Centre for the DansArts, Inc., a dance academy, in 1994.

Tidwell teaches at Parkview Arts and Science Magnet High School in Little Rock and has implemented the dance curriculum at Horace Mann Magnet Junior High School. He has also taught at the University of Arkansas at Little Rock and Philander Smith College.

Tidwell has received the Arkansas Martin Luther King, Jr., Commission "Salute to Greatness" Award, the Arkansas Black Hall of Fame Founder's Award, and the Governor's Individual Artist Award. He was also appointed to the Arkansas Arts Council Advisory Board by Governor Mike Beebe.

2016

Ambassador June Carter-Perry

Gregory A. Davis

Judge Mifflin Wistar Gibbs

Estella and Knoxie Hall, Sr., and Family

Judge Richard L. Mays

Cynthia M. Scott

Ambassador June Carter-Perry

(1943–)

June Carter-Perry is a former educator, diplomat, and U.S. State Department official. Her lengthy and multi-faceted diplomatic career included service as the U.S. ambassador to both Lesotho and Sierra Leone.

June Carter was born on November 13, 1943, in Texarkana, Arkansas. Her mother, Louise Pendleton Carter, was a Peace Corps volunteer in Malaysia. June Carter graduated from Loyola University in Chicago, Illinois, in 1965 and earned a bachelor's degree in history. She earned a master's degree in European history from the University of Chicago in 1967. She soon married Fredrick M. Perry, who served as an official with both the United States Agency for International Development (USAID) and the Peace Corps. The couple has two children.

Carter-Perry served as director of public affairs for WGMS/RKO Radio Corporation in Washington, D.C., from May 1972 to October 1974. In that position, she had both editorial and programming responsibilities while she was also involved with development and event planning. While at RKO, she started the WGMS-FM Art Auction, a project that utilized prominent Washingtonians for fundraising. She also raised money for the Kennedy Center by broadcasting the National Symphony Orchestra. In October 1974, she became special assistant in the Community Services Administration, a national anti-poverty agency. That experience was followed by her appointment, in September 1976, as public affairs director of ACTION. In that post, one she held until 1982, Perry oversaw public relations for both the Peace Corps and its domestic counterpart, VISTA.

Carter-Perry began her career as a State Department Foreign Service officer in 1983. Over the course of over twenty-five years in the State Department, she worked at U.S. embassies in Lusaka, Zambia; Harare, Zimbabwe; and Paris, France. Early in her career, Carter-Perry served as deputy chief of mission in both Madagascar and the Central African Republic. She also served as a senior advisor to the Africa Bureau's assistant secretary. In addition, she served as director of the State Department's Office of Social and Humanitarian Affairs, where she was responsible for U.S. policy related to the United Nations Commissions dealing with issues relating to women and human rights. She also served as deputy director for public policy and planning in the Political and Military Affairs Bureau, and assistant to the deputy secretary of state. Carter-Perry also did a stint in the State Department's Africa Bureau.

Appointed ambassador to Lesotho in 2004, she was the American chief of that mission from 2004 to 2007. While in Lesotho, she initiated the first Lesotho–U.S. trade mission in 2005. Carter-Perry's work in Lesotho earned her an appointment as ambassador to Sierra Leone, and she served as head of that mission until 2009. During her years as head of the Sierra Leone mission, she oversaw the successful return of the Peace Corps to the country while also helping to start a U.S. government program that provided a $13 million grant for agriculture and infrastructure development. This initiative represented a major advance for the nation's economy and offered major support for the country's developing private efforts. Carter-Perry's distinguished efforts in the State Department were recognized with a number of accolades, including the Diplomat-in-Residence of the Year Award and the Superior and Meritorious Honor Awards.

Carter-Perry retired from the State Department in 2010. In 2011, she served as the Cyrus Vance Visiting Professor at Mount Holyoke College in Massachusetts. She had served as the diplomat-in-residence at Howard University in 2001. She also taught at the University of Maryland at College Park and North Carolina A&T State University. In 2013, she taught at the University of Missouri, where she delivered the Distinguished Monroe-Paine Lecture for the Harry S Truman School of Public Affairs. In 2014, Carter-Perry served as a guest lecturer at the University of Utah's law school. She also serves on the Board of Directors of Africare, an organization dedicated to improving the lives of the people of Africa.

Gregory A. Davis

(1948–)

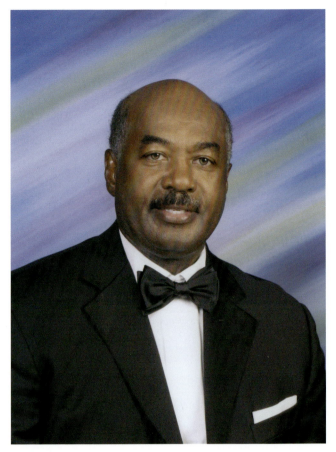

Gregory A. Davis is the founder of Davis Broadcasting, a regional media company that owns several radio stations in Columbus and Atlanta, Georgia; the stations range from urban contemporary and gospel to sports and Spanish-language formats. Davis serves as the president and CEO of Davis Broadcasting. In 2016, the company he founded celebrated its thirtieth anniversary.

Gregory Davis was born in Fort Smith, Arkansas, in 1948. His mother was an educator at the local black school, and his father worked in a bakery before opening a shoeshine parlor. He attended twelve years of Catholic school and graduated from St. Anne's Academy, where he was the first African American to participate in the school's athletic program. Although he had been encouraged to pursue the field of broadcasting by the owner of a jewelry store where he had worked during the holiday break one year, he instead played basketball and earned a degree in biology at Lane College in Jackson, Tennessee. He subsequently served in the U.S. Army and then went to Eastern Michigan University. He earned a master's degree in educational leadership.

As Davis later recalled in an interview with Columbus's *Ledger-Inquirer*, he was working as an assistant principal at an elementary school when the school nurse, with whom he shared an office, talked him into meeting her husband, who worked at a local television station. He recruited Davis to a position in sales—with double the salary he was currently earning. From 1974 to 1986, Davis embarked on a career in sales that took him to such cities as Chicago, Illinois; Los Angeles and San Francisco, California; New York City; and Detroit and Flint, Michigan. He was working as a sales manager for WLW-TV in Cincinnati, Ohio, when he decided to make his first television station purchase. He traveled to Columbus, Georgia, to buy the local NBC affiliate, then up for sale. The owner of the station backed out at the last moment, but finding that there were local radio stations up for sale, Davis changed his plans.

Davis purchased two radio stations in Columbus, along with two in Augusta, Georgia, owned by the same company. This was the start of Davis Broadcasting. Throughout the years, the company also bought and sold stations in Macon, Georgia, and Charlotte, North Carolina. In 2004, Davis

Broadcasting began the first Spanish-language FM station in Atlanta. The company also hosts a number of philanthropic events, including a yearly Christmas party for needy children.

Davis and his wife, Cheryl, have three children. After they spent time in their own independent careers, two began working for the family business. Davis has served on the boards of many organizations, including the Columbus Chamber of Commerce, the National Association of Black-Owned Broadcasters, and the Georgia Association of Broadcasters. He was the first African American appointed to serve as chairman of the Columbus State University Board of Trustees.

Judge Mifflin Wistar Gibbs

(1823–1915)

Mifflin Wistar Gibbs was a Little Rock, Arkansas, businessman, a politician, and the first elected African-American municipal judge in the United States.

Mifflin Gibbs was born on April 17, 1823, in Philadelphia, Pennsylvania, the eldest of four children born to Jonathan and Maria Gibbs. His father, a Methodist minister, died when Mifflin was a child, and his mother worked as a laundress.

Gibbs learned carpentry through an apprenticeship. He read widely and attended debates at the Philadelphia Library Company of Colored Persons. He had a chance to practice his own oratory in the 1840s when Frederick Douglass invited him to help conduct an abolitionist lecture tour.

Journeying to California soon after the gold rush of 1849, he became a successful retail merchant and a leader of the growing black population in San Francisco. He was a founder of the first black newspaper west of the Mississippi River, *The Mirror of the Times* (1855). He left San Francisco in 1858 to escape growing racial prejudice on the California frontier.

Gibbs settled in Victoria, Vancouver Island, British Columbia. Once again, he found business opportunities and was soon among the colony's black elite. In 1866, he became the first black man elected to the Victoria City Council.

It is unclear why Gibbs abandoned British Columbia, where his economic fortune was assured and where he had found a modicum of political success. In 1870, he returned to the United States and settled in Oberlin, Ohio. He was restless, however, and the placid college town could not hold his attention for long. In 1871, he headed south.

His brother Jonathan C. Gibbs was serving as secretary of state in Reconstruction Florida, where Gibbs visited him. Then he attended a freedmen's convention in Charleston, South Carolina, where he met William H. Grey, Arkansas's state commissioner of immigration and lands. At Grey's urging, Gibbs set off for Arkansas.

Gibbs crossed the Arkansas River into Little Rock in May 1871. He liked the city and settled in quickly. He read law with some local white Republican lawyers, and as soon as he had passed the bar examination in 1872, he opened a partnership with Lloyd G. Wheeler, a well-known black attorney and leader in the Pulaski County Republican Committee. In October 1873, Gibbs accepted the Republican nomination for Little Rock police judge. He was allied with the "regular" Republicans, the faction controlled by U.S. Senator Powell Clayton. Gibbs won the election in a tight race and served as police judge from November 1874 to

April 1875, when the Democrats defeated him at the end of Reconstruction.

The restoration of Democratic hegemony in 1874–75 did not end black political participation. Gibbs continued to be a power in the Republican Party, serving for a decade as secretary of the state GOP central committee. He was often a delegate to national conventions.

His success within the Republican Party reflected his close affiliation with the iron-willed Clayton, who used Gibbs and other black leaders to keep the black party leadership pliant and dependable. Gibbs's loyalty brought patronage jobs. In 1877, President Rutherford B. Hayes named Gibbs registrar of the Little Rock district land office. President Benjamin Harrison named him receiver of public monies in Little Rock in 1889. Finally, President William McKinley named him U.S. consul to Tamatave, Madagascar, in 1897.

Gibbs never abandoned business endeavors despite his federal employment. He started a real estate agency in his law office in 1874, and he invested widely, using profits from his California and Canadian ventures. In 1903, Gibbs, at age eighty, commenced his most ambitious business effort, the creation of the Capital City Savings Bank. It was the second black-owned bank in Arkansas. Organized with a capital stock of $10,000, by 1905 its deposits reached $100,000. Shortly after the bank opened, a health insurance division, the People's Mutual Aid Association, was added.

On June 18, 1908, the bank failed to open amid rumors that it was insolvent. Efforts to save the bank were fruitless, and the chancery court appointed a receiver. It became public knowledge that the bank had been poorly managed, its records unorganized. That year, a grand jury began investigating the bank management. In January 1909, Gibbs and other bank directors were indicted for knowingly accepting deposits in an insolvent bank. In May, Gibbs reached a settlement in an out-of-court decision on the $28,000 in claims against him. The amount of the settlement was not announced, but it is clear he was able to save the bulk of his personal fortune.

Little is known of Gibbs's personal life. He married Maria Alexander in 1859, and they had five children. In his autobiography, Gibbs hardly mentions his family. After a prolonged period of declining health, Gibbs died on July 11, 1915, at his home in Little Rock; he is buried in the Fraternal Cemetery on Barber Street in Little Rock.

Estella and Knoxie Hall, Sr., and Family

Operated by the Hall Family, K. Hall and Sons is a longstanding black-owned business on Wright Avenue in Little Rock, Arkansas. Originally founded as a produce store, it now also encompasses a restaurant and a wholesale food distribution business.

K. Hall and Sons was founded by Knoxie Hall, Sr., and Estella Marie Crenshaw Hall. Knoxie Hall was born on September 13, 1924. Estella Hall was born on November 24, 1927. They married on December 16, 1944, and had seven children. Knoxie Hall owned and operated several different businesses, including a carwash and detail business and a farm. His experience operating the carwash convinced him of the need to be independent, for at the peak of his operation's success, his white landlord canceled their rental agreement, only to open a carwash at the same site himself soon thereafter.

In 1973, Knoxie Hall purchased a former gas station to use as a storefront for selling produce from his Wrightsville farm. He remodeled the building and named it Hall's Produce. Estella Hall managed the store while Knoxie oversaw his other business enterprises. In 1984, their children entered the family business and expanded it to include wholesale food supply; the name was changed to K. Hall and Sons Produce. Ten years later, the family shareholders established a holding company, K. Hall and Sons Enterprises, Inc.

Knoxie Hall died on August 21, 2009; Estella Hall died on November 27, 2013.

In addition to wholesale produce supply and direct sales, K. Hall and Sons also includes a restaurant. As David Hall noted in an interview with the Rock City Eats website, the restaurant came about by accident: "Most of the food that we cook now, we actually started out cooking for ourselves. And people would come in and say, 'Hey, is that for sale?'" K. Hall and Sons is well known for its hamburgers, as well as for the weekly seafood boils that attract customers in droves.

Judge Richard L. Mays

(1943–)

Richard L. Mays was an early civil rights attorney during the struggles to integrate public facilities and end bias in Arkansas courts and law enforcement. He was in the first group of African Americans to be elected to the Arkansas General Assembly in the twentieth century and became the second African American to serve as a justice of the Arkansas Supreme Court. Governor Bill Clinton appointed him to the court in 1979.

Richard Leon Mays was born on August 5, 1943, in Little Rock, Arkansas, the younger of two sons of Barnett G. Mays and Dorothy Mae Greenlee Mays. Although the family lived in an integrated neighborhood on the southeastern edge of Little Rock, his father operated a restaurant and a liquor store in North Little Rock and developed

and managed real estate there. Mays occasionally worked in his father's café while he was in high school and during summers while he was a student at Howard University in Washington, D.C.

He attended Little Rock's still-segregated schools, though he spent the third grade in integrated classes at Tucson, Arizona, where his mother was being treated for tuberculosis. He graduated from Horace Mann High School in 1961 with Mahlon Martin—who became the first black city manager of Little Rock, director of the state Department of Finance and Administration, and head of the Winthrop Rockefeller Foundation—and Henry Jones, who became U.S. magistrate for the Eastern District of Arkansas.

Mays received a bachelor's degree at Howard University in 1965. He was the only African American in his law school class at the University of Arkansas (U of A) at Fayetteville that fall, and in 1968 became the first black law graduate in over ten years. Mays would say many years later that he faced little discrimination in the law school, although a landlord who contracted with the university to provide housing tried to deny him an apartment after learning that he was black, saying he did not want his building bombed. After his first year of law school, he married Jennifer Winstead, who had been his high school girlfriend.

The U.S. Justice Department hired Mays as a trial attorney in the organized-crime section after law school in 1968. A year later, he returned to Little Rock as a deputy prosecutor under Prosecuting Attorney Richard B. Adkisson, who later was elected chief justice of the Arkansas Supreme Court. Mays was the Sixth Judicial District's first full-time black prosecutor—and perhaps the first in the state. In this position, he suffered many experiences of racial discrimination within the courtroom.

Mays was an intern for the NAACP Legal Defense Fund. One of his first cases was a federal suit against the Arlington Hotel in Hot Springs, Arkansas, for discriminating against black employees under Title VII of the Civil Rights Act of 1964. Black employees were always porters, but white employees were always bellhops, who received higher pay. Judge Oren Harris ruled against Mays, but the Eighth U.S. Circuit Court of Appeals reversed the order and ruled for the black workers.

In 1971, Mays joined the state's first racially integrated law firm, which was headed by John W. Walker, a stalwart civil rights lawyer who filed scores of civil rights suits in the second part of the twentieth century and into the twenty-first.

Another class-action lawsuit (*Phillips, et al. v. Weeks, et al.*), filed in 1972, alleged that Little Rock police engaged in a systematic pattern of brutality against blacks, who often were arrested, held for days on "suspicion" without charges being filed against them, and subjected to physical abuse. The trial lasted more than a month, but Judge G. Thomas Eisele did not rule for twelve years, by which time most of the practices had ended under a new police chief. Still, the judge granted some relief from the remaining practices.

When Mays went to Arkadelphia, Arkansas, in 1972 to represent African-American high school students who were arrested following a major disturbance at Arkadelphia High School, the judge fined him for contempt of court for continuing to ask witnesses the race of people they were talking about. When another lawyer from the firm arrived to help Mays, the judge barred all members of the Walker law firm from ever practicing in Clark County. Oscar Fendler, a Blytheville, Arkansas,

lawyer, represented Mays and the other lawyers in an appeal to the state Supreme Court, which said the judge acted unconstitutionally and set aside his order.

After the state reapportioned seats in the legislature in 1972 to equalize representation and give a voice to African Americans, Mays and three other African Americans were elected to the Senate or House of Representatives, the first black lawmakers since 1893. His first bill, which required common carriers to have uninsured motorist coverage, was blocked by House members when, by agreement with the speaker of the House, he brought it up during the morning hour, which was reserved for noncontroversial bills that required no debate. "Mays can't have a noncontroversial bill," Representative Paul Van Dalsem of Perryville protested to the House. It was explained to Mays that he could get bills passed if everyone was assured they had nothing to do with race. The legislature passed his common-carrier bill, but his bill creating a state civil rights commission never passed the House.

Seeing no real political future, he quit after three terms to devote himself to his law practice and businesses, including a chain of fast-food restaurants. In December 1979, Governor Bill Clinton appointed Mays to succeed the retiring Justice Conley Byrd on the Arkansas Supreme Court. He served on the court for a year. Mays was the second black justice after George Howard, Jr., who was appointed to finish a term in 1977.

The biggest case the court addressed that year was a challenge to a business installment debt, which ended with the Supreme Court declaring that service charges that businesses typically included in installment loans should be counted as interest. It meant that all such loans were usurious if the interest and service charges exceeded the state constitution's ten-percent limit on interest on any debt. The suit (*Superior Improvement Co. v. Mastic Corporation*) was decided four to three. Mays joined the dissenters. The decision panicked merchants and lending institutions, and the legislature referred to the voters in 1982 a constitutional amendment lifting the ten-percent ceiling. Voters ratified the amendment.

After his term on the court ended in January 1981, Mays returned to his private law practice and business interests. His political activities did not wane. He supported three successive governors, Clinton, Jim Guy Tucker, and Mike Huckabee, the latter a Republican. He served on a number of major state commissions: the Arkansas Ethics Commission (created by an initiated act in 1988), the Arkansas Economic Development Commission, the Arkansas Governor's Mansion Commission, the state Bank Board, and the Claims Commission.

Mays worked full time for Bill Clinton in his 1992 campaign for president, raising more than a million dollars. He joined a lobbying and business-development firm in Washington, D.C., for the eight years of the Clinton administration. He also did extensive business development in Africa.

His first wife died of cancer in 2000. In 2012, he married Supha Xayprasith. His son and daughter became partners in his law firm.

Cynthia M. Scott

(1951–)

Cynthia Scott is a Grammy-nominated jazz vocalist known for her work as one of Ray Charles's "Raelettes" and for her subsequent solo career. She was named Jazz Ambassador for the U.S. Department of State in 2004 and was Wynton Marsalis's choice for the first person to give a concert in the Lincoln Center's Rose Room.

Cynthia Scott was born on July 20, 1951 (some sources say 1952), to the Reverend Sam Scott and Artelia Scott in El Dorado, Arkansas, the tenth of twelve children—six boys and six girls. She began singing at age four in her father's church but exposed her ear to secular music by sneaking over to her older sister's house, where she enjoyed, as she said, "a different set of rules." As a teenager, she joined a band called the Funny Company featuring the Sisters of Soul, a girl-group modeled after the Supremes, and performed locally for proms and homecoming celebrations. A month after graduation, Scott secretly entered the annual Miss El Dorado pageant, which was then exclusively for white contestants. Scott performed with fellow Sisters of Soul Jeanette Malone and Carolyn McDuffie for the talent competition and wore a pink bikini she had purchased at the local dollar store. She won

second runner-up, an achievement she later sought desperately—and successfully—to document after finding that the library was missing the microfilm depicting the day she made the front page of the *El Dorado News Times*.

In 1971, Scott moved to Dallas, Texas, where she became one of American Airlines' first African-American stewardesses and spent her leisure time performing with Dallas jazz regulars such as James Clay, Claude Johnson, Roger Boykin, Onzy Matthews, Marchel Ivery, and Red Garland. The following year, she received an early morning call from Ray Charles, who asked her to perform with him. She performed as a Raelette for two years, touring the world on Charles's private plane. After reporting sexual harassment from Charles, Scott was fired, which she described in an interview with Jim Newsom: "We co-hosted the *Mike Douglas Show* for a week, and John Bond, who was working with AFTRA [the television union], said, 'Don't be one of the Raelettes who let Ray.' I have six brothers so I kinda knew what he was talking about. But it was a good thing that he planted that in my mind—Ray wasn't a bad looking man and he was a little bit suave, but if he didn't get his way he could be treacherous. I got fired because I didn't play ball with him."

Scott went on to sing with a few of Charles's

band members: Hank Crawford, Marcus Belgrave, Leroy Cooper, and David "Fathead" Newman. Scott performed in Dallas until the late 1980s. Asked to perform at Chelsea Place in Manhattan, Scott hired a then-undiscovered Harry Connick, Jr., as her pianist. What was supposed to be a four-week engagement lasted three years. After Scott moved to New York City, she completed her bachelor's and master's degrees from the Manhattan School of Music. She headlined at New York City venues the Birdland, and the Iridium, and she was the featured vocalist at the Supper Club in Times Square for ten years. She worked with Lionel Hampton, Cab Calloway, and Wynton Marsalis. Scott sang at the Women in Jazz Festival at Lincoln Center and the International Women in Jazz Festival, and sang the music of Johnny Mercer in the musical *Mid-night in the Garden of Good and Evil*, for which the *Syracuse Herald* lauded her interpretation as having "haunting artistry and superb talent...singing 'Satin Doll' and 'Moon River' into suave musical mono-logues."

Scott released five albums: *I Just Want to Know*; *Boom Boom: Live in Japan with Norman Simmons Trio*; *A La Carte: Live at Birdland*; *Storytelling: Live at Birdland*; and *Dream for One Bright World*, the last of which included "Did I Know You," Scott's depiction of her mother's struggle with dementia and Alzheimer's disease. She also wrote and performed a biographical one-woman musical, *One Raelette's Journey*.

Scott taught at City College of New York until 2009 and The New School until 2012 as a vocal coach. She continues to perform widely.

CONTRIBUTORS

Betty Sorensen Adams, Cindy Albright, Bobby Ampezzan, Celia Anderson, Jeff Bailey, John Bellamy, C. L. Bledsoe, Kwadjo Boaitey, Sarah Bost, David O. Bowden, Gloria Boyd, Cary Bradburn, Jimmy Bryant, Terry Buckalew, Art T. Burton, Kevin D. Butler, Bil Carpenter, Central High School National Historic Site, Bruce A. Chabner, Paul Ciulla, Richard B. Clark, Arlene Corsano, Jimmy Cunningham, Michael J. Dabrishus, Edmond Davis, Tom W. Dillard, Michael B. Dougan, Christyne M. Douglas, Ernest Dumas, Diana Fisher, Greg Freeman, Robbie K. Gill, Kay C. Goss, Rebecca Haden, Nancy Hendricks, Rachel Hoge, Adam R. Hornbuckle, Mary Margaret Hui, Jajuan Johnson, Kyle L. Jones, Janis F. Kearney, Barclay Key, Thomas E. Kienzle, Judith Kilpatrick, John A. Kirk, Stephen Koch, Barry E. Lee, Linda McDowell, Patricia Washington McGraw, William K. McNeil, Mary Menefee, Matthew Mihalka, Wendell Miller, Ronnie A. Nichols, Bill Norman, Michelle Parks, Joshua R. Pate, Debra Polston, Mike Polston, Eugene Porter, David Prater, William H. Pruden III, David Ragsdale, Leland L. Razer, Stephen L. Recken, Brent E. Riffel, Bryan Rogers, Yulonda Eadie Sano, Nikki Scott, Raymond D. Screws, David Sesser, Deborah Sesser, Jeanette Shead, Stephanie Smittle, Grif Stockley, Joshua Switzer, Thomas A. Teeter, Katherine Teske, Steven Teske, Georgia C. Walton, Jonathan J. Wolfe, Colin Woodward, and Joshua Cobbs Youngblood.